THE
LAST
DROP

THE
LAST
DROP

Operation Varsity, March 24–25, 1945

STEPHEN L. WRIGHT

STACKPOLE
BOOKS

Published by
STACKPOLE BOOKS
5067 Ritter Road
Mechanicsburg, PA 17055
www.stackpolebooks.com

Printed in the United States of America

10 9 8 7 6 5 4 3 2 1

FIRST EDITION

Library of Congress Cataloging-in-Publication Data
Wright, Stephen L.
    The last drop : Operation Varsity, March 24–25, 1945 / Stephen L. Wright.—1st ed.
        p. cm.
    Includes bibliographical references and index.
    ISBN-13: 978-0-8117-0310-9
    ISBN-10: 0-8117-0310-X
    1. Operation Varsity, 1945. 2. Great Britain. Army. Airborne Division, 6th—History.
3. United States. Army. Airborne Division, 17th—History. 4. Great Britain. Army—
Airborne troops. 5. United States. Army—Airborne troops. 6. World War, 1939–1935—
Aerial operations, American. 7. World War, 1939–1945—Aerial operations, British.
8. World War, 1939–1945—Regimental histories—Great Britain. 9. World War,
1939–1945—Regimental histories—United States. 10. World War, 1939–1945—
Personal narratives. I. Title.

D757.W75 2008
940.54'2135534—dc22
                                                          2007038943

This book is dedicated to the men of the
British 6th and U.S. 17th Airborne Divisions,
and to those who delivered them
to their drop zones and landing zones.

CONTENTS

PREFACE

When Kevin Shannon and I wrote *One Night in June* (Crowood, 2000), we told the story of Operation Tonga, the initial assault by the British 6th Airborne Division into Normandy, through the eyes of those who were there. We used only enough of our own words as were necessary to allow the narrative to flow.

The story of Operation Varsity has been briefly told within a few books. Only one has been dedicated entirely to what still remains the largest single-lift airborne operation in history. That book, *Die Luftlandung und das Kriegsende im Gebiet der Städte Hamminkeln und Wesel* (1997) by Johann Nitrowski, has not been translated into English, however.

My aim with this book was to use the same anecdotal format as in *One Night in June*. To that end, I have received more than fifty accounts from American, British, and Canadian veterans and been granted permission to use others published in books. The men who wrote the accounts were paratroopers, gliderborne troops, glider pilots, RAF and troop carrier crews, and war correspondents. Their words add poignancy and vividness to the account of this operation. Veterans from both sides of the Atlantic have given me much encouragement to write the book. For those veterans of the 17th Airborne Division, I have a particular gratitude. Several of them have told me how tired they are of having to tell people that they *did* see combat—in the hell of the Ardennes and then in the Rhineland. As far as possible, I have compared and contrasted the words of eyewitnesses with those of others and also with the official pre- and postoperation reports.

In certain cases, the actions of some units are described in more detail than others. I would have liked to have given the same consideration to all units but was prevented from doing so because reports or personal accounts for some units do not exist or have been unobtainable. Where greater detail does exist, this was generally made possible by contributors who supplied unit reports as well as their own accounts. Unless otherwise stated, all quotes are from personal accounts that I received.

This book begins with chapters on planning, training, and getting airborne for the operation, after which the experiences of each division on 24 March have been separated into two sections, with the order of the narrative following that in which the various divisional units landed. The divisions worked largely in isolation, although there were both planned and unplanned linkups. I have therefore chosen this method of relating the events in an attempt to add clarity to the story and to paint a picture of each division's endeavors. Finally, the actions of both divisions on 25 March are brought together in one chapter.

Operation Varsity was the result of many months of planning and involved the delivery behind enemy lines of two airborne divisions. In one day, two Medals of Honor, a Victoria Cross and the British Army's first and only Conspicuous Gallantry Medal were won.

ACKNOWLEDGMENTS

My thanks, first of all, to the veterans and relatives who have provided personal accounts of the operation: Ronald "Andy" Anderson, Edgar Bartlett, Charlie Bentley (for his father's story), Everett Bullard, Norbert Burger, Bob Butcher, Denis Cason, John Chester, Capt. Hugh Clark MC, Harry Clarke, Simon Cooper (for his grandfather's account), Michael Corboy, Jake Dalton, Ellis "Dixie" Dean, Thomas E. Denham, Jan de Vries, Eugene G. Dickens, Richard Dunkley, Ted Eaglen MM, Patrick Edmonds, Denis Edwards, Jack Finch, Charles O. Gordon, Michael Ham, H. G. "Sam" Hardy, Andrew Harper (for his father's account), Bill Highfill, Howard Holloway, Irvin Holtan, Eugene Howard, Stan Jarvis MBE, John Johnson, John Kern, Joe Kitchener, John G. Kormann, Brian Latham, Clive Laurence-Peckham (for his father's account), Tony Leake, John Love DFC, Bill Lusk, Dr. John Magill Jr., Steve Marande (for his father's account), Robert W. Mortimer, Robert F. Nicholls, George Nye, John O'Grady, William O'Rourke, Des Page, Bob Patterson, Gordon Procter, James "Joe" Rheinberger, William R. Scurlock, Arthur Shackleton, Mrs. Barbara Slater (for her husband's account), Alan Stredwick, James E. "Jimmy" Taylor, George Theis, David Tibbs MC, Bill Tom, Vespucci B. "Butch" Traini, Barend "Barry" Volkers, Fred Waggett, Tom Wallis, Ken Ward, Peter Young, and Louis J. Zoghby.

For providing tireless support, as well as answering numerous questions and queries, my thanks go to Denis Edwards, Randy Hils, Michael

Ingrisano, Tony Leake, and Joe Quade. Several authors graciously allowed me to quote from their books: George F. Cholewczynski, Peter Harclerode, Randy Hils, Michael Ingrisano, Patrick K. O'Donnell, and Ron Tucker. My thanks also to George Stefanski and Bonnie Hicks, from the Airborne and Special Forces Museum in Fayetteville, North Carolina; the Reading Room staff at the National Archives, Kew, Richmond, and Lt. Col. Derek Armitage at the Museum of Army Flying, Middle Wallop; Chris Anderson, Editor of *World War II* magazine, for Frank J. O'Rourke's account; the BBC for permission to use the reports of Richard Dimbleby and Stanley Maxted; David Brook for permission to quote from *The Eagle*; Charles O. Gordon for permission to quote from his report; and Capt. J. Knox (Retd.) for permission to quote from the Royal Ulster Rifles' History.

CHAPTER 1

The British 6th and U.S. 17th Airborne Divisions

Go, go, go!" the jumpmaster yelled, placing a helping hand on the back of each man, as the two sticks of heavily loaded U.S. 513th Parachute Infantry Regiment (PIR) troopers launched themselves out the two doors of the Curtiss C-46 Commando and into airborne history.

The jerk of the canopy opening was a reassuring sensation. Not so reassuring was the storm of small-arms and artillery fire that roared up from the ground. The troopers had already been shaken around in their aircraft by the buffeting of antiaircraft shells striking the fuselage. One engine was burning, and the pilot was fighting to keep his aircraft flying straight and level. Now the troopers were descending through a maelstrom. "Hitting dirt" had never seemed such a wished-for conclusion.

The troopers were part of the U.S. 17th Airborne Division, and this was their first combat jump. Some fifteen minutes earlier, fellow U.S. troopers from the 507th PIR and others from the British 6th Airborne Division had landed two miles to the southwest and northwest, respectively. All these men, along with their gliderborne comrades had trained hard for this moment, and they were ready to do their job: seize, clear, and secure German-held positions east of the River Rhine. It was Saturday, 24 March 1945, and Operation Varsity was under way.

The previous year, the British and American Armies had not managed to cross the Rhine, though it was not for want of trying. Over three days, 17–19 September 1944, the greater part of three Allied airborne divisions, 1st British and U.S. 82nd and 101st, had landed along a line of three Dutch towns, Eindhoven, Nijmegen, and Arnhem. Their job was to capture and hold a series of bridges and thus create a corridor for the British XXX Corps to drive a wedge through the German occupying force, thereby opening a route into the industrial heartland of the Ruhr.

By the end of August 1944, the German Army was fighting on the defensive along a general line of the Rivers Roer and Maas between the Dutch towns of Nijmegen and Duren. Earlier in the month, XXX Corps had made a significant advance from the Albert and Escault Canals, between Antwerp and Maastricht, north toward Nijmegen. As Chester Wilmot describes it in *The Struggle for Europe*, "With this one sabre stroke Montgomery intended to cut Holland in two, outflank the Siegfried Line and establish Second Army beyond the Rhine on the northern threshold of the Ruhr."

On the night of 26 September the "sabre" was broken, as less than 3,000 weary members of the 1st Airborne Division, the British Glider Pilot Regiment, and Polish Independent Brigade Group were evacuated across the Rhine near to Arnhem. Close to 12,000 had arrived by glider or parachute.

Ground forces continued to pressure the German Army; XXX Corps cleared the area south of the Maas and Waal Rivers and made a successful amphibious assault on Walcheren. This opened up the valuable port of Antwerp and created the chance for British 21st Army Group to start a buildup of troops and supplies.

Then, on 1 October, the Germans launched a major counterattack against the XXX Corps salient: 2nd SS Panzer Corps from the north, 12th SS Corps from the west, and 2nd Parachute Corps from the east across the Groesbeek Heights. The offensive was heavily defeated after five days by Allied firepower.

The 21st Army Group began a series of assaults against the northern flank of the Siegfried Line in an effort to clear the Germans from the west bank of the River Rhine between Nijmegen and Dusseldorf. At the same time, Lt. Gen. Omar N. Bradley moved his 9th Army to his left flank with the intention of crossing the Rhine between Emmerich and Wesel. A close study of this area showed that it was eminently suitable for an airborne operation.

Two months later, German troops commanded by Generalfeld-marschall Gerd von Rundstedt, broke through Allied lines in the Belgian Ardennes. Thus began the offensive that has gone down in military history as the battle of the Bulge.

The situation soon required further support, and the Allies decided that the British 6th and U.S. 17th Airborne Divisions would be committed. The former had been rotated out of Europe in the first week of September, after fighting through Normandy since June. The latter, except for members of the 507th PIR, had not yet seen combat. As they entered the cauldron of the Ardennes, little did the men of these divisions know that within a month of being withdrawn, they would be flying, and jumping, into another hell.

1ST ALLIED AIRBORNE ARMY

Following the Normandy campaign, Eisenhower established the 1st Allied Airborne Army (FAAA), which was commanded by Lt. Gen. Lewis H. Brereton and had two corps: the British I Corps commanded by Lt. Gen. Frederick A. H. "Boy" Browning and then Maj. Gen. Richard S. Gale, and the U.S. XVIII Corps commanded by Maj. Gen. Matthew B. Ridgway. The former comprised the 1st and 6th Airborne Divisions and the latter the 13th, 17th, 82nd, and 101st Divisions.

6TH AIRBORNE DIVISION

The 6th Airborne Division began to take shape in May 1943, under the command of Major General Gale. For the previous twelve months, Gale had been deputy director of air in the War Office. Before that, he had commanded the 1st Parachute Brigade. He therefore brought a lot of experience to his new post, and he looked forward to the job of pulling together the constituent parts of his new division: two parachute brigades, an airlanding brigade, and divisional troops from the Royal Armoured Corps, Royal Artillery, Royal Army Medical Corps, Royal Signals, Royal Electrical and Mechanical Engineers, Royal Engineers, Royal Army Ordnance Corps, Intelligence Corps, and Corps of Military Police.

Delivered to Normandy on D-Day, 6 June 1944, the 6th Airborne fought determinedly through the ensuing campaign. The intensive fighting took its toll. The 3rd Parachute Brigade's 1st Canadian Battalion lost twenty-four of its twenty-seven officers. In the Airlanding Brigade, Company D of the 2nd Battalion, the Oxfordshire and Buckinghamshire Light Infantry, only 40 men out of 180 came home.

After reequipping and reinforcing, the division was soon ready again for action, this time with some new leadership. Maj. Gen. Eric Bols DSO replaced Richard Gale, who had been promoted to command the 1st Airborne Corps and act as Ridgway's deputy. Brig. Hugh Bellamy took command of the Airlanding Brigade.

Airborne Troops

The 6th Airborne Division's airborne commitment for Varsity was the 3rd and 5th Parachute Brigades and the Airlanding Brigade.

3rd and 5th Parachute Brigades

The 3rd Parachute Brigade was commanded by Brig. James Hill DSO MC, who had been a regular soldier since before the war and had seen action in France, where he was awarded the Military Cross (MC), and in North Africa, where he commanded 1st Parachute Battalion and won the Distinguished Service Order (DSO). His brigade comprised the 1st Canadian, the 8th (raised from 13th Battalion, the Royal Warwickshire Regiment), and the 9th (10th Battalion, the Essex Regiment) Parachute Battalions.

The 5th Parachute Brigade's commanding officer, Brig. Nigel Poett, had been a regular officer with the Durham Light Infantry. His three parachute battalions were the 7th (raised from 10th Battalion, the Somerset Light Infantry), the 12th (10th Battalion, the Green Howards), and the 13th (2nd/4th Battalion, the South Lancashire Regiment).

Airlanding Brigade

The Airlanding Brigade consisted of three gliderborne battalions: 2nd Battalion, the Oxfordshire and Buckinghamshire Light Infantry (OBLI), and 1st Battalion, the Royal Ulster Rifles (RUR), both formerly of 1st Airborne Division; and 12th Battalion, the Devonshire Regiment (Devons). Its third CO, Brig. Hugh Bellamy DSO, took up his post in February 1945.

Divisional Troops
In addition to its airborne elements, the 6th Division had further support.

6th Airborne Armoured Reconnaissance Regiment
The commitment of the 6th Airborne Armoured Reconnaissance Regiment (AARR) was its 4.2-inch Mortar Troop and two tank troops of eight American Locusts, instead of the usual British Tetrarch.

Royal Artillery (RA)
The Royal Artillery contingent in the Airlanding Brigade had 6-pounder antitank guns in the support companies of each battalion, but it was also given extra support.

The 53rd (Worcestershire Yeomanry) Airlanding Light Regiment RA (Light Regiment) was reorganized from three to two batteries, each of six 75-millimeter howitzers. In addition, for Varsity, it was also responsible for two 25-pounders, which would fire colored smoke to mark targets for supporting fighter aircraft.

Two of the 2nd Airlanding Anti-Tank Regiment RA's three batteries, the 3rd and 4th Airlanding Anti-Tank, went by air. Each battery had four troops, of which three had 6-pounders and the fourth 17-pounders.

The 2nd Forward Observation Unit RA (2FOU) consisted of a headquarters and three sections, No. 3 manned by Royal Artillery personnel and Nos. 5 and 6 by Royal Canadian Artillery personnel. Nos. 3 and 5 Sections were assigned to the 3rd and 5th Parachute Brigades and No. 6 Section to the Airlanding Brigade. In addition, four fire liaison parties worked alongside the supporting army artillery. The unit was equipped with jeep-mounted sound ranging, radar and radios, and man-pack radio sets.

Air Support Communication was organized through two Forward Visual Control Posts (FVCPs), with a third as a spare.

Royal Army Medical Corps (RAMC)
The 224th and 225th Parachute Field Ambulances RAMC supported the two parachute brigades, respectively. Each ambulance contained a headquarters, two surgical teams, and four clearing sections. The 195th supported the Airlanding Brigade and was organized along similar lines.

In addition, each divisional battalion was assigned a medical officer and platoon.

Royal Engineers (RE)

The usual assignment of the 3rd and 591st Parachute Squadrons RE was to the respective parachute brigade. For Varsity, the 3rd provided one troop and the 591st two, one of which went in by glider in support of the coup de main.

Royal Army Service Corps (RASC)

The 716 Light Composite Company RASC was the unit responsible for collecting and distributing stores and ammunition to the division. Its two gliderborne platoons went on Varsity. Its motorized transport consisted of jeeps, each with two trailers, and Bren carriers.

Royal Signals

Members of the Royal Signals unit's No. 1 Company worked at divisional headquarters while those of No. 2 Company were posted throughout the division, providing wireless and line communications between the brigades and headquarters.

17TH AIRBORNE DIVISION

The men who would become the 17th Airborne Division arrived at Camp Mackall, North Carolina, where they were placed under the command of Maj. Gen. William M. "Bud" Miley. Like his British counterpart, Miley was an experienced paratroop commander who had followed the traditional route of army service. In 1940, he was given command of the 501st Parachute Battalion, thus becoming the first American officer to command a designated airborne unit. After time with his battalion in Panama, he returned to the States in 1942 to take charge of the 503rd PIR. Three months later, he was promoted to the command of the 1st Parachute Brigade. He served for a short time as assistant division commander of the 82nd Airborne Division before taking command of the 17th.

The constituent units of the 17th were somewhat different from those of the 6th. At the time of its first review in England, the division comprised two parachute infantry regiments, two glider infantry regiments, four artillery units, engineers, medics, ordnance, and signals.

The fighting and the conditions in the Ardennes had been brutal and bitter. General Miley sums it up in the foreword to his report on Varsity, "17th Airborne Historical Report of Operation Varsity":

> The Division had just completed the most rigorous campaign the American Army had ever fought, casualties had been so heavy that some rifle companies had less than 40 men of their original strength and some were without officers. The Division was about 40,000 officers and men under strength. . . . Much equipment had been lost or turned in and the remainder was in need of complete overhaul.

The decision was made to completely reorganize the division with new tables of organization and equipment—i.e., its mission, capabilities, and structure were changed. For Varsity, it was fielded in three combat teams, two parachute and one glider, with additional supporting artillery plus the existing signals, engineers, and medical units.

507th Combat Team
507th Parachute Infantry Regiment

The 507th Parachute Infantry Regiment (PIR) was assigned to the 17th Airborne Division in the post-Ardennes reorganization, and until that event, it was the only unit of the 17th to have seen action. It was activated in 1942 at Camp Toccoa, Georgia, under the command of Lt. Col. George V. Millett Jr. After jump training at Fort Benning, the regiment was assigned to the 1st Airborne Brigade. The regiment arrived in England in March 1944 and was attached to the 82nd Airborne Division for the invasion of Europe.

Much has already been written on the fate of American paratroopers during the drop into Normandy. Suffice it to say that the 507th was scattered over an area some twenty miles wide. Lieutenant Colonel Millett was taken prisoner on 8 June. Once his capture had been ascertained, General Ridgway, then CO of the 82nd, passed command of the 507th to Col. Edson Raff, who had fought through to Ridgway's position. A veteran of Operation Torch when he led the 509th PIR, Raff led the 507th ("Raff's Ruffians") through the remainder of the war.

464th Parachute Field Artillery Battalion
The 464th Parachute Field Artillery Battalion (PFAB) arrived in the divisional area on 14 March. It had four batteries of 75-millimeter howitzers.

513th Combat Team
513th Parachute Infantry Regiment
The CO of the 513th Parachute Infantry Regiment, Col. James W. Coutts, was the former assistant commandant of the Fort Benning Parachute School. In March 1944, the 513th was relieved from assignment to the 13th Airborne Division and formally assigned to the 17th.

466th Parachute Field Artillery Battalion
As with its counterpart, the 466th Parachute Field Artillery Battalion (PFAB) also had four batteries of 75-millimeter howitzers.

194th Combat Team
194th Glider Infantry Regiment
The reorganization placed the remnants of the 193rd Glider Infantry Regiment (GIR) and the 550th Airborne Infantry Battalion (activated in Panama in 1941 as America's first airborne battalion and attached to 17th Airborne for the Ardennes campaign) as the third battalion of the 194th GIR (Companies G, H, I, K, L, and M). The 194th's CO, Col. James R. Pierce, who had been with them from the start, remained in command. The 193rd's executive officer, Maj. David P. Schorr, now became XO in the 194th.

681st Glider Field Artillery Battalion
The 681st Glider Field Artillery Battalion (GFAB) also had 75-millimeter howitzers and was increased to three batteries. It was to support the 194th.

680th Glider Field Artillery Battalion
The 680th GFAB was also increased to three batteries and was converted onto the 105-millimeter howitzer. It was to provide general support and answer any specific calls from the 3rd Battalion of the 513th.

155th Anti-Aircraft Battalion

The 155th Anti-Aircraft Battalion (AAB) fielded four batteries to support the three infantry battalions. Batteries A, B, and C were equipped with British 6-pounders while E had .50-caliber machine guns and 57-millimeter antitank guns. It was one of three heavy weapons batteries. Ten days before the operation, Batteries B and C each gave up one 6-pounder to be replaced with a 75-millimeter recoilless rifle. According to Cpl. Eugene Howard of Battery C:

> [The 75-millimeter] looked a lot like a fancy bazooka. It had a 7-foot-long rifled barrel mounted on a yoke, with a pin on the bottom of the yoke to fit onto a .50-caliber machine gun tripod. The rifle weighed about 175 pounds and the tripod weighed about 65 pounds.
>
> The gun was fitted with a new electronic sighting device that made it more accurate than the sight on the 57-millimeter [recoilless rifle]. In one respect it was like a bazooka: When the gun fired, a blaze of hot gases came out the rear of the gun with an equal force to the projectile coming out of the muzzle. It had an effective range of about 1,500 yards.
>
> The jeep was modified to carry the gun. The tripod mount was secured to the floor of the back section of the jeep. A cradle for the barrel was welded to the front bumper of the jeep. One of the advantages of the gun was that it could be fired from the jeep. It could even be fired with the jeep moving. Since we did not have to pull the 57-millimeter we would get a jeep trailer to haul ammunition. This meant we could haul more ammunition than we could for the 57-millimeter.

The 155th as a whole was seen as the 17th's heavy weapons battalion. It had enormous firepower and could lay down a tremendous field of covering, or attacking, fire.

517th Signals Company

As in 6th Airborne Division, signals personnel, from the 517th Signals Company, were posted throughout the 17th.

139th Engineer Battalion

The 139th Engineer Battalion was organized in three companies and, unlike its British counterpart, worked independently, although it was involved in similar work, such as cleaning up landing zones (LZs) and drop zones (DZs), mine clearance, obstacle removal, and demolition.

224th Airborne Medical Company

The 224th Airborne Medical Company provided divisionwide medical support but was also supplemented by combat medics, assigned to the various units, and medics-at-large.

9TH TROOP CARRIER COMMAND (TCC)

The U.S. 9th Troop Carrier Command (TCC) provided paratroop transport for both divisions and gliders for the 17th. Activated in England in October 1943 to carry the U.S. 82nd and 101st Airborne Divisions to Normandy, the 9th was initially composed of only six officers, who were still in the United States. Within a short while, a troop carrier wing of three groups was transferred from the 8th Air Force. By the time of the Normandy invasion, it had three wings with a total of thirteen groups. On 1 September 1944, it was reassigned to U.S. Strategic Air Force for administrative control and the 1st Allied Airborne Army for operational control.

Much has been written about the role of the 9th's transport pilots during the Normandy operation. After speaking to British veterans who were carried to Germany by the 9th, I believe that the TCC's pilots were far from incompetent, but rather were held in the highest esteem.

38 AND 46 GROUPS ROYAL AIR FORCE
TRANSPORT COMMAND

Transport Command was formed in 1943. The function of 38 and 46 Groups was to deliver the 6th Airborne Division by parachute and glider, and then resupply it.

The origin of 38 Group was as No. 38 Wing, which was formed in January 1942 for army and RAF training and operations and put under the command of Group Captain Sir Nigel Norman with its headquarters at RAF Netheravon. Less than two years later, the role of the airborne forces had developed enough for the wing to be redesignated as a group, with Air Vice Marshall L. N. "Holly" Hollinghurst in command. The group comprised ten squadrons, which were based on five airfields.

The second group, 46, was formed under Transport Command in January 1944, with its headquarters at Harrow on the Weald. Because 38 Group had operational control, an advanced headquarters for 46 Group was set up in Netheravon. This group comprised six squadrons, which all flew the Douglas C-47 Dakota.

THE GLIDER PILOT REGIMENT (GPR)

The Glider Pilot Regiment (GPR) provided the transport for the Airlanding Brigade. Formed in 1942 with one battalion, the GPR was an all-volunteer regiment, with its headquarters and training depot at Tilshead on Salisbury Plain. Its members came from regiments throughout the army and had been trained to fly and to fight. The regiment's second commanding officer, Lt. Col. George S. Chatterton, described his men as "total soldiers." As Major Chatterton, he was second in command to Lt. Col. John F. Rock, a former Royal Engineer. When the 2nd Battalion was formed, Chatterton was promoted to lieutenant colonel as its CO. Rock was fatally injured in a night-flying accident in September 1943, and Chatterton became the new CO, with the title of commander glider pilots.

In January 1943, the regiment was formed into wings, squadrons, and flights. Each wing corresponded with a lightly armed infantry battalion. Eventually there were seven squadrons, each with four operational flights and a headquarters flight. Six squadrons flew the Airspeed Horsa, and the seventh the mighty General Aircraft Hamilcar. The lowest rank held by a trained member of the GPR was sergeant, and every aircraft commander was, at the very least, a staff sergeant.

The GPR had taken great losses in Operation Market Garden around Arnhem. At the roll call that followed the regiment's return to England, Claude Smith reports in *The History of the Glider Pilot Regiment*, "it was found that 229 members had been killed and 469 wounded or made prisoners of war. This appeared to be a deathblow to the Regiment for the recruiting and necessary flying training of so many replacements looked like being an impossibility."

All of these airborne troops and crews would be brought together, and would train hard, for what would become history's largest single-lift airborne landing.

CHAPTER 2

Planning for Varsity

Following the Allies' success in the Ardennes, the advance toward the Rhine continued, and Montgomery's plan was to establish a firm bridgehead in the Emmerich-Wesel area and, as he put it, "to thrust into the northern plains of Germany." Staff at FAAA prepared plans for operations that, they hoped, would assist this continued advance: Varsity, supporting Montgomery's crossing opposite Wesel; Choker II, to support Lt. Gen. Alexander M. Patch's 7th Army's crossing at Worms; and Naples II, in support of Bradley's now-intended crossing between Cologne and Bonn.

As early as the previous November, the first Planning Staff Study for the operation that would be code-named Varsity had been published and distributed. The operation was planned for late January. Naturally, the Ardennes offensive put this on hold. As things stood by the end of January, however, Naples II was abandoned, and all efforts were concentrated on the remaining two operations.

Brereton had given Richard Gale the responsibility for the planning of Varsity and had also made him the provisional operation commander. This decision did not sit well with Montgomery and Gen. Miles Dempsey, commander in chief of the British 2nd Army. They insisted that Ridgway should be in command. Eisenhower added his voice to this, during a brief tour that included Ridgway, by informing him of the plans for Varsity and Choker II and saying that it was his wish that Ridgway command both operations. It was then Ridgway's turn to be uneasy. He preferred Gale to have oversight of Varsity so that he himself could concentrate on Choker II. He continued to try to have himself relieved of this command and handed over all the planning to Gale. It was all to no avail. (On 22 March, however, Choker II became redundant with the crossing of the Rhine at Mainz.)

The original intention for Varsity was to launch it simultaneously with Plunder, the river crossing. Dempsey was all for the airborne phase following the ground phase. Montgomery concurred. They also decided that a third airborne division would be added, prompting the addition of the U.S. 13th, an inexperienced division only recently arrived in France. (As the problem with aircraft resources became clear later, the 13th, as the least experienced American division, was stood down.)

On 14 February, Ridgway met with Dempsey, who gave him a broad outline of the overall plan to cross the Rhine. Dempsey also presented Ridgway with a prepared airborne plan, rather than seek the advice of the experienced airborne commander. This did nothing to endear the British general to his American counterpart, who strongly believed that Dempsey's lack of aggressiveness had been one of the reasons for the failure at Arnhem.

The area chosen for the operation has seen little change. It is flat agricultural land that forms part of the Rhine floodplain and is dominated by a feature known as the Schnepfenberg. Standing some 100 feet in height, the Schnepfenberg lies opposite the point at which British XII Corps crossed the river and is topped by the thick Diersfordter Forest. Through the wood runs the main road from Wesel to Rees and Emmerich. The River Issel runs along the eastern edge of the landing area. Though not a particularly wide river, the Issel's steep banks were a natural tank trap.

A daylight landing into the heart of a defended area would, of course, limit any element of surprise. The fact that the enemy was expecting landings from the air was well known, however. Indeed, the overall planning of the operation had been greatly influenced by a German document that had come into the Allies' possession in December 1944. This was an appreciation of the mistakes made in Operation Market Garden. The document highlighted the failure to put down the maximum force possible on 17 September, slowness in building up forces following the first lift, keeping to the same route in resupply missions and a concern to over-protect the immediate drop zone area rather than put pressure on German forces. This last failure allowed the Germans to concentrate troops and organize rapid counterattacks. Following their findings, they put measures into place that would seek out areas most likely to be chosen for large-scale airborne landings. Antiaircraft and mortar defenses would be concentrated on these areas. Air raid precautions would be improved and new mobile patrols trained for antiairborne defense and capable of mobilization at twenty minutes' notice would be created.

Taking note of the points raised in the captured document, the Allies decided not to use Pathfinder troops, as in Normandy and Holland. Careful study of the photographic reconnaissance of the area showed that suitable landing and drop zones were available adjacent to the immediate objectives. In an attempt to disperse the enemy's attention and fire, the Allies chose ten zones: seven for the 6th and three for the 17th.

Following Varsity, further evidence of German intelligence of the anticipated landing was gathered during the interview of the captured CO of the 84th Infantry Division, Generalmajor Heinz Fiebig.

> [He] claimed that the Germans were not unaware of our preparations for an airborne operation in support of the Rhine crossings and appreciated that no fewer than four allied airborne divisions were available, although he confessed he had been badly surprised by the sudden advent of two complete divisions in this particular area, and throughout the interrogation reiterated the shattering effect of such immensely superior forces on his already badly depleted troop, which did not number more than 4,000 in all.

Fiebig had no exact advance information about times or landing and drop zones, although he had fully appreciated the likelihood of a landing somewhere in his area. He rather expected the landing farther from the Rhine, in the area east of the River Issel, and thought it would take place either at dusk before the land assault or else simultaneously with it.

For the first time, glider troops would be landing on unsecured zones. For this reason, the gliders were to execute tactical landings. The

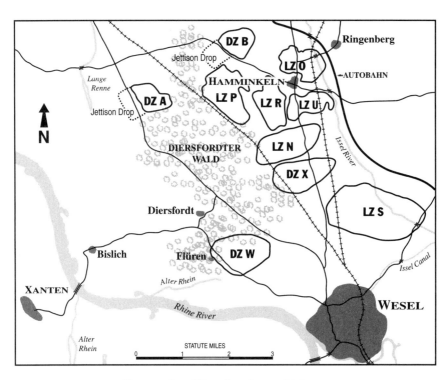

Operation Varsity Assault Area

idea had been proposed by Colonel Chatterton and required the use of a number of smaller areas into which individual groups of gliders would land. The intention was to confuse the defenders about the direction from which the main attack would come. Further, to enable troops to capture their objectives in the shortest time, gliders would land as close as possible.

The 6th Airborne would be required to land on the northern edge of the Diersfordter, on the outskirts of the village of Hamminkeln and beside two road bridges across the Issel Canal. The parachute brigades would take care of the first area.

On 6 March, Major General Bols briefed his brigade and battalion commanders at Bulford. Using a large-scale model and photographs of the landing area, Bols pointed out the task of each brigade. Lt. Col. Napier Crookenden, CO of 9th Parachute Battalion, writes in *Airborne at War*: This briefing "sent us all away . . . in a cheerful and confident mood. [We] . . . were also privately delighted by the way in which our own brigadier, James Hill, had explained his plan and tasks, stealing the show by his decisive and eloquent delivery."

As reported in Peter Harclerode's *Go to It: The Illustrated History of the 6th Airborne*, Brig. James Hill was given a choice of drop zones: "a small DZ . . . located in a clearing . . . amongst enemy positions manned by German parachute troops . . . [or] a more ideal DZ some three miles away but with the prospect of fighting all the way to our objective. The choice was simple—land on top of the objective."

Two days later, Brigadier Hill took Crookenden and Lt. Col. Paul Gleadell, CO of the Devons, to a briefing at 17th Airborne headquarters in Rheims. Crookenden met Colonel Miller of the 513th's 2nd Battalion, whose final position would be near to his own. The two men arranged where and how they would meet up after the landing: "It had been a good day," says Crookenden, "and we were impressed by the Americans."

The Airlanding Brigade would secure Hamminkeln and capture two road bridges and one railway bridge.

In a repeat of the initial landing at Normandy, the Oxfordshire and Buckinghamshire Light Infantry's (OBLI) Company B and the Royal Ulster Rifles' (RUR) Company D would execute a coup de main, landing on the bridges. As Lt. Hugh Clark, a new arrival in the OBLI, describes it:

The gliders allotted to our company, each with a chalk number, were Nos. 1 to 8. No. 17 Platoon [No. 1 glider] commanded by Jimmy Cochrane MC, No. 18 Platoon [No. 2
glider] commanded by Bob Preston, and No. 19 Platoon [No.
3 glider] commanded by myself were to land on the east bank
of the river as close to the bridge as possible. Our task was to
take the bridge and form a small bridgehead. No. 16 Platoon
[No. 4 glider] commanded by Jack Trafford would land on
the west bank.

The plan was to fly in pairs, and the company was in the
lead gliders in a column of 440 British gliders. We were told
in the briefing that although there were a number of German
antiaircraft guns in the landing area, we need not worry, as
what the British artillery did not take out the RAF would.
The whole tone of the briefing filled us with confidence. The
company was to fly from the nearby Gosfield airfield.

The four remaining gliders were to land in a field on the west side
closer to the Hamminkeln road. The company commander, Maj. Gilbert
Rahr, would be in No. 5 glider, his second in command, Captain
Nicholson, in No. 6; and two groups of engineers in Nos. 7 and 8. These
last two gliders would be carrying explosives to mine the bridge after
capture.

The remainder of the RUR would take and hold the station area
and level crossing and create a defensive perimeter linking all three of
the battalion's objectives. The OBLI would concentrate on the area of
the road junction north of Hamminkeln, the railway bridge and an
adjoining group of farm buildings. Links were to be made with the
Devons, in Hamminkeln, and troops of the 5th Parachute Brigade. The
Devons were to seal off Hamminkeln, to prevent any movement in or
out, and then seize and hold the village.

The town of Wesel and its environs would be the main objective of
the 17th. The parachute regiments were to drop to the south and east of
the Schnepfenberg and secure the area east of Diersfordt. The gliderborne elements were to land to the north of Wesel. Tasks included seizing a bridge over the Issel, protecting the right flank of the landing, and

establishing contact with the British 1st Commando Brigade, which should by then have captured and secured Wesel.

Throughout the planning, one of the overriding factors was the single delivery of the three airborne divisions. For the protection of the ground forces, it was out of the question to extend the landing over two days. It was as late as 5 March before the planners knew they had the capacity to do this, and that capacity could not stretch to three divisions. They decided to drop the 13th and reassign it to Choker II.

A total of twenty-three airfields, eleven in England and twelve in the Paris region, would be used. The plan was that from England, the 38 and 46 Groups would tow all 6th Airborne Division's gliders. This meant that U.S. aircraft would be needed to carry the division's paratroopers. The task was given to the 61st, 315th, and 316th Troop Carrier Groups (TCGs). The first two groups had previously carried British 1st Airborne paratroopers to Holland as part of Operation Market Garden. From the French airfields, TCGs would carry the 17th Airborne Division in Douglas C-47s, Curtiss C-46s, and WACO CG-4As.

There were enough Horsa and Hamilcar gliders to carry the 6th Airlanding Brigade, but the RAF could provide only 320 towing aircraft. This was not enough. The matter was taken up with Major General Ridgway and Air Vice Marshall J. R. Streatfield CBE, CO of 38 Group. As a result, the number of towing aircraft was increased to 440. This involved raising the squadron unit establishment, the number of operational aircraft, from twenty-four to thirty-four, and bringing in twenty aircraft from 38 Group's Operational Refresher Training Unit (ORTU). Crews that had just completed courses at heavy conversion units, learning to fly bombers, plus a fast-track two-week glider-towing course were tasked to fly the ORTU aircraft on the operation. The crew strength of each squadron was also increased to thirty-one by keeping tour-expired crews on the active list. Additionally, 46 Group used some ORTU aircraft.

The 9th Troop Carrier Command (TCC) had available 1,264 C-47s, 117 C-46s, and 1,922 CG-4As. In round terms, the C-46 was equal to two C-47s. The final agreement for the 17th Airborne was 226 C-47s and 72 C-46s for the paratroops, and 906 CG-4As towed by 610 C-47s for the airlanding units. The vast majority of the gliders would be double-towed, a technique that had been used in Burma the previous year, with mixed results.

In total, 2,942 aircraft—1,819 U.S. and 1,123 RAF—carrying some 8,000 men of the 6th Airborne and some 9,000 of the 17th, would lift off for Germany. The sight of this huge armada would have a deep effect on the men who saw it from their gliders and paratroop transports.

One month before the landing, the RAF and the U.S. 9th Air Force would undertake an intensive bombing campaign. The intention was to isolate the immediate landing area by cutting communications, road, rail, and telephone, and rendering ground and air reinforcement unworkable. Airfields would also be targeted, particularly the jet-fighter fields in northwest Germany.

Three days before the operation was due to go, air activity would be intensified. Since the Germans knew about the massing of Allied troops on the western bank of the Rhine, any assault would not be a surprise. So the plan was to keep German troops on constant alert, and thus deprived of sleep and rest, through day and night bombing raids on barracks and other military sites within a thirty-mile radius of Wesel. The vast majority of these targets would be well outside the assault area, and therefore not a threat to the airborne divisions, but the idea was to keep German morale as low as possible. In the immediate area, Wesel was an important communications center and therefore heavily defended against airborne assault. The town would be heavily bombed the day before the operation.

Plans were now complete, and those who had worked hard to make sure all possibilities were covered could only hope that their efforts would be justified. Montgomery set the date for Varsity as 24 March, but he wanted to be certain that the operation could be mounted quickly in the event of a breakthrough near Wesel. FAAA told him that it would need a week's notice for this to happen. The issue came to nothing, as the Germans continued to fight hard.

Following the push to the Rhine, the Allies were faced with the remains of the 1st Parachute Army, 84th Infantry Division and their supporting armor, and the 47th Panzer Corps, which had under its command the 116th Panzer and 15th Panzer Grenadier Divisions. On 10 March, the German forces crossed the Rhine, using a heavy rainstorm as cover, and blew the last bridge behind them. At this time, the Allies estimated that the Germans had lost some 40,000 killed and more than 50,000 captured. The armored divisions had also been badly mauled by the intense assault of the combined Allied presence. Estimates of the number of enemy troops occupying the crossing and invasion area vary: 7,500 to 12,000 with 100 to 150 armored fighting vehicles and their crews available in support. More significantly, and proving that the Germans expected an airborne landing, approximately 800 antiaircraft guns were noted in the week running up to the operation.

In overall command was Generaloberst Alfred Schlemm, CO of the 1st Parachute Army. Using what time he had, Schlemm ensured that defensive works were constructed to secure or cover all areas that could be used for waterborne or airborne landings, height advantage, or speeding movement through and beyond the defensive zone. Farmhouses and suitable farm buildings were also turned into strong points.

CHAPTER 3

Training

During the first week of February, Lt. Col. Lyle McAlister and Lt. Col. Edwin Messinger, the 17th Airborne Division's G2 (intelligence) and G3 (operations) officers, were ordered to attend a briefing at FAAA headquarters near Paris. Here they were told the overall plan for Varsity, and details such as units and availability of aircraft and airfields were discussed. The division as a whole began to leave the Our River zone on 10 February, and all units were established in a rest and reorganization center in the Châlons-sur-Marne area four days later.

In an article in the April 2004 issue of *World War II* magazine by Pvt. Francis J. O'Rourke, Mortar Squad, Company C, 1st Battalion, he remembers the changes:

> Some 40 days later, we were pulled out of the Bulge and settled in at a camp outside Châlons-sur-Marne, France, to be reorganized and refitted. As a result of the casualties the division had suffered, the 193rd and 194th Glider Infantry regiments were combined into one regiment, while the 507th and 513th Parachute Infantry regiments received hundreds of replacements from the States to fill out their depleted ranks.

The 6th Airborne Division's training for an airborne crossing of the Rhine had begun in the autumn of 1944. The 3rd Parachute Brigade ran two exercises: Fog on 9 and 10 October and Eve on 21 November.

Exercise Fog should have commenced on the eighth, but it was delayed for twenty-four hours because of poor visibility. The objects of the exercise were to practice in preparation for a large-scale drop on a brigade drop zone, practice movement by night, and practice the evacuation of casualties. The "enemy" was located in and around the Wiltshire village of Shrewton, which the brigade was to seize and hold.

The 1st Canadian Parachute Battalion's Training Company was given the task of acting as the enemy and jumped from Stirlings. Unfortunately, eight casualties were sustained on the jump when the men were given the "Go" at 150 feet.

The brigade emplaned at 1645, in aircraft of the 315th Troop Carrier Group (TCG), which had flown down from its base at Spanhoe to Netheravon. The planes took off at 1700 and were over the drop zone at 1849. The brigade was clear of the drop zone in twenty minutes and headed for the rendezvous. Here Brigadier Hill quickly conferred with his battalion commanders, and then the march to Shrewton began. The men reached the outskirts of the village an hour and a quarter later. Small parties of "enemy" had been encountered on the way but were swiftly dealt with. "Enemy" troops in Shrewton were quickly overcome, and the battalions dug in at their defensive positions.

The following morning, a two-and-a-half-hour route march brought the brigade back to its barracks, where officers and men began a thorough debrief and review.

Exercise Eve was classed as a full rehearsal for a drop over the Rhine. This time the brigade took off from airfields in East Anglia and as before was carried by the 9th Troop Carrier Command (TCC). The drop zone was flat open ground, near the River Thames at Wittenham Clumps near Abingdon, Oxfordshire. No casualties were suffered, and the exercise was considered a great success.

Not all training that autumn went so smoothly. Lt. Delbert Townsend, executive officer, Company A, 1st Battalion, 194th Glider Infantry Regiment (GIR), recalls a fatal training accident that took place three weeks later:

> In preparation for possible commitment across the channel, we continued our small unit and glider training. We used mainly the U.S. CG4A gliders that would carry some thirteen soldiers,

a jeep and four men or a 75-millimeter howitzer and a crew of four. Both a "single tow" and a "double tow" were used in training. As part of our training we were cross training with the British Horsa glider. I completed Parachute School in Camp Forrest, Tennessee, and was not required to take a glider flight for pay purposes. Those individuals who did not complete the jump training in Tennessee were required to participate in a glider flight every three months for pay purposes.

On 12 December 1944, thirty-one members of the 17th Airborne Division (mostly from Company C, 194th Glider Infantry Regiment) gathered at the Greenham Common Air Base for a Horsa glider flight for training and pay purposes. The flight ended in a horrific crash, killing all thirty-one members plus the two pilots.

I personally knew three of the victims quite well. Maj. James Klock was the 194th regimental surgeon. During my early days at Camp Mackall, Major Klock treated me for an allergy to poison oak and kept me from being thrown out of the army. CWO Ira Smith was an assistant adjutant to Capt. William Hunter. Lt. Charles Albury was a platoon leader in Company C, 194th GIR, whom I saw almost on a daily basis.

In his article, O'Rourke also recalls the accident:

There were six gliders sitting in a row on the tarmac when we arrived. Because there were enough of us for seven loads—and I was in the seventh group—I didn't get to fly. Annoyed because it meant I would have to stay over and fly the next day, I went back with the others to the tents and waited.

The company commander called us out and read the names of the guys in the glider. We lost one mortar squad, one machine gun squad, one rifle squad and some from company and battalion headquarters. Together for more than a year, we knew each other as intimately as we knew members of our own families. That night we stripped the beds of the men from the machine gun squad in our barracks and packed up their personal possessions.

A few days later we went by bus to a cemetery outside Oxford to bury those men. Their graves had been dug by German prisoners, who stared at us as we passed. They seemed, as fellow soldiers, to share our sadness.

During January and February, 9th TCC crews were involved in formation flying and glider towing, with some 21,000 hours spent in the former and more than 9,000 hours in the latter. It was further required that all Glider Pilots complete five landings a month.

With the return of the 17th Airborne from the Ardennes, it then became possible to include the troopers in any flying training. Three weeks of intensive training began in March. Due to end on the twentieth, ten days before the operation, with a full-scale rehearsal, the training period instead was terminated on the fifteenth.

The 313th TCG was the only complete group to be involved in joint training. Its acquisition of the Curtiss C-46 Commando meant that its pilots and passengers had to become familiar, in a very short space of time, with this unfamiliar aircraft. The original intention of Gen. Paul Williams was to have two parachute infantry regiments (PIRs) trained on the C-46, but this was not possible. The 313th did not complete its move to Achiet until the tenth, and the pilots were also completing their transition training. So from 15–20 March, the 513th PIR had its familiarization period on the C-46. Cpl. John Magill, a forward observer with the 466th Parachute Field Artillery Battalion (PFAB), describes what the men faced:

The parachute infantry and the artillery forward observers would jump from the two-door C-46, while the parachute field artillery and the parachute support troops would jump from the old workhorse, the single-door C-47. Once the decision was made to jump from the C-46, briefings on the jumping procedures had to be conducted immediately, to be followed by an actual training jump with full field equipment.

The advantages to jumping from the C-46 would be several: More men would leave the plane more quickly by the two doors, creating less spread when we hit the ground. Small units could therefore group up much more readily and keep better visual contact with our own equipment bundle. As a result, the troopers could clear the drop zone of enemy troops and move off on their specific mission or objective. In addition, by using C-46s and C-47s, it meant that our entire division would be dropped within hours, not days.

My reaction to the thought of jumping from the C-46 was keen. The training to exit from the single (right) door of the C-47 had been so intense and so complete that it had become almost second nature to me—I could almost recite it verbatim: "Snap fastener and static line over the left wrist as the jumper shuffles toward the tail. Then, pushing the line, he abruptly turns (right) into the open door. He kicks out with the right leg, ducks his head, grabs his reserve, and counts."

Now the unfortunate men in the left stick of the C-46 would have the snap fastener and static line over the right wrist, would turn into the left door, and with full combat equipment, would try to kick out into the prop blast in the hope of getting a reasonable body position. The seasoned troopers knew that many parachute malfunctions were due to bad body positions on the exit. In combat, a malfunction could be fatal, because the low altitude would almost rule out getting the reserve chute open in time.

Thinking about this drastic change in technique bothered me more than I liked to admit. I knew that a training jump with full equipment from the left door would be rough, but jumping the left door in combat, in the midst of heavy flak, would be much worse. While I struggled with my own internal fears, however, I hid all semblance of the emotion from the young replacements. This was part of the "duty complex"—to help those whose psychological transition was still in the early, precarious stage.

A second innovation was handed the troopers of the 17th. We would use the quick-release parachute harness for the training jump and the subsequent combat jump. The quick-release had several good features. It would allow the jumper to release the chest strap and leg straps simultaneously upon landing. Previously, the jumper had to struggle to release the chest strap, then each of the leg straps, in a time-consuming process. With the quick-release, all straps fit into a circular, metal disk in the chest area. When the trooper hit the ground, he gave the disk a quarter turn and struck it with his hand to release all straps. This could mean precious moments to him, which in combat could mean the difference. The quick-release also reduced the chances of being dragged by a high wind, and it would help somewhat in getting out of a tree, although that was still almost a death sentence in combat. My one fear concerning the new device was a remote one. What if, in the process of leaving the door with full equipment and a bad body position, the shattering opening shock caused the disk to turn 90 degrees and release all the straps that held the jumper?

The day of the practice jump arrived. As Magill recalls:

The jump schedule was released; my section was assigned to the left stick, and we would exit from the left door!!

We had a new radio operator in the section—just a boy, so to speak, barely nineteen years of age. The youngster's concern over the pending training jump was apparent. He had completed only six jumps in his youthful career—the five qualifying jumps and one additional training jump in the States. I continued to be nonchalant about the upcoming venture; to have given evidence of my own misgivings would have placed the young neophyte in a very difficult position.

It was strange to enter the bulkier C-46 from the left side while the other stick entered from the right. The whole routine of standing up and hooking up placed two columns down the center of the plane, each column with its own cable. As the green light flashed over the double doors, men shuffled forward—the right stick gracefully, the left stick much more clumsily. My body position going out the left door was poor; I couldn't seem to get the "left-side kick." The opening shock with 80 pounds of equipment was terrible, delivering a severe injury to the right groin area, but the sight of the billowing chute was most welcome. The division training mission was successful. The 17th Airborne Division was ready!

S.Sgt. J. C. "Jake" Dalton, 1st Battalion, describes the training in this new aircraft:

> While regrouping and getting back in shape physically and mentally, we made a practice jump from C-46 airplanes. All of our jumps prior to this were from C-47s. The C-47 had one door for entry and exit, and that was on the right side of the plane. So all through jump school, prior to actually jumping out of a plane, we used mock-ups that required standing in the door, stepping out, and turning left to face the tail of the plane after exiting.
>
> The C-46 had doors on both sides, so theoretically a planeload of troopers could exit in half the time. If you were in the stick on the left side of the plane, however, you had to remember to do the opposite of what had become rote after about fifteen practice jumps.

S.Sgt. R. L. "Lendy" McDonald notes the positive side of using the C-46, however:

> The practice jump from the C-46 went well. Jumping from both doors greatly reduced the time by jumping two sticks at one time, which kept our landing area shorter in distance. This cut our assembly time.

At the beginning of March, the 6th Airborne took part in Exercise Mush I over eastern England. Pvt. Denis Edwards OBLI had been in the first glider to land at Pegasus Bridge, had fought his way through Normandy, and was now recently returned from the Ardennes. He describes his experiences in *The Devil's Own Luck*:

> In full combat condition my platoon was loaded into a Horsa.... In flight over Cambridge the tug plane developed an engine fault and suddenly we were in real trouble.

The Horsa had half a dozen portholes along either side and I was peering out of one of these to see what was happening. Already we were just a couple of hundred feet above the ground and losing height rapidly. . . . I was horrified to see a passenger train passing from right to left and directly in front of our flight path. I saw the passengers looking up at us as we swept over their heads just a few feet higher than the roofs of the carriages. A few seconds later, we were skidding in to a perfect landing in a field on the outskirts of March in Cambridgeshire.

The local folk treated us like heroes, made us really welcome, took us into their homes and shared their meagre rations with us. When the pubs opened, people were lining up to buy us drinks! We were having such a good time that when our Platoon Officer informed us that transport would shortly be arriving we quickly hatched a plan to allow our unscheduled holiday to continue. Some of the lads went to the outskirts of the town and misdirected the truck drivers. When they finally arrived they were not too pleased with their wild goose chase. I don't recall anyone being put on a "Charge" for these antics.

According to Lt. Hugh Clark, OBLI:

Included in the training was one full-scale divisional flying exercise. We moved to a camp in Essex, where we flew from a nearby airfield. This was my first experience of a glider flight. It was a perfect day and we had a smooth takeoff towed by a Halifax. As I remember, we flew west in a large formation as far as Bristol, when we turned back east. On the flight back toward Essex, we flew right over my parents' house in Hertford. When we arrived over Essex, a mist had come down and we were unable to land, so we flew back to an airfield near Oxford, where we landed and returned to Bulford. The flight had lasted for over three hours. We found out later that the exercise had been a rehearsal for the Rhine crossing.

Although these exercises were second nature to the airborne men, there was one group for whom this was a new experience. The Glider Pilot Regiment (GPR) had suffered grievously during Operation Market Garden, and with the ensuing airborne operation leaving too little time to train new pilots from scratch, RAF pilots were brought in, a total of 1,500 arriving by various routes. Some that I have interviewed regard their posting to the GPR as having been more by foul means than fair. Be that as it may, they all played an important role in the GPR at that time.

Sgt. Pilot Eric Ayliffe had learned to fly in Arizona and was one of these pilots:

> Together with other RAF Pilots I was sent to the HGCU [Heavy Glider Conversion Unit] at RAF Peplow in November 1944. The heaviest plane I had flown to date was a Harvard. The Horsa glider looked gigantic, with its wingspan of 88 feet. After six tows behind a Dakota, I was "converted." Another twenty-eight tows in a Horsa II and five tows in a Hadrian glider, and I was fully trained and almost enjoyed diving onto the airfield.
>
> We then went to Uxbridge and were issued with tropical kit for India. At the last minute, a few of us were taken off the draft. I was sorry to leave my old friends, several of whom had been with me on Course 18 at Falcon Field in Mesa, Arizona.
>
> I was posted to Fargo Camp on Salisbury Plain and spent a very cold December and January training to be an infantry soldier. To my surprise I enjoyed it, especially organizing raids on the nearby American coal dump when our fuel supplies ran low!
>
> At the end of January 1945, I was posted to RAF Broadwell, to F Squadron of the Glider Pilot Regiment, under commanding officer S/Ldr. V. H. Reynolds. I teamed up to fly with Flight Lieutenant Ince, who was in charge of No. 16 Flight. Army and RAF pilots worked, played and trained together during the following weeks and a terrific esprit de corps developed. Most of our time was spent on maneuvers, but we

included eight tows on local flying and four tows on night flying. The night flying was hair-raising as the instrument that
indicated the glider's position in relation to tug aircraft—
colloquially called the "angle of dangle"—was operated by
a piece of elastic running from the nose of the glider to the
tow rope. We found it easier to follow the exhaust ports of the
Dakota. Landing was a different matter; no one was injured but
one crew wrapped a Horsa around a steamroller that had been
left on the perimeter track.

In March 1945 we practiced two Balbos, which meant flying in huge formations, followed by all the gliders landing in
one small space. On 14th March we did our longest tow to
date—two hours.

RAF WO Len Macdonald relates his experiences in the April 1995
issue of *The Eagle*:

Having completed my flying training with the RAF flying
Fairchild PT19 and North American AT6 training aircraft at
No. 3 British Flying Training School, Miami, Oklahoma, it
never was my intention to fly military gliders.

However, fate plays funny tricks and in mid October 1944,
I found myself in the company of some 200 RAF pilots on
parade at 0830 hours on the car park of the Majestic Hotel
in Harrogate. Roll call completed we were addressed thus by
the officer in charge of the parade, who even at this stage, for
the sake of his personal safety, must remain nameless. "You
lot," said he, "you lot have just volunteered to fly gliders." He
said this with a certain amount of relish, happy at being shot
of, at a single stroke, some 200 bods whom neither he nor
the RAF quite knew how to keep gainfully employed at that
time.

Then followed in quick succession a glider course at 21
EFTS on Tiger Moths, Heavy Glider Conversion on Horsas
at 21 HGCU Brize Norton and Operational training at 21
HGCU Brize Norton and Operational training at Hampstead

Norris, which was the ORTU [Operational Refresher Training Unit] for 38 Group RAF.

Apart from the odd run-march and night march armed only with a compass, with the rendezvous at some God-forsaken pub in Berkshire, very little time was spent on turning me into a soldier. Along the way, however, I gained the knowledge that the Tare Weight of the Horsa as flown at Brize Norton (including 2 pilots with parachutes, all seats and modifications carried out BUT less the skid) was 8900 lbs. I also learnt that the maximum permissible payload was 6900 lbs, 100 lbs of which could be carried in the wings. As we never saw parachutes it was comforting to know that a small WAAF might be carried without exceeding the prescribed all-up weight. As the Brize Whitley Tugs were only cleared for towing 15250 lbs I have sometimes wondered what would have happened if we had attempted a take-off with a fully laden Horsa . . . 8900 plus 6900 = 15800 lbs, always less the skid, a small matter of 550 lbs over the permissible all-up weight.

Also at Brize I was taught something that was to prove very useful indeed at a later date. This was the method of loading and evenly distributing the load around the CG Datum Point of the Horsa and also the Hadrian.

Then followed eight weeks at Rivenhall in Essex with A Squadron where I remember more about off-duty trips to Chelmsford (7 up in a small standard saloon) than I do about the actual work on the Camp. Next came a posting to Tarrant Rushton ostensibly to transfer to the Hamilcar. That I never did fly the Hamilcar was probably a blessing in disguise. Tarrant was great fun in early 1945. The flying was straightforward and there were excursions to Blandford, Wimborne, Bournemouth and the "Get Knotted Inn" at Tarrant Keyneston, sometimes known as "The Lover's Knot"; but best of all were the nights in the Nissen huts listening to tales of Sicily, D-Day and Arnhem landings by both sung and unsung heroes of the Regiment. Earlier advice given by RAF Regiment

instructors whilst attending a battle course at Whitley Bay
in August 1944 was both repeated and amplified. The impor-
tance of DCOSF (Down, Crawl, Observe, Sight and Fire) was
heavily underlined.

Sgt. Pilot Brian Latham had been trained at an Empire Training
School. On his return to England, he was posted to Harrogate, in York-
shire, to await further training. Volunteers were sought to be seconded to
the GPR:

Very few volunteered, because we wanted to fly Spitfires and
Mustangs. We were read the riot act and told that if we did
not volunteer, then we would never fly again. So we became
voluntary conscripts and very "Bolshie."

Off then to Bridgnorth, to the RAF Regiment depot. We
were put through weapons training and shown how to dig slit
trenches. This lasted for two weeks, and then we went to Brize
Norton. This was the Heavy Glider Conversion Unit, where
we flew Horsa and Hadrian gliders.

The Hadrian was an American one. It was smaller than the
Horsa and made of steel tubing covered in canvas. The Horsa
was quite large—as big as a Wellington—and made out of
plywood (as was the Mosquito). We were towed by Whitleys.
They were ex-bombers and pretty well used.

We were still in blue and used the sergeants' mess. We were
drilled by the regiment, and the senior regiment man was
RSM Briodie, ex-Irish Guards—a great man.

After two weeks, we went to Hampstead Norris, where we
were towed by the Albemarle, a twin-engine aircraft built by
Armstrong Whitworth. Here we practiced mass landings, but
with not many aircraft. Home then for Christmas leave before
joining my first squadron.

I joined F Squadron, Glider Pilot Regiment, at the beginning of January 1945, at RAF Broadwell, Oxfordshire. Broadwell was a wartime station. Lots of Nissen huts and two
Dakota Squadrons, 512 and 575. Each squadron had fifteen

Dakotas, and we had about twenty Horsas. I was the first RAF pilot to join the squadron and was met at Brize Norton and Bampton station by a squadron truck and delivered to our part of Broadwell. I was shown a hut, and there were two staff sergeant glider pilots huddled over the iron stove with which every hut was equipped. They were very welcoming and insisted on one of them taking me to the mess for a meal. They were Gerry Moorcraft and Geoff Collins. They had been on both the D-Day and Arnhem operations. Gerry had been on the coup-de-main party on Pegasus Bridge. When I got back to the hut, my bed had been made

The following day, I was kitted out in khaki. Of course, we were to keep our RAF uniforms and wear them off the station and for social occasions. However, we were to have our army battle dress fastened up to the neck, khaki stripes to be blancoed, and horror of horrors, army wings to be worn instead of our RAF ones. I asked to see the station commander, a group captain, and told him about these orders, and he told me not to worry, he would sort this out. He did, and we were still to wear collars and ties, blue tapes, and our RAF wings.

More RAF people now joined us, and we were made to train hard for what we knew would be a crossing over the Rhine. The army pilots were determined that we would not be passengers. They took it upon themselves to make us as capable as they were. They were all from other regiments and had volunteered to become glider pilots, and the Glider Pilot Regiment was considered a corps d'elite on a par with commandoes and Special Forces. We were taught to ride motorbikes; drive jeeps, 15-hundredweight trucks, and Bren gun carriers; handle explosives; fire all types of small arms; and be able to act anywhere on a 6-pounder antitank gun. In fact, we were to be able to operate with any of the troops we may carry.

We did 10-mile run marches with Bergen rucksacks. We were dropped at night off trucks in the wilds of Oxfordshire and had to make our way to a rendezvous, with Paras out to stop us. We spent spent hours on the ranges and learned to handle the Horsa under all conditions, night and day.

Now of course, we were treated as operational aircrew. The food was very good in the mess. Eggs and bacon when we had flown. Leave every six weeks. Chocolate, chewing gum, and dried fruit given out with our pay every two weeks. There was always a churn of fresh milk in the dining room, and meal-times were very flexible.

The Dakotas were operating over to the continent and bringing back wounded, so it was a busy place, with aircraft arriving and departing by day and night.

Our off-duty time was often spent in Oxford, and one of the army pilots and I joined a dance class. Coming back in the train was pleasant. We shared the train with Brize Norton people, and the walk back in the dark along the lanes was companionable.

Pilot Officer John Love was also at Harrogate:

Because of the heavy losses at Arnhem, the GPR desperately needed trained pilots. To train replacement pilots for the regiment would take far too long, so they asked for volunteers from the RAF that had, because of the success of the Commonwealth Training Plan, a surplus of fully trained pilots.

I put my name forward and was sent to Glider Training School at Croughton and then to Seighford, where I flew Horsas. This was followed by a week's intensive military training at Bridgnorth. I was then posted to C Squadron at Tarrant Rushton.

Love's first sight of his new aircraft was on 10 February 1945:

My first impression was, "My Gawd, what a size!" However, after a spell at the controls, I was amazed at how easy it was to fly. After half a dozen tows, I went up with my copilot, Sgt. Bill McEwan, a fellow Scot and another volunteer from the RAF. From then until 17 March, we spent our time on ten-minute circuits and bumps. Some light relief came in the form of two mass lifts, on February 25th and 27th, and two final exercises, Riff Raff I and Riff Raff II.

Sgt. Pilot Peter Young would also be flying a Hamilcar:

> I had my first flying lesson in a Hamilcar on 1st February. My instructor was Sgt. Dennis Cason. We managed three tows. Four days later, my logbook records that I flew as second pilot to my friend Sgt. Ken Williams.
>
> On 11th February, the weather was very unpleasant, with a strong wind and low clouds. There was no flying in the morning, and in the afternoon Ken and I with our second pilots were playing snooker when we were called to the flight line.
>
> I was first to fly and completed a stormy circuit and into-wind release. On returning to the flight line, I was told there would be no more flying, as Ken had disappeared off the end of the runway. Later we found that he had hit a tree and been killed by a branch.

The crash inquiry report said that Sergeant Williams was flying with a pilot under training, who took control after takeoff but got into difficulties. The towrope broke and Sergeant Williams instructed the trainee to land the glider in a field. Unfortunately, the pilot overshot the field he had chosen, and after a last-minute tight turn, the glider crashed into a tree near the village of Spettisbury. Williams was killed, and the trainee pilot was injured. Inspection of the Hamilcar showed that its flaps had not been lowered for the landing. Part of the inquiry's conclusion said that the pilot "had been converted onto the Hamilcar after insufficient experience on Horsa."

Flying Officer Gordon Procter corroborates the statement about the amount of training RAF pilots received:

> My training time was seventeen hours in the air. This was accomplished in a period of twenty-four days, spread over six weeks. Not one fully loaded landing prior to Varsity.

S.Sgt. George Nye was a GPR veteran from Normandy. He was involved in providing military training for the RAF pilots at the Iving-hoe Range near Dunstable, Kent, and says:

> The RAF glider pilots were subjected to a strict, hard, and demanding course involving live ammo and explosives, which for them made the course realistic. In the evening, we returned to HQ, and after a shower and meal, a period of question and answer occurred, and we tried to instruct, not scare. Eight hundred RAF GPs had to be put through training, and other courses were set up in the southeast.

Acting Flight Lt. Jack Finch had passed out of the Advanced Flying Unit with an above-average rating. He asked to be posted to operational flying but was sent back to flying school as an instructor. On 30 September 1944, he recalls:

> I was promoted from flying officer to acting flight lieutenant to be flight commander of night flying, and therefore responsible for instructors and pilots undergoing the final stage of their training at No. 3 Advanced Flying Unit. At twenty-one, it was the most responsible task I'd been assigned to and was the brief but utterly enjoyable and memorable part of my instructor task of fourteen months.

But Finch still yearned for operational flying:

> Around 10 October, I was opening flight mail, and one was an invitation for squadron leaders or flight lieutenants to volunteer for operational glider flying overseas. I had heard about gliders being used behind Japanese lines in the Southeast Asia war and assumed that this is what it was. I applied, and it must have been a signal of urgency, as I was posted almost immediately. I was headstrong in those days, and I suppose it was precocious of me not to take into account that I was only acting flight lieutenant!

Over the next four weeks, Finch learned to fly gliders. On 15 November, he was posted to ORTU Hampstead Norris, near Newbury, where he became a victim of a training accident:

> We were doing weapons training, using dummy grenades, to become used to battle noise. One of the grenades had not gone off, and a few of the lads started to throw bricks at it in an attempt to detonate it. This worked, and Bakelite from the casing hit me in the face and my finger was smashed by a ball bearing. I was sent to Newbury Cottage Hospital, where my finger was put in plaster. From there I was transferred to the RAF hospital at Wroughton. As my finger had developed gangrene, it was amputated.

Jack Finch returned to flying duties in February 1945, but he was not selected for the Rhine crossing. Instead, he trained for the expected operation to cross the River Elbe. As several of those pilots with whom he had shared training flew to Germany, Finch traveled to Blakehill Farm to take up a new post as flight commander in N Squadron.

The ground situation of the American glider pilots was given more consideration than in previous operations, and they were issued compasses, entrenching tools, and lightweight sleeping bags. For the majority of pilots, their infantry role remained confined to noncombatant tasks such as guarding prisoners and collecting supplies. But on this operation, there was to be an exception.

The 435th TCG's gliders would be carrying the 3rd Battalion and Regimental HQ Company of the 194th GIR, the two batteries from the 155th Anti-Aircraft Battery (AAB) that would be supporting the 194th and the entire 680th Glider Field Artillery Battalion (GFAB) contingent. In all the reorganization, the 194th was still short one company. Capt. Charles O. Gordon, glider operations officer with the 435th TCG, explains in his report on his pilots' training for their role in Varsity what happened next:

> Gen. William Miley called all group glider pilot operations officers of the 53rd Wing to report to his headquarters. After

being assembled in his private office, Gen. Miley revealed the plans for a new airborne operation to cross the Rhine River at Wesel, Germany. Gen. Miley stated that the 194th Glider Infantry Regiment was in need of an additional infantry company in order to complete their battle plan. He asked for one group to volunteer to take this infantry assignment after landing in the DZ and in so doing, they would receive extensive training by the 194th. I made an immediate decision that the 435th glider pilots could handle this assignment based upon my knowledge of their previous combat experience and the use of various weapons.

Gordon also recalls:

Captain H. K. Lyerly of the 194th was assigned as Liaison Officer to assist me on this mission. Immediately, trucks and personnel of the 194th arrived daily at A-48 [Bretigny] to provide two weeks of infantry training and the use of various weapons including light machine guns, bazookas, rifle grenades, BARS, sub-machine guns, grenades, so forth.

During this period, I had a difficult problem with our group commander, Col. MacNees, because I could not give him any details of operation "Varsity" or the date of the operation or why our glider pilots were involved. I was even threatened with the possibility of court martial. However, Gen. Beach, commander of the 53rd wing, came to my rescue.

There had been plenty of time to train for the inevitable crossing of the Rhine, and it had been used wisely. Both veterans and newcomers felt more confident as they waited to be sent.

CHAPTER 4

Final Preparations

In a letter to his fiancée published in *Valor without Arms*, Sgt. Michael Ingrisano, 440th Troop Carrier Group (TCG), ponders on the future: "Sitting on the threshold of March, I wonder what it has to hold."

For many, like Cpl. Robert Patterson, 2nd Battalion, 513th Parachute Infantry Regiment (PIR), it would be a time of new faces and new friends. After being rotated out of the Ardennes region in February, Patterson had found training difficult because he was not feeling too well. He checked in at the camp hospital and was diagnosed with hepatitis. He was feeling much better after a few days of good food, a comfy bed, nice nurses, and no duty, so on 19 March, he climbed through a window and made his way back to his unit. He found his kit laid out for him and was soon heading toward the marshaling area for Varsity. He had been promoted to sergeant and made a squad leader:

> My squad were newly arrived replacements, all but one college students, reassigned to active duty. Fortunately they were sharp young men who had volunteered for the paratroops and before being sent to us had completed basic training and jump school.

S.Sgt. William D. Lusk tells of his own experience:

I was wounded on January 7 and was in the hospital at Reims France until March 22. A jeep came by the hospital, and the driver presented sealed orders for my release and to go with him. I asked where we were going, and he stated he could not tell. Later we approached a barbed-wire fence, and once inside I was taken to the 194th Glider Infantry Regiment A Company and was made a platoon sergeant of the 2nd Platoon. My old CO, Captain Stuhrman [from 193rd Glider Infantry Regiment], was in command, and Lieutenant Henderson was my platoon leader.

Lt. Delbert Townsend had also been wounded in the Ardennes:

I returned from my stay in the hospital in England and rejoined my old unit, Company B, 194th GIR, around 18 or 19 of March 1945. After greeting the few "old-timers" that were still around, I was sent to the 1st Battalion headquarters, where Lieutenant Colonel Barnett informed me that I was being transferred back to Company A. As a result of the battle of the Bulge, the 193rd GIR was deactivated and the personnel moved over to the 194th GIR, where the regiment was reorganized to a three-battalion unit. Capt. Jerry Stuhrman and his first sergeant, Kepler, were moved from the 193rd to Company A, 194th. I was assigned as the executive officer. One day after joining Company A, the unit moved into the marshaling area in preparation for Operation Varsity.

The marshaling area was a new experience for me. It was "tent city," surrounded by a very heavily guarded barbed-wire fence. The exit and entrance were very rigidly controlled. We spent many hours in detailed briefings and equipment maintenance and inventory. Individual soldiers spent considerable time on personal hygiene, including haircuts and laundry.

One incident of note that caused the troops to smile while the command frowned on the action is worth repeating. Lt. Tyrrel Devolin was a platoon leader in Company A. He was an excellent leader and his men would do anything to please him.

Tyrrel thought it would be great if every man in his platoon received a Mohawk haircut. As a result, every man in his platoon, including Lieutenant Devolin, had Foster Lickliter, our company barber, give each individual a Mohawk haircut. Both sides of their head were shaved, with about a one-inch-and-a-half strip down the middle about an inch long. The troops in the marshaling area thought it was great, but Lieutenant Colonel Barnett thought differently. As a result, Lieutenant Devolin was disciplined, and every man in his platoon had his head shaved to eliminate the Mohawk appearance.

Pvt. Jack Trovato, whose description is recorded by the Drop Zone Virtual Museum, was a replacement in the 155th Anti-Aircraft Battalion (AAB):

I was eighteen years old and an eager volunteer for the 17th Airborne Division. I was assigned to 1st Squad, A Battery, 155th Battalion, in Chalons-sur-Marne. They had been in the battle of the Bulge, with everyone killed or wounded except the squad leader. After two weeks of torturous physical training, interspersed with piling in and out of airplanes and gliders, I received my wings and a raise in pay. Within three days, our unit was in a marshaling area looking over maps of a little town named Wesel and a bridge that crossed the Rhine River into Germany.

Gunner Tom Wallis was among those new to the 6th Airborne:

Having completed a total of eleven months training as general-purpose gunners my chum Pat Rock and I found ourselves the only two from our course who had not been posted to a service unit. After a couple of days, we decided we would volunteer for an airborne unit. As luck would have it, the newly formed 2nd Airlanding Anti-Tank Regiment needed two drivers/wireless operators, and within two days we'd be interviewed by the colonel, accepted, and transferred to Bulford. Within less than a week, we were on our way to a guarded security camp somewhere in East Anglia, where the plan was revealed and we were briefed for the operation to take place the next day.

As the operation drew closer, security was stepped up. Sgt. Fred Waggett's unit, 796th Military Police Battalion, was on attachment to the 17th Airborne Division:

> We were in the eastern section of Belgium and widely spread out. My platoon was sent to Poix, France, west of Amiens. We were sent back to check the airstrips and to provide security when the 17th AB [Airborne] arrived. Technically we were told that the 17th was in charge and we were to do whatever they needed/requested for security. Where I was could be described as 2 miles from nowhere, but we were to keep any civilians away and troopers in.
>
> Having been an interpreter, I knew from the few times we went to the small town nearby that they had no idea there was an AB camp close by. I told a 17th AB officer this one day, and he said, "That means you are doing the job we wanted done." The irony was that Axis Sally was broadcasting taunts to the 17th and what they were going to run into when they jumped. The joke among the troopers was that "Axis Sally knows we are coming, and we know she knows but she doesn't know when." Again, we must have done our job.

Life being what it is, though, there was bound to be someone who was out to spoil Waggett's hard work:

> One first lieutenant decided he was going into town with a uniform bearing 17th insignia on it. I stopped him and he proceeded to give me a ration of———. No EM [enlisted man] was going to tell him what to do!
>
> A lieutenant colonel from the 17th stopped by at that moment and listened to both sides of the story. Looking sternly at the lieutenant, the lieutenant colonel said, "That

soldier has his orders to shoot, if you refuse to follow your orders about not leaving the camp. Why do you think these Intels and security are here?" End of trip into town for the lieutenant—big smile from the lieutenant colonel.

With security as tight as it was, it seems rather odd, then, that a reconnaissance flight of tugs and gliders was sent along the planned route for Varsity. RAF Glider Pilot Alan Stredwick explains:

I was based at Great Dunmow airfield. My copilot and I always flew with 190 squadron tugs. Exercise Token was a secret exercise and, by my recollection, involved six Horsa/ Stirling combinations: two from Great Dunmow and four from two other airfields. All this took place March 17th.

My copilot was Flying Officer A. S. "Tiny" Ledbrook, and our glider was RN923 (the same one which we flew on Operation Varsity). The glider was ballasted with concrete, the occupants being only FO Ledbrook and myself. Unusually, we were required to wear parachutes, "Mae Wests," and carry side arms with fifty rounds of ammunition.

At our initial briefing, we were told to record the flight as "Operation Token," and this appears in my logbook, written at the time before Varsity took place. However, the Record Office, Kew, lists the flight as "Exercise Token," and this difference arises, probably, from a moot point as to how one defined an operation.

The requirement was for the two combinations from Great Dunmow to rendezvous with the other four and proceed across the Channel, over Cap Gris Nez to the Rhine, in the neighborhood of Xanten, and return. We had a high-altitude escort of fighters, and the trip was quite uneventful—no enemy fighters, no flak, not a shot. We did not fly over occupied territory, but we were in the area where we could be "bounced" by hostile aircraft—hence an RAF fighter escort above us. So it becomes an "exercise."

At the time, I was only aware that two aircraft flew from my own airfield—Great Dunmow—and we had no contact with the other crews who were briefed for the flight. It would seem that there were individual briefings, but no collective briefing—as far as my memory recalls. The object of Token was to test the timing, fuel consumption, and the special beacon system that had been set up in preparation for Varsity. These beacons were also used by American aircraft towing CG4As from airfields in southwest France. I have no information as to whether or not American aircraft flew a similar check flight. As the aircraft combinations flew "loose," it was natural that not every aircraft flew exactly to a scheduled turning point.

The official order is marked "TOP SECRET" and bears the comment "Crews for 'Token' should be those who will lead serials for 'Varsity.'" When we returned to Great Dunmow, we knew that the enemy would certainly be expecting us when Operation Varsity eventually took place. My logbook shows the flying time for Token as 4.00 hours.

Stredwick's colleague Jim Davies was also involved in Token and under the impression that each flight provided a glider.

B Squadron, Glider Pilot Regiment, at Earls Colne provided the other combinations. The Squadron War Diary has the following entry:

From Earls Colne—Exercise TOKEN—2 heavy and two light loaded Horsas on "Cross Channel" flight.

Sgt. John Hebden was a pilot in one of the "light" Horsas and writes in the April 1987 issue of *The Eagle*:

[Our] tugs were Halifaxes. There were three GPs [glider pilots] in each, as those in authority apparently thought to spread the load. I flew with Captain Norton and a Lieutenant. I do not recall that we had ballast or wore parachutes.

The exercise, or operation, was carried out without any problems, and as secretly as possible. Nevertheless, there was a widespread belief that the Germans were ready for the landings.

Final briefings took place during the last two or three days. In *Valor without Arms*, by Michael J. Ingrisano, Lt. John W. May, a pilot with the 44th Troop Carrier Squadron (TCS), 316th Troop Carrier Group (TCG), recalls Lt. Col. Peter Luard, CO of the 13th Parachute Battalion, at RAF Wethersfield, Essex:

> We were a bit anxious about their jumping time—on practice missions last Spring, they were a bit slow. Well, Colonel Luard proved with his contagious humour that we had nothing to be afraid of. [He] was confident of success and full of courage—a good-humoured man, a hard taskmaster, a man a fellow would want to follow. He was convinced that this mission was to be a fox hunting do—he intended to catch German fox.

As reported in Pater Harclerode's history of the 6th Airborne Division, Brig. James Hill gave a rousing final briefing fillip to his men:

> Beaten and demoralised . . . what would you think if you saw a horde of ferocious, bloodthirsty paratroopers, bristling with weapons, cascading down from the skies? . . . If by any chance you should happen to meet one of these Huns . . . you will treat him, gentlemen, with extreme disfavour.

Lance Cpl. Richard Dunkley, Mortar Platoon, 12th Devons, describes his unit's briefings:

> We were briefed as to our exact landing point across the Rhine and what was expected of us after landing. This was first to fight our way to the church in Hamminkeln, where we were to set up our mortars and help with a defensive position to the northeast of the church.
>
> As in the Normandy campaign, we were issued with army "funny money," given a lecture on the nonfraternization orders, and issued with grenades. I know I was very wary about the phosphorous grenades. I think the top brass felt the

same way, because they always left the grenade issue to the last
because of the strong possibility of accidents and the phos-
phorous/smoke grenade (No. 77) was a real nasty.

I do not remember anyone around me being at all appre-
hensive, and certainly there was no sign of fear. For my part, I
felt that our military power was such that I was a little sorry
for the Germans.

Our last briefing was late afternoon on the 23rd March,
when we were told that all the local A.A. [antiaircraft] positions in our landing area were taken care of, and we believed
it. We were given a meal and told we could go to the big tent
and eat whatever we wanted. Not much choice, just cheese or
corned-beef sandwiches, but miracles of miracles, as much tea
as we wanted—not a good idea if you were flying in a glider
in a few hours.

Sgt. Jake Dalton was ranking NCO in the 513th PIR's 1st Battalion
Intelligence Section:

My S-2 job was to prepare a sand table of the drop zone
assigned to the 1st Battalion. To do this, I was given an army
map with our DZ circled and several low- and high-altitude
reconnaissance photos. We did this on a sheet of plywood
with 6- or 8-inch sidewalls filled with about 4 inches of sand.
The tent in which we built the sand table was large enough
that we could get a couple of squads around it for a close look
and for any necessary explanation. One of the features that I
remember pointing out was a power line that could be seen
from the air on the way down and would help immensely
with orientation.

According to Edgar E. Bartlett, HQ Company, 2nd Battalion, 194th
GIR:

We were to land in a triangle formed by the River Rhine,
River Issel, and Issel Canal. We were told that the area had
lots of houses and barns built together. These buildings were

occupied by German soldiers. We were told to burn them down as soon as possible to force the Germans out.

Cpl. John Magill, 466th Parachute Field Artillery Battalion (PFAB) recalls:

The briefings were held in a large tent capable of holding several hundred men at a sitting. Crucial landmarks, including the huge power line in the drop zone and landing zone, were pointed out. Every man had a general sense of familiarity about the entire prospective battle scene.

Each briefing added to the apprehension. Ever-increasing concentrations of antiaircraft guns were confirmed by air photos taken of the area. Antiaircraft fire was the dreaded nemesis of the airborne soldier. The concentrated fire would take a heavy toll of airplanes and gliders as they moved across the Rhine into enemy-held territory. Then, as the pilots would slow the planes down to release their human cargo in the mass jump, the toll would be even greater. Finally, the exploding shells would create a hell-like inferno for the descending paratroopers and glidermen. There was a feeling of powerlessness against the exploding shells. The 17th could cope with the enemy soldiers, but they would be helpless for those few critical moments while they descended in the midst of flak.

The continued briefings also stimulated rumors among the troopers: "The Germans are committed to hold or die." "Old men, women, and children have been trained to maim or poison members of the invading army." "Sharpened sticks have been set up to run us through as we land." "Wide areas have been wired to detonate when the landings are made."

But for now, rumor had to be put aside as, briefings completed, loading, lashing, and manifests became the priority tasks. Eugene Howard, 155th AA Battalion, describes loading one of the gliders:

The WACO glider could lift a maximum cargo of about 7500 pounds. Everything was carefully weighed. Each individual was weighed. I weighed 139 pounds stripped; fully clothed, with combat gear, rifle, and steel helmet, I weighed 174 pounds. The jeep, gun, and trailer were weighed. The weight of the gun crew, jeep, jeep trailer, and gun were added. We found that we could carry about 120 rounds of ammunition for the 75-millimeter to make the 7,500 pounds. A fleeting thought occurred to me about the ability of the glider to carry two and a half tons of cargo. Jim Calebs and I had never qualified as glidermen.

We found that the load had to be strategically located in the glider for it to fly as it was designed to do. Each piece of equipment, supplies, jeep, trailer, and gun was assigned an exact spot. Each person was assigned an exact spot. On March 22nd, we began to load the glider.

The WACO glider was a USA product. It was hinged at the top front so the whole front end folded back over the top and exposed the cargo bay. Cleats and eyebolts were everywhere for lashing and securing the cargo. Rope was everywhere. Suddenly I was back in my element. I still knew how to tie more knots and secure the cargo better than all of the rest of the crew put together.

Pete [S.Sgt. Peter I. Piergiovanni, section leader and gunner] wanted to know where I had learned how to lash and secure cargo. I told him that knowing how to do that was what had caused me to be at Utah Beach. Lieutenant Gray brought Captain McCrory to look at the way the cargo had been lashed. Both were pleased with the space utilization. I explained the theory of space utilization as I had learned it in basic training back at Indian Town Gap, Pennsylvania.

The experience of WO Len Macdonald appears in the April 1995 issue of *The Eagle*:

I was detached to "G" Squadron, then at Great Dunmow where I found that I was crewed for Varsity with one Staff Sergeant Penketh. There was a problem however as nobody really knew where he was. Eventually after considerable detective work I found that he was in the Station sick bay and I paid him a visit on March 20th. He was recovering from a fairly minor complaint and was given the choice by the medical officer to either stay in sickbay or be released for the pending operation. He chose the latter option but decided to stay in sickbay until the last possible moment. So on March 22nd I loaded Horsa Mark II Glider, chalk number 397 with one Royal Signals Jeep, one trailer and two motorcycles, then went to the sick bay to obtain a progress report on my co-pilot. He was in good shape and it was agreed that he would report to Glider 397 on the runway on the morning of Saturday March 24th at 7.15 am.

CHAPTER 5

Takeoff

At 1600, on 23 March, Brereton made the decision for Varsity to go ahead the following day. Five hours later, Operation Plunder, the river assault, began as the 51st Division headed for Rees, 12 miles downstream from Wesel. The division met fierce opposition and was held throughout the twenty-fourth. Though it was not able to help the airborne divisions, it nevertheless kept a good part of the German contingent occupied and well away from the landing area.

British XII Corps had crossed opposite Xanten. By 1000, the 15th (Scottish) Division had made good progress and was ready to move up to the aid of the airborne troops. Members of the British 1st Commando Brigade made a crossing 2 miles downstream from Wesel and quickly moved toward the town. At 2230, 195 Lancasters and 23 Mosquitoes, from Bomber Command, dropped 1,100 tons of bombs on German positions in the northwest corner of Wesel. The targets were just 1,500 yards from the commandos. The bombing caused widespread damage and confusion, but not enough to prevent the German *Wesel Division*, a mixed group of antiaircraft units, from putting up a strong defense.

The airborne helped the commandos on the twenty-fourth. Following are descriptions of the differing experiences of the 6th and 17th Airborne Divisions.

6TH AIRBORNE DIVISION

In England, reveille for the 6th Airborne Division was at 0245. The men of the parachute and airlanding brigades were served a hearty breakfast of porridge, bacon and fried potatoes, bread and marmalade. This was somewhat different for those who had participated in the Normandy invasion when the order had been for a fat-free meal.

Daylight came as the men were taken by truck to the various air-fields. It was a clear day with excellent visibility. Sgt. R. F. "Andy" Anderson, Company B, 1st Canadian Parachute Battalion, was in a reflective mood:

> After packing my own gear, I visited with the men in the platoon. Everyone is noticeably excited and perhaps a little nervous. Most men are cracking jokes, while at the same time checking equipment, ammo, grenades, and small arms. It suddenly occurs to me that for perhaps 50 percent of this group, none had seen action in Normandy, and perhaps a further 20 percent did not join us until after the Ardennes. Therefore, it might be said that for many, it is a totally new experience. One reassuring factor, and a comfort to me, is that I have complete confidence in the leadership and experience of the section sergeants, and every man, I am convinced, is in top mental and physical form. If ever a fighting unit was ready for anything, this had to be it. My personal concern is that I can measure up, and not let anyone down.
>
> From the day we entered this staging area, it has been impressed on us, in every briefing, that this Rhine crossing is the final and most decisive phase of the war. It contains the elements of a full breakout into the heartland of Germany, and an early and fast close to the war in Europe. Our battalion objective is to capture the town of Wesel, and of course seize and contain the bridgehead. It is estimated that we will be relieved by waterborne forces at the close of the first day. That remains to be seen. There are always risks and the unexpected. Many "old sweats" have memories of Ardennes, which was badly planned, conceived, and executed.

Pvt. Doug Jilks, 2nd Forward Observation Unit (FOU):

The planes were already warmed up but we stood alongside for quite some time, smoking and having a last-minute check of our equipment. Finally we boarded ours just as everything was becoming visible around the airfield. We taxied about the field, more or less queuing up to run down the takeoff strip. The motors roared and the ground became a blur, and the next thing I knew we were off the ground and sliding back to our respective seats. I looked across at Don; he was No. 9 and I was 10 in our stick of 18. He was grinning and said to me, "Well, we can't go back now." I tried to manage a grin but it was quite forced, believe me. The copilot came back through the plane and passed out gum and oranges. One guy pulled out a magazine and commenced to read. I saw London below, next it was the chalk cliffs of Dover, and then the Channel and England passed from the picture.

Pvt. Tony Leake had dropped into Normandy as a member of the 8th Parachute Battalion. Now he was on attachment to his old unit as a medic with the 224th Parachute Field Ambulance:

We drove to the airfield, where we put on jumping jackets over everything, then life jackets each with an emergency light on the shoulder, followed by parachutes. We felt like pregnant elephants when we emplaned carrying our bundles or kit bags.

On board we hooked up our parachute static lines to the webbing strops by strong D rings. The strops were attached at the other ends by similar D rings to a wire hawser which ran along the length of the aircraft under the starboard side seats. It was attached at each end, fore and strong point.

We checked each other's hooks and made sure their locking pins were in place, then fitted our kit bags or stretcher bundles, equipped with quick-releases, to our right legs and tied the top end of their ropes to our parachute harnesses.

The door of the Dakota, which was at the rear of the plane on the port side, had been removed for parachuting and its hinges taped to prevent the static lines getting caught on them. As No. 2, I sat opposite to the open doorway, and our CO, Lieutenant Colonel Young, as No. 6, sat next but one to me.

For those who were to fly from Wethersfield, the reception was not one that was expected, as Lt. Ellis "Dixie" Dean, 13th Parachute Battalion, explains:

Wethersfield seemed deserted, and we drove directly to the dispersal point, where the Dakotas were parked. At Keevil, on the evening of 5 June, the aircrew had been there to welcome us—a move much appreciated, but now there wasn't a soul about. There was still time to go before chutes were to be fitted, and so, as if we wanted to delay such actions until the last possible minute, we hung around and watched as a mighty armada of "Flying Fortresses" collected overhead.

At last things couldn't be delayed any longer. The door had been removed from the plane, but we required the ladder to enable someone to get inside and hand the chutes down. We all gathered round the door, and Frank Kenny was given a leg-up into the fuselage, on the floor of which were several bundles. These came to life and revealed the crew, who hastily dressed. Then one said, "Gee fellas, what about chow?" and they disappeared across the tarmac in search of their breakfast.

Some time later, the crew rolled up in a jeep, leaped aboard and busied themselves for takeoff. In no time flat, the C-47 was rolling along the runway.

Capt. David Tibbs MC was medical officer of the 13th Parachute Battalion and in the HQ aircraft:

[Our] pilots looked at the load we were carrying and said, "What are those?" We explained that they were Bangalore torpedoes and that we were carrying them for the engineers. The pilots asked if the torpedoes would explode if they were hit. I said, "Probably not, but they could." The pilots muttered something and then got aboard. We settled into our seats and waited for takeoff. Then, suddenly, the whole plane lifted. You felt it go up. We were puzzled, until I realized what had happened. Our load had been dropped. With the signals officer, who sat next to me, I got off to see what had happened. We looked under the plane, and there were the torpedoes lying on the ground, but still attached to the plane. If we had tried to take-off with them attached like that, we would have had to abort. Now, I knew nothing about loading these, nor did my companion. But we found that we could lift them and saw that the fitting was a hook. We managed to click them all back into place. I clearly remember that we waddled round to the front of the plane and shook our fists at the pilots. One of them put his head out of the window and gave us a wave as if to say, "Sorry, guys, we won't do that again."

Airborne Troop Carrier Three One Five Group, by George Cholewczyn-ski, describes the experiences of the 315th TCG at Boreham, where it was preparing to carry the majority of 5th Parachute Brigade. The 315th's CO, Col. Howard B. Lyon, recalls that "while the combat crews had breakfast, the dance band, The Dakotans, played music. We knew the war would soon be over and we were in good spirits." According to Capt. Richard L. Adams, 34th TCS, 315th TCG: "Everybody thought that everything was going to be all right. We were talking about a lot of things. We weren't talking about the mission. I figured 'It's a day's work.' I wasn't a fatalist." In the 43rd TCS, 315th TCG, 1st Lt. Charles Voeglin was somewhat less certain: "I'll never forget the night before. You know you're supposed to get crew rest, and we all had these crews, 15–20, sleeping in one room. All of us were frightened. Someone would wake up, light a cigarette at 2:00 in the morning, and say 'I can't sleep.' Then nobody would sleep, and here you've got to take off on a mission in a few hours."

Pvt. Bob Butcher was in the Mortar Platoon of the 12th Parachute Battalion:

Dawn was just breaking as we left for the airfield, and on arrival, we had an hour or so to make final preparations, have a cup of tea, and attend to the wants of nature. While waiting to board, we saw bombers preparing to land at another airfield, presumably returning from a mission. Some fired flares, which I think indicated that they had wounded on board. Then we boarded our planes, hooked up, took up takeoff positions—and the airborne crossing of the Rhine was about to be launched.

I don't think that any of us was actually scared—tense and excited but very confident would, perhaps, best sum up our states of mind. Some of the tenseness was due to the feeling that we always got immediately before a practice drop, for the acute shortage of aircraft meant that we were never able to make sufficient jumps to enable us to accept them with equanimity. For my own part, the worst time was when the engines revved up to take off; after that I was more or less composed.

Tom Wallis, 2nd Airlanding Anti-Tank Regiment, recalls:

At the crack of dawn, we were on our way to the RAF station (location unknown) [most likely Earls Colne], where lines of Horsa gliders were parked alongside the runway in readiness for the Halifax bombers to pick up the towlines. It was about 06:00 am when the group started to take off with a large number of RAF personnel to wave us off. Our glider, with two army staff sergeant pilots, with its cargo of Lt. Col. W. Allday [the 2nd's CO], Captain Argent, an SAS liaison officer, and the RSM (Royal Horse Artillery) at the front, followed by Jeep, trailer with radio, and one bombardier and two gunners at the back.

This, for the boys at the back, was our very first flight, which went very well with little turbulence, except when the pilots changed towing position from above the Halifax to below the slipstream. Having spent most of my time peeping out of the tiny circular window in the sliding rear door, with regular attendance to the tundish with drainpipe to relieve the call of nature, the trip was quiet and pleasant watching the scenery roll by as we flew at about 2,000 feet at a comfortable 150 mph.

Lt. Hugh Clark, in the Oxfordshire and Buckinghamshire Light Infantry (OBLI) coup-de-main party, was flying from Gosfield:

> At the airfield, the gliders and Dakota tugs were lined up, ready to be pulled into position on the runway. We left our trucks and moved to our individual gliders. Each glider load had been supplied with flasks of hot tea for the flight. There were also tea wagons handing out cups of tea while we waited in the dark. Just before boarding our gliders, a lot of the chalk slogans were put back on the side. We boarded our glider full of confidence, but with a good deal of apprehension. On my own glider, I chalked the name "Mary," that of my fiancée, just by the forward door. At 0530 hours, we were all in our gliders with the tension mounting as we waited for takeoff to start at 0600 hours. Although still dark (the clocks were set to double summer time), it was a fine clear morning. Takeoff was to be at one-minute intervals, and we were due to go at 0602.
>
> As soon as glider No. 2 started down the runway, we moved into position and linked up with our tug. We could just make out the dim taillight of the tug. At that precise moment, the roar of the tug engines increased, and we started on our way. (This was only the second time I had flown in a glider.) I have since learned that we were towed by a Dakota of 512 squadron crewed by S./Ldr. P. A. Clarke, Flt. Lt. A. D. Burt, Flt. Lt. W. R. James, and F/O H. M. Anderson (RCAF). We flew roughly north to a turning point somewhere in the area of the Wash before turning back south. This was to enable the following gliders to form up behind us. We had been flying for an hour, and it was just beginning to get light. I looked down and we must have been over Essex again, and I saw gliders still taking off. As the sun rose in a clear blue sky, we continued south, crossing the Thames and heading for the Kent coast in the region of Dover and Folkestone. To prepare for any emergency caused by a broken towrope, we all wore life jackets for our flight over the Channel.
>
> We realized at this point that gliders Nos. 1 and 2 were not in position ahead of us. I asked the pilots to call up the tug

through the intercom to see if they could find out what had become of them. The reply came back that there was radio silence and they could not help. As we were relying on the support of the troops in the leading gliders once we reached the ground, I called the section commanders together and rebriefed them on our action when we landed. However, just as we reached the French coast, gliders 1 and 2 came up on our left and took their place in the lead, resulting in a loud cheer from my platoon. We therefore reverted to our original plan. The flight continued very smoothly in glorious sunshine and it was reassuring to see our fighter escort flying round the column. We continued in a northeasterly direction and saw the transport planes of the parachute troops pass below us. We also saw the tugs and gliders of the American 17th Airborne Division flying on our right. Our flying height throughout the trip was 2,500 feet.

I have often been asked since the operation how I felt on the flight and I have to say that one felt resigned to the situation, as there was not much we could do about it at that stage. I suppose my feeling was a mixture of apprehension, excitement, and nervousness wondering how I would cope when under fire.

Sgt. Pilot Brian Latham was in the group right behind the coup-de-main gliders:

My load was a mortar section of the Oxfordshire and Buckinghamshire Light Infantry, with their jeep and trailer, a motorbike, and one officer and seven men. We were to deliver them and then to meet up at a farmhouse with other glider pilots from the squadron.

Takeoff was at 0600 on Saturday, 24th March. The Dakota taxied onto the runway, the towrope connected, slack taken up, throttles opened up, and off we went to war! We were seen off by the station personnel, who lined the runway and waved.

At Birch, Sgt. Pilot Stan Jarvis, now a member of E Squadron Glider Pilot Regiment (GPR), was carrying Denis Edwards and his mates from the OBLI:

> I was positioned about fifth in order of takeoff and was towed by Squadron Leader (later Group Capt.) Alex Blyth from No. 233 Squadron. As we gathered speed down the runway. the towrope broke and takeoff was aborted. I cleared the runway quickly by steering onto a perimeter track, and the other combinations roared ahead. Alex Blyth meanwhile had managed to supply sufficient brake power before his Dakota ran out of runway!
>
> After the other fifty-nine combinations had departed, we were hitched up with a brand new towrope, and then successfully took off without further incident. I carried twenty-six airborne troops of the OBLI Light Infantry, together with a handcart of ammunition, etc., and it goes without saying that they were not best pleased about the mishap with the towrope.
>
> Alex Blyth realized that we would be in a very vulnerable position when we reached the Rhine, as we would not land with the other airborne troops, who had been detailed to jointly capture Hamminkeln railway station, close to the River Issel. In the circumstances, he decided, after discussion with me over the intercom, to cut across the continent. His navigator worked out a dogleg course, and we flew across the continent in splendid isolation for about three hours, not seeing another aircraft. As we approached the Rhine, the airborne armada stretched in front of us, and we got closer and closer, and to my amazement we entered the airborne stream within a few combinations of the position held originally at RAF Birch. This was an excellent example of the navigation and airmanship, for which I was extremely grateful.

Capt. Michael Graham was a former artillery officer and had joined the GPR only the previous May. Despite various delays to his continued

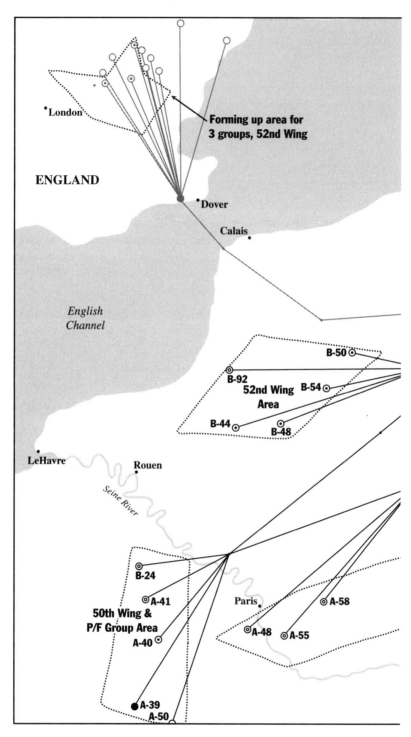

Routes Taken by Airborne Forces

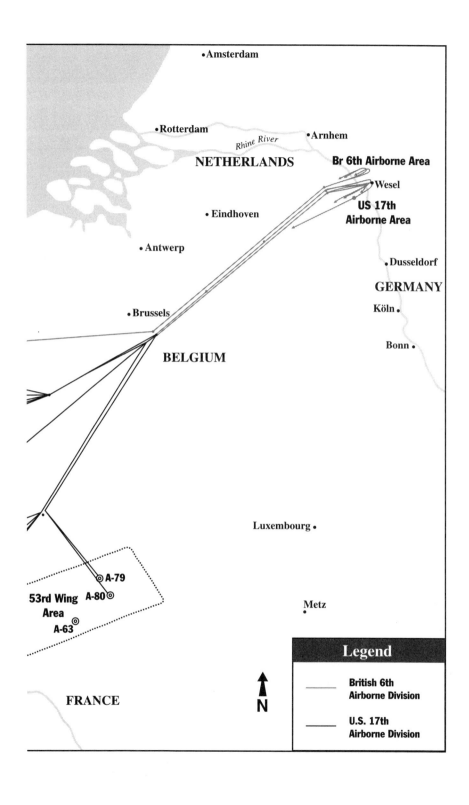

Amsterdam

Rotterdam
Rhine River
Arnhem
NETHERLANDS
Br 6th Airborne Area
Wesel
US 17th
Airborne Area
Eindhoven

Antwerp
Dusseldorf
GERMANY
Köln
Brussels
BELGIUM
Bonn

Luxembourg

A-79
53rd Wing A-80
Area
A-63
Metz

FRANCE
N

Legend

———— British 6th
       Airborne Division

———— U.S. 17th
       Airborne Division

flying training, he had gained his first pilot's wings during December. As reported in the December 1985 and April 1998 issues of *The Eagle*:

> In February I was teamed up with Sergeant Dennis Hardy and we spent the early part of March ferrying Horsas to Birch.
>
> On Varsity our glider was badly loaded, hopelessly nose heavy and the nose wheel was only persuaded to rise from the runway by the tug lifting to clear the perimeter fence. In the calm conditions at no. 30 in the stream, we had no difficulty on the way over, though the stick was well aft to keep the nose up.

Flight Lt. Patrick Edmonds was second pilot to Lt. John D'Arcy-Clark and recalls:

> We were both lieutenants, but John had more flying experience, so he was first pilot. We were friends. He was very much an individual, an artist wearing his red beret like a French peasant! In spite of numerous reprimands by senior officers, he continued to enjoy upsetting the establishment. This we both had in common, so this is maybe why we contrived to fly together.
>
> After we had checked that everyone was correctly seated and the loads were secure, it was time to strap ourselves in the cockpit. Whilst waiting for takeoff, we had time to survey the scene. A great deal of activity and noise surrounded us as the tow planes moved forward up the runway to be attached to their glider ready for take off. The combinations were becoming airborne at frequent intervals, and our turn was rapidly approaching. Two airmen attached the towrope to the wings with a locking device. With a thumbs-up and a wave they vanished, and our tow plane took up the slack rope.

Capt. H. J. Sweeney, OBLI, had been a platoon commander on the Pegasus Bridge coup-de-main. Now he was in charge of the Mortar Group. He reflects in the December 2004 issue of *The Eagle*:

After circling we headed over the Thames Estuary. As we flew over Canterbury I looked down from the cockpit of my glider to see if I could spot the house where my wife and baby daughter were no doubt fast asleep. The previous year, in September 1944, having been wounded in Normandy, I had been walking over the Old Park at Canterbury when a vast aerial armada came over our heads. It was part of the airborne force on its way to Eindhoven, Nijmegen and Arnhem. I had pointed out to my wife at that time that this was no doubt an Airborne Division or Divisions on their way to an operation. So as she awakened and looked out that morning in March she realised that another airborne division was on its way to yet another.

According to Cpl. John Cooper, a medic in the 195th Field Ambulance:

The glider that I was to travel in carried a jeep and fifteen men. The jeep occupied the center of the glider, with nine men at the front and six men at the rear, the jeep effectively cutting off communication between the two parties.

Pvt. Leonard Waller, HQ Platoon, Devons, recalls:

The group I was to fly with included the adjutant, Captain Bowman, and Private "Ray" Raeburn, whom I knew well. Ray had originally joined the Intelligence Section with me in September 1940 but was later transferred to the orderly room. I was pleased to be flying with Captain Bowman, who was a big man, over six feet tall and weighing nearly fourteen stone, who would thus be a great help when it came to unloading speedily the jeep and trailer which we were taking with us.

As the battalion took to the air on this very fine morning, we had the feeling that we were on a holiday trip, or at worst, an ordinary training flight, with the potential problems of unloading our equipment temporarily forgotten. We reached the south coast without seeing any incident. The copilot announced that we were now at the point of no return and soon to cross the Dutch coast. It was then I felt the holiday feeling ebb away, and soon we were bang slap back into the war.

Lance Cpl. Richard Dunkley, Mortar Platoon, Devons, describes his experience:

My seating position was on the port side under the wing, which I believe was the best position to fly in.

We had a full glider, along with our two handcarts holding all our mortar equipment. I think we had twenty-three men aboard but one thing of which I am sure was that we had the battalion padre sitting up front.

At about 0630 hours, the copilot shouted back, "Hold tight!" Then, after a long wait, we quite gently started to rumble along the runway, gathering speed quickly. It was at that moment in my life, more so than with the Normandy "do," that I realized that my life may soon come to an end. However, I just looked around at all my friends and felt reassured. I imagine that's how men go into battle, not that I could have done anything about it anyway.

The moment of liftoff was always quite memorable, because I usually felt sick on long flights, but I never was in fact. The noise inside the glider was more of a drone than a roar and really felt quite smooth. I believe we leveled off at 3,000 feet, and although I had a window behind me I could only see one glider and tow. This was because my small pack and the necessity to hold on to my rifle restricted any twisting around, and we were never allowed to walk the aisles. In fact, the whole aircraft was very crowded.

We soon broke through into brilliant sunshine, and I have since been told that we leveled off at 0640 hours. Whenever the glider tilted to starboard I could see the magnificent gardenlike countryside of Kent and remember being told we were over Canterbury.

The next I remember is the copilot shouting back something about, "You will never see so many aircraft in flight again, so just look out your windows," which I did with the help of my friend Jimmy Bick from Gloucester. It was a magnificent sight, even though I could only see a little of this great armada. There were 860 aircraft from the British stream alone in the air over Belgium, and I am told that the American 17th Airborne effort coming in from the Paris area was even bigger. Then I really thought the war would be over in a few days and that the landing would be a pushover.

The April 1995 issue of *The Eagle* reports that as promised, Staff Sergeant Penketh joined Len Macdonald:

As we walked out to the glider the Staff Sergeant confided in me that he had not flown for about nine months and suggested that in the circumstances that it would be better perhaps if I did the take-off. Having bedded down our complement of 7 Royal Signallers and established that our Tug skipper was a New Zealand Squadron Leader we set off down the runway at the usual smart pace that was customary on these occasions.

S/Sgt. Penketh, obviously satisfied with the take-off and the first five minutes or so of flight, enquired whether I would mind, "If I had a kip." I remember thinking that this was a somewhat strange request, but as I could think of no reason why he should not, I said "Go ahead." The redoubtable Staff Sergeant then dipped into his rucksack, pulled out a blanket, placed it right over his head and promptly went off to sleep.

The senior signaller who I believe was an RSM was somewhat uneasy about this but was reassured when I said that I would soon wake up my co-pilot if the need to do so arose. He did however make quite a number of trips forward to enquire as to our well being. With 397 practically flying 'hands-off' we had no problems and Varsity turned out to be one of the smoothest glider flights I ever experienced.

Bob Mortimer, a wireless operator with No. 2 Forward Observer Unit, had initially qualified as a paratrooper but was now sitting in a glider flown by two pilots from D Squadron:

The Horsa carried my wireless, jeep, trailer, and two motorcycles. A gunner and I sat in the tail facing forward. Up front
was a captain in our unit.

At Woodbridge, the forty-eight gliders of the GPR's C Squadron
were hooked up and ready to roll. Third in line, in Chalk 241, were Sgt.
Pilots Peter Young and Neville Shaw, with a load for the 3rd Airlanding
Anti-Tank Battery's No. 4 Troop. Young recalls:

> Our load was a 15-hundredweight truck and a 17-pounder
> antitank gun, with a crew of eight soldiers, seventy rounds of
> ammunition, and spare petrol. The total weight was around
> 17,800 pounds.
>   We have the distinction of completing the shortest flight.
> On takeoff, the Halifax got into a tangle in the slipstream of
> the aircraft in front and cast me off. There was no choice but
> to put down in the overshoot. There was a spare loaded glider
> but it was decided not to use this.

Young never learned the reasons, and none of the official docu-
mentation throws any further light on this event. It therefore remains a
mystery.

Four Hamilcars were tasked to land on Landing Zone P in support
of the light regiment. Two carried 9 tons of petrol and the other two 9
tons of artillery shells. Their tailfins and rudders were painted yellow for
quick reference. All four gliders arrived safely, and their loads were
brought into use.

S.Sgt. Denis Cason and Sgt. Raymond Jenkins, in Chalk 271, were
carrying a 716th Company Royal Army Service Corps (RASC) Bren
carrier and its crew of four. Cason recalls his experience with the crew's
officer, a major:

> He had never been in a glider before. I remember he came
> over to us to introduce himself, and he asked me if this was
> my first trip. When I replied, "It's my fourth," his face lit up
> and he returned to his men. "We're all right, lads," I heard him
> say, "It's his fourth op."

All the Hamilcars were airborne in twenty-eight minutes.

More than 200 fighters of RAF Fighter Command escorted the UK contingent of tugs, gliders, and C-47s to the Rhine. Air Sea Rescue launches were on standby in the English Channel and rescued crews and passengers from two ditched gliders.

One week later, the 31 March *Folkestone, Hythe and District Herald* carried the following comment:

> Mighty to behold shall we ever forget that mighty armada of the skies that passed over our heads on Saturday morning; that vast airborne army that filled the heavens and set our ears throbbing with the roar of the great four-engined machines that carried our parachute troops and towed gliders.
>
> I do not think in all of my life I have seen a sight that so stirred me. As the great winged army passed in steady procession across the skies it seemed as if a veritable canopy had been placed over this England of ours, a canopy that moved along and yet seemed never to be completely ended.
>
> And we thought, you and I, that it might have been the other way. Those hundreds and hundreds of machines might have been coming from Germany, bringing the enemy to our land. We have but to look back such a little way to realise how possible it might have been.

17TH AIRBORNE DIVISION

In France, the troopers and crews of the 17th Airbore Division were roused at 0530. As did their British and Canadian comrades, they ate well before enplaning. Cpl. John Magill, 466th PFAB, describes their meal:

> We ate a heavy, somewhat unmilitary breakfast. I understood the reason for the heavy breakfast; it might be the last prepared food for some days, until the ground troops would reach us. I didn't understand why the apple pie was included in the menu; was it the grand flourish before the grand finale? Was it the last meal for hundreds of young American boys?

Cpl. Howard Huebner, Company C, 507th PIR, had broken his leg during a training jump from a C-46 a week earlier. He had been in the hospital since, thus missing the Ardennes, but was discharged in time to get to the airfield near Prosnes:

> The regiment was moving out to the airfield when I arrived. My company commander told me to take charge of the company, as I was a noncom corporal, the only rank there at the time. I told him I would, but a fellow I knew came back out of the hospital, and I told him what to do to keep the company going. I then went with the motor pool and got caught miles down the road, as I was a stowaway. The motor pool officer let me go along. The day my company jumped, we were about 50 miles from the Rhine. The next morning, we crossed the Rhine on a bridge, and I hooked up with the company. The next day, the lieutenant that told me to take care of the company saw me and said, "Huebner, you so and so, you're going to get a general court-martial." I told him, "I trained with these guys, and I am going to fight with them or die with them."

Also discharged from the hospital was Sgt. Irvin Holtan, Company D, 2nd Battalion, 507th PIR. During the fighting in the Ardennes, he had been blown off the back of a jeep by a mine. Though understandably dazed and disoriented, Holtan managed to get back to his unit. He had sustained no physical injuries except a sore ear. As he was not suffering too much, he did not report this until just before leaving the zone, when a medic examined his ear and told him it was blown out. Holtan was sent straight to the hospital. On catching rumors of the Rhine crossing, he asked to be discharged and reports:

> I spent only one night in camp before we moved to the airfield. This gave me enough time to check out an M1 rifle, but nowhere, or time, to fire it or zero it in.

The first of the lead serial's C-47s took off from Chartres at 0725. Its pilot was the Pathfinder Group's CO, Col. Joel Crouch, and one of its passengers was Colonel Raff. Crouch had led his Pathfinders on the operations into Italy, Southern France, Normandy, and Holland. His forty-six-aircraft serial was airborne in less than five minutes and was so well organized that it flew over the airfield in formation just ten minutes after the last aircraft had taken off.

The 513th PIR was ready in its C-46s. As Jake Dalton, Intelligence Section, 1st Battalion, describes:

> The morning of March 24 was an ideal day for the jump— not a cloud in the sky, warm, with unlimited visibility.

According to Bob Patterson, Company E, 2nd Battalion:

> We were up early, had a great breakfast, and then loaded up. We were all carrying around 100 pounds, some even more. It was a beautiful, clear, and sunny day.

But it was also windy at the Achiet airfield. Crosswinds of 10 to 15 miles per hour caused some difficulty for the C-46 pilots. One aircraft swerved and crashed and only the lightning reactions of those piloting the following aircraft prevented a major pileup. Even so, these pilots still struggled to get their planes off the ground. Other than those injured in the crash, all other troops from the aborted aircraft were transferred to substitutes, which were away only some thirty minutes after the end of the serial. Not all the other aircraft got airborne, however. One was grounded with engine trouble, and another had a flat tire.

Cpl. John Magill, who was in the last serial, recalls the preparation and takeoff:

> We troopers moved through the line, picked up the main chute, equipped with the quick-release apparatus. The reserve chute was optional. Since it would be a low-altitude jump, it was a distinct possibility that the reserve could not be opened in time, if needed. I strapped my reserve on anyway. It was psychologically comforting to feel it on the midriff, and it could be an important buffer against flak or small-arms fire on the way down.

My forward observer section would jump with the parachute infantry in the C-46, from the left door. The entire section would be equipped with .45-caliber automatic pistols, trench knives on the leg, and hand grenades. Being equipped with the .45-caliber pistol did give me access to a weapon while descending, even though it was short range in effectiveness; nevertheless, I pinned one of my hand grenades firmly to the combat jacket for quick emergency use immediately upon landing. The fact that none in the section had long-range small arms like the carbine or M1 did not strike me at the time. My personal pack contained extra clips of ammo for the .45, extra grenades, and K rations. It was interesting to note how each trooper would debate taking an extra clip, an extra grenade, or an extra K ration, for there was only limited room. The seasoned veteran tended to carry the extra ammo or extra grenade, since his survival might depend on it.

Each squad or each section in a given C-46 would have a different-colored equipment chute. This enabled each unit to visually pick up their own equipment bundle and visually track it down through the air as we descended. Our section had an equipment bundle supported by a red cotton chute; in it would be the crucial communication equipment—radio, telephone, wire—for establishing contact with the Fire Direction Center 1 of the 466th and the huge supporting artillery on the west bank of the Rhine.

I ran the prospective mission through my head once more. "We're supposed to land at a curvature in the large power line. Watch for the towers and the high-tension lines. Check the terrain below for signs of opposing forces. Keep track of our equipment bundle. Assemble on the bundle, pick up the communication equipment, and then proceed to help clear the area of any opposition. The 466th Parachute Field Artillery Battalion will be landing in the cleared area within twenty minutes of our drop. Once the area is cleared, move off with the infantry toward the designated objective. Establish and keep contact with the artillery for supporting fire, once they have landed and are set up. Remember—we're landing on top of the enemy, so to speak. Watch for snipers and so-called civilians."

The flight north to rendezvous with the transports carrying the British airborne was peaceful and quiet. The faces across the aisle of the C-46 were pale and somewhat anxious. The "nonchalanters," those who disguised their emotions, gave a pretense of being asleep or made weak attempts at jokes. We all knew that Operation Varsity was to be the first to strike the German homeland. Invaders of the homeland would be dealt with more severely than any previous airborne troopers; the enemy knew that the Rhine was their last formidable defense line. Suddenly I added one more concern to my private collection: "My God! Would the enemy use poison gas on us as a last, desperate effort to save the homeland? We have no gas masks with us!"

Then the world's greatest single air armada turned east toward the Rhine River. Additional questions poured through my mind: "What impact is this endless string of planes and gliders having on the Allied ground troops as they watch? What will we find on the German side of the Rhine? What are our chances of success? What are my chances of making it?"

The gliders in the first eight serials were double-towed. Standard operating procedure called for a thirty-second gap between each takeoff. With the airfields at Brétigny and Melun each having two runways, the serials of the 435th and 436th TCGs were able to get off the ground very quickly.

The 194th GIR, carried in 435th TCG gliders, were at Brétigny. Lt. Del Townsend recalls:

Early in the morning, the company was treated to a gourmet breakfast of steak and eggs, a far cry from the normal menu. Following this hearty breakfast, we went back to the tent area to gather up all of our personal gear and made those last-minute checks. We loaded up on the trucks and headed for the airfield. The time for action had arrived.

The airfield was a beehive of activity. We found the CG-4A gliders were parked in a column of twos—one on either side of the runway with the short tow on the left. My particular glider was a "short-tow." My manifest included the company first sergeant, Robert M. Kepler, and eleven other enlisted men from Company A. The complete manifest included the glider pilot and thirteen men from Company A. The pilot was in the left seat, and I was the copilot and sat in the right seat. During many training flights, I had been in the right seat and learned how to follow the instructions from the pilot on releasing the towrope and applying the appropriate amount of flaps upon landing. We loaded up and waited for takeoff.

Pvt. Frank O'Rourke, describes the scene:

As I awoke, I thought at first that we were still in the States, and I was being called out for another day in the field, another day of running around the pinewoods of North Carolina, digging foxholes, playing at being soldier. But when the cold morning air swept over my face and I saw the first sergeant's silhouette in the tent opening, I knew this was no dream.

The pilot looked like a typical glider pilot. Wearing a wool knit cap, an old flight jacket and dress shoes, he was not outfitted for combat. His appearance was so casual that it gave me a sense of security to be in his hands.

The co-pilot, however, did not look as nonchalant. A C-47 pilot, he had been pressed into service because of the shortage of glider pilots. He looked nervous; he should have been.

According to 1st Lt. Earl Davis, 78th TCS, 435th TCG:

The dawn of 24 March revealed that A-48 was a part of the spawning of a huge new airborne invasion; objective: across the Rhine into Germany. The 78th was ready with thirty-six gliders each of which was manned by a pilot and co-pilot. At approximately 0830 hours, the first tow-ship took off with its gliders.

Disaster touched the 78th on take-off. The glider in which Flight Officer Heelas and Flight Officer Hyman were flying became entangled in the long rope of their tow, causing serious damage to the elevator. When they cut-off, the glider plunged instantly to earth, killing all occupants. One other glider, piloted by F/O Cook, cut-off, but it landed safely on the field. Its load was transferred to another glider, which was tacked on to the end of the formation.

PFC Louis J. Zoghby, Company F, 2nd Battalion, tells of his experience:

> I sat next to the exit door. Obviously we were all nervous and somewhat scared. We were being towed two gliders to a C-47 and were in the air at about 7:30 A.M. The ride was a rough one, and I watched as the tips of the wings of the two gliders kept almost hitting each other. It did in some cases. Not mine.

S.Sgt. Charles Everett Bullard was the crew chief of Roger the Dodger, a 440th TCG Dakota, which had a glider in tow. He spent much of the flight in the doorway of his plane, as he describes in *Little One and His Guardian Angel*:

> It was a beautiful sight to look out at planes and gliders on all sides. The gliders flew so gracefully at the end of their ropes, swinging up and down and from side to side. It is a sight no cameraman could capture, and a sight relatively few people have ever seen. I had a constant moving seat to observe what was going on.

Jack Trovato was in one of those gliders:

> The ride got bumpy and I could feel my stomach turning. I fought this feeling until I saw Murphy throwing up, followed by the rest of the squad and myself. It was one big stinking mess.

The 17th Airborne lift was escorted by aircraft from the 9th and 29th Tactical Air Command, and ahead of the whole armada ranged more than 1,200 Mustangs and Typhoons of the 8th U.S. Army Air Force. The flight to the Rhine went smoothly, with no navigational problems. The patrolling fighters had little to do, as not a single German aircraft came within sight of the armada.

CHAPTER 6

The 6th Airborne Lands

At 0820 on 24 March, artillery units of medium, heavy, and super-heavy guns, dug in on the west bank of the Rhine, began a one-hour bombardment of the German positions. At 0930, a similar setup began a half-hour antiflak bombardment. Because of an error in timing en route, however, the lead aircraft arrived nine minutes early, causing a sudden cease-fire from the artillery support.

As the aircraft appeared, a huge cheer went up from the spectators on the ground. Amongst them were Winston Churchill and Field Marshals Alan Brooke, Lord Alanbrooke, chief of the Imperial General Staff, and Bernard Montgomery. Alanbrooke recalls in *War Diaries, 1939–1945: Field Marshal Lord Alanbrooke*, edited by Alex Danchev and Daniel Todman:

> [The aircraft] arrived punctually up to time and it was a wonderful sight! The whole sky was filled with large flights of transport aircraft. They flew straight over us and on over the Rhine. Unfortunately they disappeared into the haze before dropping their loads of parachutists. The flak artillery could be seen bursting amongst them before they disappeared.

Alanbrooke's "haze" was, in fact, a huge smokescreen created by dozens of smoke canisters that had been activated by members of the

Pioneer Corps. The ground troop generals had taken no chances when they launched the river crossing. But unfortunately, this action was to have a telling effect on the airborne contingent.

Captain Sweeney, Oxfordshire and Buckinghamshire Light Infantry (OBLI), who watched the paratroop transports on their run-in to the zones, describes what he saw in the December 2004 issue of *The Eagle*:

> As we neared our objective, the parachute planes, which had taken off slightly later than us because they were faster flying aircraft, passed below, their camouflage markings showing up as they flew about 1,000 ft underneath our tugs and gliders. As we got closer and closer we could see a cloud of black smoke and dust in front of us. Through it we could glimpse the flashes of the German anti-aircraft guns as they began to open up on the parachute planes, which were now in front of us.

3RD PARACHUTE BRIGADE

The 3rd Parachute Brigade was carried in aircraft of the 61st and 316th Troop Carrier Groups (TCGs), the 61st providing the bulk of the transports.

The drop zone was on the northwest edge of the Diersfordter. Brig. James Hill had taken the risk of landing his 1,920 men on top of the enemy, rather than an "Arnhem-style" march to his objective. Peter Harclerode reports in his history of the 6th Airborne that "a bad drop did not occur as the American pilots performed brilliantly." The German defenses had not been subdued for long and began a steady and accurate fire as the troop carriers approached, crossed, and turned away from the zone.

Pvt. Doug Jilks, 2nd Forward Observation Unit (FOU), was part of this drop:

> Don and I were chattering away to each other—nothing in particular, but just killing time—when France loomed below us. Gosh, it was a big country, I thought as we wheeled north. Next came Belgium.

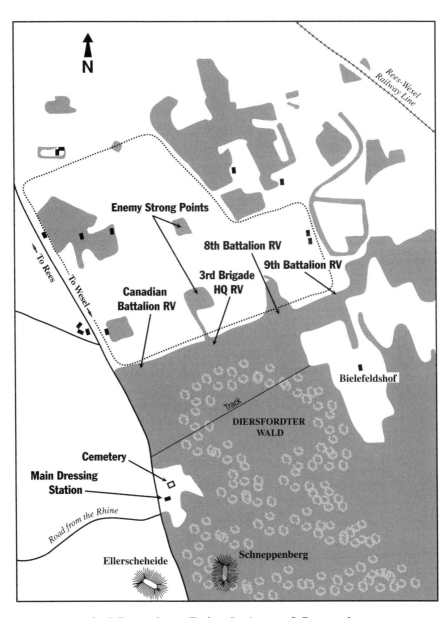

3rd Parachute Brigade Area of Operations

I could see columns of transport below. I was wondering what they were thinking about down below; it certainly must have been impressive-looking sight, as looking out the door, I could catch glimpses of fighters buzzing past and also see the endless-looking caravan of planes flying in the distance. I could make out the Stirlings towing the gliders. Yes, this would be a black day for "Herman." Time was getting shorter now. We were told to hook up. Having done this, I tightened the straps of the kit bag to my leg.

I began to perspire now, and I could feel a sudden coldness in my stomach. It was only a matter of minutes now, I thought. One of the fellows shouted, "Look, there's the Rhine!" I looked out of the little window back of me to take a look at this river which we had journeyed so far to cross; it was just like a ribbon of silver as the sun shone on it. Flak was beginning to creep up at us now. Everyone was tensed. The red light above the door was on; that meant we had four minutes to go. The major said, "Well, this is it men. Don't stand up until we have a minute to go, and then it won't seem so long." The dispatcher was at the door with his flak suit on in case any fragmentation found its way through the open door.

Next thing we were up, and the green light was on; everyone lurched for the door in single file. No. 3 man slipped and the dispatcher shoved him out. Just as I fell through the door, I saw flak hit the tail; later I learned that the man after me, No. 11, was the last man out alive. My parachute opened and I yanked the release pin and my kit bag slipped away. I couldn't control the fall of the 30 feet of rope, and it snapped. Down went all my equipment, including my machine gun. There was a bright flash just above my head, but I wasn't hit.

However, my chute had a gaping hole in it. Down I went; it was only a matter of seconds, and I hit the ground at above normal speed due to the flak. Gosh, I thought, someone had knocked the wind out of me. Just to my right, a fellow paratrooper scrambled to his feet as I was lying on my back gathering my wind; a machine gun stuttered and he sank down slowly. I drew my fighting knife, as that was all I had left except my grenades, and I would have to be pretty close to be able to use them. Just about 40 yards to my front, Jerries had a machine-gun set up in the front part of a house; the only thing that saved me was a slight rise or crest between myself and house, plus the fact that due to having the breath knocked out of me, I hadn't jumped up. I wormed up to the crest just in time to see two "Tommy" paratroops rush in the backdoor of the house. Next thing, out came four Jerries; they had a terrified look on their faces. Through talking to the two "para" boys I found out that we were about 3 miles from where we should have landed, but due to the intensity of the flak, the pilot had to drop us here.

Well, we had the Jerries to push into the clearings, so we headed back. Every clearing or field we had to cross we shoved them out first. On the way back, I managed to get a machine gun, and our gathering of prisoners increased as the Hun was throwing in the sponge, as there seemed to be British paratroops everywhere now, as more planes droned over and dropped their load. I paused for a second to watch a Dakota go screaming by overhead with its rear portion in flames. The gliders were slated to land fifteen minutes after we had landed, and they were coming down now. God, the mortars were getting worse now. The gliders were easy targets, and I saw a couple of horrible sights just now.

The Jerry artillery seemed to have found us now, and it seemed like hell had broke loose. The ground erupted around us. A glider was burning fiercely right in front of the woods I was in; the poor chaps hadn't managed to even get out of their seats. I dug feverishly with a shovel one of our fellows wouldn't need anymore. I made a bit of a hole and flopped in it. Just then I saw Don. I yelled but he didn't hear me. (Later when I met him, I found out that he had shrapnel in both elbows and a splinter in his leg.)

After a few minutes, I pushed on. Gosh, it seemed like I had been walking for hours; then I saw my rendezvous, the crescent-shaped woods. In a few minutes, I located my officer. The mortars were landing about 15 yards in front of the woods, so we started to dig in again. I was in a gully of slime so I didn't have much digging to do this time, as it was up to my knees before I started.

Word had been passed down to prepare ourselves to take our first objective. It was a clump of houses about 1,000 yards away. We certainly had to leave here anyway, as the shelling was too intense. We took the houses by storming both sides, without any casualties. The colonel of the battalion I was attached to gave orders to dig in. God, I wasn't going to dig again. The prisoners were being herded outside the houses, so I went over and got three of them and put them to work digging my trench, The Jerry artillery seemed to be concentrating on the gliders, which were sitting targets. However, all the personnel and equipment would be out of them by now, so it didn't matter.

My officer told us to lie down and get a little sleep, but after lying down, I found that even though I felt out on my feet, I still couldn't sleep. By this time, everyone had Jerries digging them slit trenches. The camp was shaped in a circular fashion, as the land army hadn't linked up with us as yet and may not even make it the next day. There wouldn't be much sleeping tonight in case of a breakthrough.

We were all ready for any Jerries that would try to counterattack, but they didn't, and the only thing that broke the lull of the night was fresh prisoners coming in after being captured by our patrols. Well, the "op" was over, and I had spent a day on German soil and was still intact, so I guess I was pretty lucky.

8TH PARACHUTE BATTALION

The 8th Parachute Battalion's task was to seize and clear the drop zone and establish a brigade rallying point in a tongue of wood on its eastern edge. Sgt. Ted Eaglen, Company C, had been wounded in the Ardennes and had arrived back with the 8th just in time for Varsity:

Approaching the DZ [drop zone], we were under heavy anti-aircraft fire. It was a lovely clear day, and I thought, "Let's get out of the bloody plane before it gets blown out of the sky." I certainly was not frightened. I expected I would get killed sooner or later, and that this time my luck had run out.

I remember someone shouting, "Red light on!" We got on our feet. Two or three of our stick got out, then a loud bang and the plane shook. Sergeant Keeble fell over. Sergeant Major Burns stood on him, followed by those behind, including me.

On my way down, I felt the draft of a shell as it went by. All hell was let loose. I was looking where I was going to land. It was going to be among barbed wire.

It seemed ages before I could get out of my parachute. The bullets were hitting the barbed wire and whining. It seemed endless. I could not believe that they were not hitting me.

Eventually I got free and ran about 50 yards to some trees, which I dived behind for cover. I landed near another para, who had been killed. I slowly put my head round the tree. There were three or four Germans, with their backs to me, on the ground firing. I gave them a burst of my Sten gun at the same time as someone else.

Companies A and C took their sections of woodland relatively quickly, and brigade headquarters was established in Company C's rendezvous. Company B and the Machine Gun Platoon had had a somewhat disorganized landing, and men were coming into the rendezvous in dribs and drabs. Two platoons of German paratroopers had dug in to the hatchet-shaped woods and were putting the British under heavy fire. As reported in Harclerode's *Illustrated History*, Brigadier Hill spoke to the CO of Company B, Maj. John Kippen, telling the major "to collect some men and eliminate the enemy position, which he proceeded to do with considerable gallantry."

Kippen managed to gather a platoon and led the attack from the northeast. Throwing smoke grenades and covered by fire from the rest of the company, the small force advanced along a trench. In contact with the enemy, the paratroopers now threw standard grenades and fired their weapons. The fight ended in a hand-to-hand struggle. Sadly, both Kippen and the platoon commander were killed. A considerable number of the enemy were also killed and twenty-seven prisoners taken.

The Anti-Tank Platoon stick also found itself contesting the owner-
ship of a house. Because of jump light problems, the platoon had landed
to the east of the drop zone. Working its way back toward the rest of the
battalion, it came under fire from a house occupied by a German signals
unit. In a short, sharp engagement, the Germans were overpowered. The
antitank troops arrived at the drop zone with sixteen prisoners and a 3-
ton truck. The vehicle was put to great use when zone clearing began
after the arrival of the glider element.

The gliders began landing at about 1100. The 8th's CO, Lt. Col.
George Hewetson, had too close a call with one glider, which landed
out of control. He describes the experience in Harclerode's *Illustrated
History*:

> [I was] briefing my Intelligence Officer. Two sergeants, one
> from 9th Parachute Battalion, were standing a few yards away.
> Suddenly, with a terrific crash, a glider came through the trees
> and I found myself lying under the wheel of a jeep. I managed
> to crawl out from under the wreckage of the glider. The crew
> had been killed and my Intelligence Officer [Lt. John England]
> and the two sergeants were also dead.

Lt. Col. Napier Crookenden was standing some yards away and witnessed the crash. He writes in *Airborne at War*:

> We ran over to find it was our medical glider. My Medical
> Sergeant Millot and his two orderlies were dead; their jeep
> and trailer, full of medical stores, were smashed and George
> [Hewetson] was crawling out from under the wreckage, alive
> but badly bruised.

Despite a concerted effort by German mortar and artillery crews to
force battalion members back to their trenches, the drop zone was all but
cleared by 1200 hours. The 8th was then called back into reserve but left
one platoon from Company C to finish the job. The men encountered
two 88s on the way, and some casualties were caused by tree bursts. The
battalion attacked the guns and killed their crews. After reaching its new
position, it settled into a defensive role.

About 1830, Brigadier Hill arrived at the battalion headquarters and ordered Hewetson to move his men into a position covering the rear of divisional headquarters. The battalion set off through the woods. There were numerous tracks, darkness was falling, and the enemy was becoming quite active. It wasn't long before the 8th became completely lost. Hewetson decided that it would be better to stay put until daylight.

Enemy activity increased over the next few hours, and several minor skirmishes ensued. Hewetson learned later that this fighting had been a concern to divisional headquarters and had resulted in a stand-to being ordered for the remaining hours of darkness.

The battalion liaison officer had to return to brigade headquarters, and the chaplain decided to go with him so that he could visit the casualties being cared for by the 224th Parachute Field Ambulance. The two men were not too far into their mission when they were ambushed and killed by a German patrol.

As daylight came, the 8th Parachute Battalion found that it had actually arrived at its intended position.

1ST CANADIAN PARACHUTE BATTALION

The 1st Canadian Parachute Battalion was to move through the woodland, clearing and securing as it went, and then was to take and hold a group of houses at a road junction just on the other side. From here, it was to move east along the road to the hamlet of Bergefurth, where the church had been designated as the brigade's main dressing station.

Company C jumped while the 8th was still clearing the drop zone. Pvt. Jan de Vries had spent the flight to Germany finishing a book he had been reading. Soon his turn came to jump:

> I made a great exit from the plane and saw the air filled with parachutes—2,000 paras out in eight minutes. That was just our brigade.
>
> As I drifted down, I heard some vicious cracking sounds. Looking up, I saw a number of bullet holes in my chute and sure wished I was already down. As I neared the ground, I could see where I was going to land—so I thought.
>
> I had my spot picked out when a gust of wind caught my chute and drifted me over the trees at the edge of the field.

I followed instructions for a tree landing: feet and knees together, arms over face, and pray. I came down fast through the branches and came to a sudden halt when the chute caught up in the top of the tree.

The sudden jolt forced the parachute harness to jam up my arms and my helmet half over my eyes.

De Vries had ended up some 6 or 7 feet above the ground. He felt fine, and not too worried, as he watched bits of tree fall past him. With the enemy in close proximity, it was time to get down. There was just one problem: De Vries found that he was unable to reach his knife. With the encumbrance of all his equipment, he found it impossible to lift his leg high enough to retrieve the weapon.

It was hard to say just how long I hung there, perhaps twenty minutes, half an hour? My underwear was still clean, but I sure sweated a lot. Thankfully, two British paras happened to come along. One boosted the other on his shoulders; he grabbed my ankles, and the weight brought me down on top of them. Gathering myself together, I headed for the rendezvous and took part in securing our area.

Maj. John Hanson, Company C's CO, missed the trees but still landed awkwardly, breaking his collarbone in the event. The company second in command, Capt. John Clancy, and two others narrowly escaped their burning plane. Clancy landed amongst enemy troops and was captured. The other two, Lt. Ken Spicer and Pvt. J. Cerniuk, landed safely, but apart. Cerniuk was carrying the company headquarters radio set. Along with his Sten gun, the radio was parted from the carrying rope by machine-gun fire. Cerniuk escaped injury and capture, however, and later linked up with the 15th (Scottish) Division. It therefore fell to two sergeants, Murray and Saunders, to organize those company members present into an attacking force. They took their objective and put a number of machine-gun positions out of action.

Company A landed on the eastern edge of the zone. Pvt. Barry Volkers recalls his jump:

As usual [I was] last out and looking to be first down. Only this time I looked up and saw holes popping in my canopy. I would be down sooner than expected! A couple of jumpers looked like they were faking death to avoid being shot at. I was too busy watching the holes opening up in my chute. A "thunk" into my kit bag woke me from my fascination with the perforations overhead. I released the bag and let it out on its line. This slowed my oscillation just as it hit the dirt, and my landing was a good one, despite the speed of descent. No stand-up landing, this; I had to get below enemy fire.

Soon I was rid of my parachute and reeling in my bag of tricks. Those two jumpers that I thought were faking death— they weren't! A little ways off, one of our Dakotas was heading earthward with a heavily smoking right motor. I hoped it wasn't ours. I liked our crew, and they had set us right on target.

There was noise and death all around. I spotted the company colored smoke and soon joined the others in the broken dash to the edge of the woods, dropping down into shell holes whenever possible. There we ran into a German slit trench. Fortunately, they had already skedaddled.

Volkers was among the two-thirds of Company A that made it to the rendezvous within half an hour of landing. Buoyed up by this, the company CO, Maj. Peter Griffiths, decided to attack a group of building designated as battalion headquarters. The men took these with minimal casualties.

The company was also tasked to take the houses at the road junction. These proved to be more of a problem. The first attacking wave was brought to a standstill. Company Sergeant Major Green took charge. He got covering fire on the houses and personally led another wave into the nearest one. It took some fierce hand-to-hand fighting to clear it, but theCanadians eventually won. They took each of the remaining houses in similar fashion. The enemy tried desperately to retake the houses throughout the day, but they were denied.

The main objective of Company B was a group of farm buildings. Sgt. "Andy" Anderson relates his experience after being hooked up and shuffling to the door:

> Am conscious of other aircraft in the vicinity, also "fire-cracker" sounds coming up from below, plus puffs of smoke. More pushing, close right up, kit bags in hand.
>
> Then green on, "Go, Go, Go!" Into the slipstream, drop like a rock. Looking up, am conscious of plane climbing out of line of antiaircraft fire. Chute cracks open, one problem down, keep busy, start letting down kit bag. All the while my subconscious picks up small-arms fire around me. Couple of holes appear in the canopy. Damn it. Seems too long to be floating up here; must have jumped out 200 feet too high. Can see, in periphery, other planes unloading, one or two on fire, heading into the deck.

Having "dropped like a rock," Anderson also describes his landing as "rocklike": something the staff at Ringway, the British Parachute Training School, would not have approved or awarded any prizes for.

> Stretched out on the ground, somewhat amazed to find nothing broken, and kit bag still intact, I unpacked my gear and started for the RV [rendezvous] point at the edge of the woods, about 200 yards away.
>
> I crouched low and ran like hell, conscious of fire coming from somewhere, and of several men lying motionless on the DZ.
>
> Obviously the area has not been totally secured. At the RV point, all section sergeants report in, amazed to find that only six or eight men are missing.

Anderson moved his platoon off toward the farm buildings. As the men were setting up their defenses, they were joined by others, including Capt. Sam McGowan, who had been put in command of the company after the CO, Maj. C. E. Fuller, had to remain at Chipping Ongar at the last minute. McGowan was bleeding badly from a head wound and was having difficulty seeing, but he was completely mobile. Anderson tried to persuade the captain to put a shell dressing over the wound, but McGowan would have none of it. He clamped his helmet on tight and pushed his men on. He did not want to delay the attack. Anderson continues:

> At the fence line on the edge of the farm, have lined up the platoon in some kind of attack order. Then with fire coming from the farm, we are off and running, firing wildly from the hip, covered by Bren fire.
>
> We overrun bunkers, toss grenades into the houses and barns, generally raise hell and take a few prisoners. The whole episode, in looking back, could not have taken thirty minutes in all. Seems too easy. I found the largest bunker outside the farm perimeter, set up a kind of headquarters, and put a guard over the prisoners, who are scared to death. One or two of them are medics, and I tried to get them to look at Captain Sam's head.

Contributing to that covering fire was the Bren gun of Sgt. Howard Holloway, from the Anti-Tank Platoon, who had joined up with four others from his stick:

> We headed across the DZ, took cover near a fence, and returned the fire towards a tepee of wooden poles close to a farmhouse. We saw five or six guys attacking the area, which soon became silent. One parachutist was wounded in the upper leg. I administered my morphine, bandaged his leg, and applied a tourniquet. He was OK and said he could release the pressure. The area was well occupied, and I'm sure there were 8th Battalion medics around.
>
> Now I had to cross a plowed field, so I jumped onto a passing jeep. Bullets were hitting the side and popping and whizzing around us. We made it to the trees and found it already occupied. We saw a chute with a man hanging in the trees. It was our CO, Colonel Nicklin.

The 1st Canadian Parachute Battalion's CO, Lt. Col. Jeff Nicklin, had landed above a machine-gun position and was shot as he struggled to get free from his harness. His second in command, Maj. Fraser Eadie, took charge of the battalion.

As the battalion settled into its defensive positions, one of its medics, Cpl. George Topham, was watching the attempts of two members of 224th Parachute Field Ambulance to help a wounded man on the drop zone. Under intense fire, the medics made a dash for the casualty, but were both killed. Without hesitation, Topham also raced out to the man. Enemy fire continued to sweep the zone, and Topham was shot through the nose. Yet despite the severe pain, he continued to give first aid. He then hoisted the man on his shoulders and carried him to cover. Topham was not yet finished. He refused treatment and went back onto the zone to help more wounded. Eventually he accepted first aid. He also refused to be evacuated, and such was his determination that he was allowed to continue on duty.

Some time later, as he was returning to his company, Topham came across the Mortar Platoon's Bren carrier, which was burning fiercely. The Mortar Platoon, under Lt. G. Lynch, had landed to the north of the landing zone, and it was during the platoon's attempt to reach battalion headquarters that its Bren carrier had suffered a direct hit. Enemy mortar fire was landing in the area, the carrier's own mortar ammunition was exploding from the vehicle, and an officer was not allowing anyone to approach. Topham did not agree and ran to the carrier. In turn, he carried each of the three occupants to safety. For his gallantry throughout the day, Cpl. George Topham was awarded the Victoria Cross. The conclusion to his citation reads: "This noncommissioned officer showed sustained gallantry of the highest order, for six hours, most of the time in great pain. He performed a series of acts of outstanding bravery and his magnificent and selfless courage inspired all those who witnessed it."

On 9 April, Brig. James Hill wrote to Lt. Gen. P. J. Montague, Chief of Staff at the Canadian Military HQ in London:

> I thought you would not mind my writing to you direct to tell you what a very wonderful show the Battalion has put up since our Operations over the Rhine on March 24th last.
>
> They really put up a most tremendous performance on D Day and as a result of their tremendous dash and enthusiasm

they overcame their objectives, which were very sticky ones, with considerable ease, killing a very large number of Germans and capturing many others.

Unfortunately the price was high in that they lost their Colonel, Jeff Nicklin, who was one of the best fellows that I have met, and was the ideal man to command that Battalion as he fairly used to bang their heads together and they used to like it and accent it. He is and will be a tremendous loss to the Battalion and of course to me. I only hope that the people back in Canada appreciate the really wonderful job of work he has done in producing his Battalion at the starting line in such outstanding form.

9TH PARACHUTE BATTALION

The aircraft from the 316th TCG's 37th and 45th Squadrons, which were carrying the men of the 9th Parachute Battalion, caught a tremendous amount of attention from the German gunners. Of the 37th's twenty-one aircraft, sixteen were hit by enemy fire.

The sixteen paratroopers in the lead aircraft, Chalk 82, exited with no difficulty. The aircraft, flown by the 45th's CO, Lt. Col. Mars Lewis, was hit by antiaircraft fire as Lewis executed a left turn from the drop zone. He held the aircraft straight and level for a few seconds, but the rudder and elevators were burning fiercely, and it went into a diving turn to the right. No parachutes were seen.

In Chalk 85, piloted by Capt. James Bramlette Jr., the crew chief, T. Sgt. William H. Hendricks, was the only survivor after the drop. The Dakota was hit heading back to the Rhine. All the crew prepared to evacuate, but only Hendricks got out safely.

Chalk 108, from the 37th, ended up, fully loaded, at Eindhoven airfield in Holland. The parachute on one of the parapacks had "blossomed" underneath the door. Attempts to bring it and its container on board were unsuccessful, and it was too dangerous for the paratroopers to attempt to jump past it. The men were returned to the front by road.

The Schnappenberg and another, smaller ridge, the Ellersche Heide, were the 9th's objectives. Col. Napier Crookenden, the battalion CO, landed in the middle of the zone. In the far corner, close by the woodland, blue smoke marked the battalion's rendezvous, and men were streaming toward it. Crookenden's batman, Lance Corporal Wilson, had jumped behind him but was now nowhere to be seen. Then, Crookenden says in *Airborne at War*, "Wilson appeared, leading two horses, one for me and one for himself."

Not all Crookenden's men had landed successfully. Sgt. Michael Corboy was stick commander for half of 11th Platoon, Company B, carried in Chalk 115. Also in his stick were the platoon commander, Lt. Gordon Lee (a CANLOAN officer) and three Royal signalers. At the stick commanders' briefing, Corboy's pilot, 1st Lt. William L. Ballard, had told him that he had trouble remembering to put the green light on, "what with having to keep station in the Vee formation, throttling back on the port engine and coping with the slipstream turbulence. So when we reach the start line, sling them out." Corboy takes up the story:

> We reached the road, which I knew to be the start line, and saw feet beginning to appear. I had five out on the red (well, it was war and not Ringway!). At this point, No. 6 fell over, and with about 100 pounds of gear on me, it was as much as I could do to stand and assist others to climb over him. When No. 16 fell as well, after No. 17 went, I stood not upon the order of my going.
>
> I was miles away from our drop zone. I ended up crossing the glider landing zone with jettisoned tow cables whistling around my ears, and half the American Army in chutes and Wacos descending all around.

Corboy may have landed far from his intended zone, but he was lucky to be alive. The two paratroopers who failed to exit the aircraft rejoined the unit thirty-six hours later and told Corboy what had happened, moments after he jumped: The aircraft's tail had been hit by anti-aircraft fire, but Ballard managed to keep her in the air and landed at Eindhoven.

Pvt. Ron Tucker, Company C, was hooked up and ready to go. He writes in *A Teenager's War*:

> The red light was on; now the green—and out goes the first lad. We lose no time and follow on very quickly. Suddenly the

plane heels over and some lads fall down, weighted heavily with equipment. It is difficult to get up quickly, but they do, and jumping continues.

As Tucker moved toward the door, he saw flames passing the windows on his left. The starboard engine was on fire and the heat could be felt through the fuselage. All of his stick exited safely, and it was a relief for him to feel the tug of his parachute opening and the cool air on his face. Less welcome were the small holes that started to appear in the canopy. Nevertheless, he made a perfect landing, then shucked off his parachute and harness and raced toward his rifle valise, which he had cut loose from its rope.

> I was conscious of a machine-gun firing and was flung like a paper bag in the opposite direction for at least three yards. Without thinking, I jumped to my feet and raced towards the rifle, diving down with my knife in my hand to cut the stitching. The machine-gun opened fire again, showering me with soil and dust as the bullets hit the ground half a yard in front of me. I had slashed a good few stitches when it fired again; this time my hand went numb, the knife disappeared completely and fragments had cut into my face—I could feel the blood running down it. At least my eyes were all right.

Expecting to die from the next burst of fire, Tucker lay completely still. Nothing happened, and he decided that the Germans must have thought he was dead. Using the arrival of 1st Canadian paratroopers as an opportunity to move, he made it to the 8th Battalion rendezvous. After his hand was dressed, he and his section Bren gunner carried on to their own battalion rendezvous.

He now had time to examine what damage the bullets had done to his equipment. His small pack had taken the brunt of the burst. His mess tin, rations, spare socks, and towel were shredded. Examining himself further, Tucker found that a bullet had passed through his right-hand ammunition pouch, through his smock, and into the right-hand breast pocket of his battle-dress shirt. The bullet had been stopped when it hit the cross he had placed in the pocket that morning.

Tucker had purchased the cross on a visit to the Abbeye de Maredsous in the Ardennes and had worn it ever since. It was normally attached to his identity disks, but in the rush to get ready for the lift, Tucker had placed the cross in his pocket. He was now convinced that he would not suffer any more injuries. During the remainder of the day, he was involved in two assaults on German gun positions, from one of which he "liberated" two Luger pistols. He did indeed suffer no further injury, and after a night in a barn, commandeered as an aid post, he was evacuated across the river.

Cpl. Reginald Knights was in the Machine Gun Platoon. He describes his experience in *Valor without Arms*, by Michael J. Ingrisano:

> I jumped No. 1 and landed exactly on target relative to the ground features. The plane was right on course and the rest of the stick and our container landed exactly where they should.
>
> Unpleasantly, on reaching the container, I looked up to see overhead a C-47 with a sheet of flame streaming from both trailing edges. Some of the stick had jumped and one was descending with his chute on fire. I could see others backed up in the doorway by the flames and could hear their screams. The flames rapidly completely engulfed the aircraft which went into a shallow descent and exploded a mile or two away. One of the sights I shall never forget.

Within forty-five minutes of landing, the battalion was almost at full strength. Maj. Alan Parry's Company A took the lead toward the Schnepfenberg. Following, with battalion headquarters, were Crookenden and Wilson on their horses. Companies B and C brought up the rear.

Small groups of enemy were encountered along the route, but these were dealt with quickly, and the men reached the Schnepfenberg without much incident. A battery of 76-millimeter guns was firing on the 15th (Scottish) Division, which had just crossed the river. Company B charged at the guns and within a few minutes had killed or captured all their crews.

By 1300, the battalion was dug in by company: A on the Schnepfenberg, B across the main road to the southwest, and C in a woodland south of the road. All seemed quiet until a German assault gun and infantry appeared on the road and attacked the positions. The vehicle drove straight into the headquarters section of Company B, scattering men as it went. The company clerk stayed out on the road and slapped a Gammon bomb onto the engine cover. The vehicle stopped, and a crewman was shot as he looked out. The rest of the crew surrendered. The vehicle, still in running order, was then crewed by two ex-tank drivers from Company B, and was part of the battalion's transport for the next week or so.

During the afternoon, Crookenden was standing at the side of the road when a jeep drove up. On board was Montgomery. Crookenden explained the situation to the field marshal and advised him not to proceed any further because no link had been made with the Americans, and his safety could not be assured. With a word of thanks, Montgomery told his driver to turn the jeep around. That was not the end of the story. Crookenden later learned that on returning to his headquarters, Montgomery had written a postcard to Crookenden's father saying that he had seen his son alive and well—a wonderful gesture by an army group commander on the evening of a major operation.

Shortly after Montgomery left, Crookenden decided to go and see if he could find any news of Colonel Miller and his men. Accompanied by Harrold, he went into the woods. The two men found the Americans, who shared a bottle of whiskey with them while they recounted the events of their misdrop and the problems they had encountered getting to their objective.

224TH PARACHUTE FIELD AMBULANCE

A detachment of the 224th Parachute Field Ambulance jumped with the brigade. It consisted of four complete headquarters (HQ) sticks and three sections in half sticks.

The unit CO, Lt. Col. A. D. Young DSO, was in HQ Stick 1, which was in the first serial with the 8th Battalion. As its members stood up, Cpl. L. F. Nicholson's voice was heard for the last time, leading the chorus of "Macnamara's Band." Instances like this were later recalled as typical of the final moments of the flight. Pvt. Tony Leake's drop was somewhat hair-raising:

> We were dropped at 1,000 feet, which was the standard height
> for American parachutists, who always wore reserve chutes.

Operationally, British parachutists jumped at 400 to 500 feet, as we had no reserve chutes. As we normally descended in less than half the time, we were a target for only about thirty seconds. As a result of the higher drop, we were fired on for over sixty seconds as we came down.

When my chute had fully developed, I found that I had twists—that is, my rigging lines were twisted up. Before dealing with that, I had to drop my stretcher bundle. But the quick-release would not come loose immediately, and then when it did unfortunately the rope ran through my hands and gave me friction burns with blistering.

I had not got time to get untwisted and landed backward, but luckily the ground was soft, being a plowed field, so I was not injured. Being dropped at 1,000 feet probably saved my life. If I had been dropped at 500 feet, I would have landed with my stretcher bundle still attached to my right leg, causing a serious injury. I would also have been unable to get off the DZ and would have been shot dead.

I ran off the DZ as fast as I could to the 224th rendezvous in the woods, near the 8th Battalion RV, on the southern side of the DZ, carrying my stretcher bundle. When I got there, I took off my life jacket and unzipped my jumping jacket and removed that too. Then I unpacked my stretcher bundle, opened the stretcher, and put the blanket on it.

The Roman Catholic chaplain, Captain Kenny, who was also in HQ Stick 1, and Corporal Nicholson were shot dead in the trees where they landed. Nicholson's fate wasn't known until a week later. His grave was found next to that of Driver Shelton RASC, who was attached to the 224th. In Normandy, Shelton had dropped into the swamp. Just before he left the aircraft over Germany, he was heard to say, "Let's hope for a better landing this time!"

Private Bamber, the unit's photographer, was in HQ Stick 2. His first photograph was of his parachute hanging from the roof of a farm building. As he made his way to the rendezvous, he turned to watch a C-47 making a shallow dive, with one engine in flames, into the building he had just left.

Capt. E. D. Anderson, in true quartermaster style, had used his privilege of being allowed out of the transit camp to buy a clothesline at the village shop. Knowing his luck, he was convinced he would land in one of the clumps of trees that dotted the drop zone. This is indeed what happened. As he was organizing the line to lower himself, however, a mortar bomb scored a direct hit on the tree trunk and so saved him the bother. None the worse for wear, he unburdened himself of his harness and made for the rendezvous. En route, as he stopped to give first aid, he was shot through the shoulder and briefly lost consciousness. After coming to, he wrapped a shell dressing around the wound and carried on. Suddenly he saw a German soldier running at him with bayonet fixed. Too weak to do anything quickly, Anderson pointed to his Red Cross armband. The soldier grinned, gave him the thumbs-up, and ran past. Anderson reached the rendezvous and apologized for being late.

As they reached the brigade rendezvous, the medics began to dig in, but they were soon needed to deal with the growing number of casualties. The unit's dental officer and anesthetist, Captain Chaundy, became a fatal casualty when he was shot through the neck while assisting a wounded man. In fact, casualties were so numerous that the supply of stretchers gave out.

When the brigade's glider element arrived, the 224th had an allocation of three, of which two landed safely with much-needed jeeps. Tony Leake was digging a slit trench and watched their arrival:

> The gliders started landing on DZ/LZ A. A Horsa glider came at high speed and crashed into the trees ending up with its cockpit about 30 feet away from me. I saw it all happen, and there were lots of other gliders crashing on LZ A too.

Leake's observation that "there were lots of other gliders crashing on LZ A" neatly sums up the situation. Twenty-three Horsas and three Hamilcars were scheduled to arrive with artillery, mortars, medium machine guns, and ammunition. Twenty Horsas and three Hamilcars landed on the zone, but because of in-flight problems and the intense anti-aircraft reception, not all the gliders were the ones intended for Landing Zone A. Half of the Horsas all but landed on top of one another, and of the Hamilcars, only that of the 8th Battalion arrived with its load of Bren carrier, mortars, machine guns, and radios intact.

With further casualties being caused by the gliders' landing, it was a relief to the medics to find that plenty of stretchers had arrived intact. Private Lenton, attached to the 8th Battalion, said he would go and get some. His Section Commander, Staff Sergeant Walsby, told him he would never make it back alive. Undeterred, Lenton and his mate, Private Downey, ran to the gliders. Not only did they make it there and back alive, but they also rescued some wounded men who had been left in the open. For this action, Downey was mentioned in dispatches, and Lenton received the Military Medal.

The men cleared and prepared Bergefurth Church, which had been damaged by artillery fire from across the river, as a main dressing station. The first patient went onto the table at 1430.

5TH PARACHUTE BRIGADE

The 5th Parachute Brigade was carried by the 315th and 316th TCGs and was to drop onto Drop Zone B, northwest of Hamminkeln on the Hamminkeln to Rees road.

The 316th's 44th and 36th Squadrons flew the first serial, B4. On the final run-in, the pilots had a good view of what awaited them on the way back to the Rhine. As one observer describes in Ingrisano's *Valor without Arms*: "About 500 yards to the north, we could see the 45th Squadron catching 'holy hell' from German mobile batteries. We knew they were flying the heading we would be flying eventually—our aircraft would catch it, if we came out that way."

Piloting the lead aircraft was the 44th's operations officer, Maj. William S. Keiser. On board were Brigadier Poett and his headquarters. Poett was first out over the drop zone, and he recalls the experience in Harclerode's history of the 6th Airborne:

> As we dangled from our parachutes we tried, in the very short time available, to pick up the landmarks. These had seemed so very clear and simple on the sand models and in the air photographs, but now they appeared somewhat different as we came down rapidly amongst the firing and into the dust and smoke

caused by the artillery bombardment, which had finished more than ten minutes earlier.

After his stick was clear, Keiser made a sharp left turn, dropped the C-47's nose for speed, and slid by under other aircraft turning above. His deputy, Capt. Dwight E. Maul, followed him down. The two aircraft leveled off and, engines pushed to the maximum, headed back to the Rhine. Most of the squadron's aircraft were hit by antiaircraft or small-arms fire, but all returned, with no injuries or loss of life.

On his first mission, Lt. William F. Ross, Chalk 134, was lucky to make it to Germany, let alone back to England. On the last leg to the Rhine, one of his engines cut out. Employing all his skill, he kept the aircraft in the air, and in formation, by using the autopilot to lock the ailerons and elevators. Managing to get the engine started, he reached the Rhine, dropped his stick past the river, and made it back to the Rhine; where the engine cut out again. He followed the same routine he had on the flight out. It was only when he reached the Channel that the engine cut in, and it turned for the remainder of the flight.

The 36th was not so fortunate. On the return leg, two aircraft went down near the Rhine. Capt. Robert E. Pace and his crew bailed out safely. Minus the crew chief, T. Sgt. John F. Keating, they returned the following day. Keating had landed in a minefield and was rescued by a British artillery unit with the aid of its mine detector. Another four aircraft made it only as far as airfields near Eindhoven. None of the crews suffered any injury.

Poett was now on the ground. As reported in *British Army of the Rhine (BAOR) Battlefield Tour*:

Once the troops reached the ground, they soon realised the difference between an opposed and an unopposed landing. Although battalions were dropped with fair accuracy the individual officers and men had considerable difficulty in identifying their exact positions and this caused some delay to the rallying.

The enemy opposition on the ground was moderate. The enemy was occupying entrenched positions and was difficult to locate. The paratroops moving across the DZ to the RV were conspicuous and vulnerable. Considerable casualties inevitably resulted. Once an enemy post had been detected, and determined action taken to deal with it, the enemy surrendered without serious fight.

13TH PARACHUTE BATTALION

The 13th Parachute Battalion was to clear and hold an area bounded by roads, a stream, and a collection of buildings.

Capt. David Tibbs, the battalion medical officer, had suffered some airsickness on the flight. Jumping at No. 2, he was by the door, and the air helped clear his head. In seat No. 1 was a good friend from the Normandy operation, Sergeant Webster of the Royal Electrical and Mechanical Engineers (REME). Tibbs's plane was on the right of the V, so the other two planes could be seen from the doorway. Back at Wethersfield there had been some discussion about the use of the jump lights. The pilot, 1st Lt. Colvin T. Smith, Chalk 146, had suggested that the troopers jump when they saw the men from the other planes jumping. Tibbs's stick had asked for the green. They reached a compromise and Smith said he would wait and see how the situation unfolded. Now his plane was getting close, and Tibbs was watching the lights.

> As the warning red light came on, I could see the broad glint of the Rhine below. Sergeant Webster and I had decided that we should not jump until we had cleared the trees and crossed a line of electric pylons and power cables just beyond the forest. To our horror, we saw that the other two planes in our V were dropping their paratroops into the woods, and our dispatcher was motioning us to go. I thumped Sergeant Webster on the shoulder to persuade him to go, but he shook his head and pointed ahead. It would, of course, be a court-martial offense to refuse to jump, but I realized that Webster was right and waited in mental agony for several long seconds more until, to our relief, the pylons came into view. With Webster jabbing a finger at them, and myself responding with a shouted "Yes!" we jumped! At this stage, flak was bursting all around us and one of the other planes had an engine on fire.

As Smith's aircraft turned for the flight home, it was hit by anti-aircraft fire. 1st Lt. Merrill J. Jackson, flying at No. 2 in the V, witnessed the strike, as described in Ingrisano's *Valor without Arms*:

> When we dropped our troops I fell behind as my troops were very long in leaving the plane. The element leader and Lieutenant Smith were diving and turning before I had dropped my troops. I was 50 to 75 yards behind [in the turn]. . . . Lieutenant Smith was . . . about 100 feet above me. I was on the deck. As we straightened out . . . I flew right over the gun which I think was firing at Lieutenant Smith. [His] ship burst into flames and one parachute came out immediately. I received hits and turned to look and see if I was on fire. As I turned my head another parachute came out at 600 to 700 feet. The plane flew along level and then nosed down in a gentle glide into the ground, exploding on contact, just short of the river.

Capt. David Tibbs picks up the story:

> We had been dropped a quarter of a mile to the east of the intended area and our rendezvous was nowhere to be seen. By some fortunate instinct, aided by hunting horns (our battalion trademark), about 300 men made for a solitary farmhouse. A dangerous congregation of men if those guns had still been active! There was a ten-minute pause before our position was accurately identified and we moved off. At that moment, a grinning Sergeant Webster appeared, driving a jeep he had captured. I loaded our mortar officer, who had been concussed, onto this, and we moved off, skirmishing with some Germans firing from the trees nearby as we went.

During final planning, senior medical officers had identified buildings for their field dressing stations. Soon after setting up the aid post in his chosen farmhouse, Tibbs and his staff rushed outside at the sound of an earthshaking crashing coming from the farmyard. Tibbs continues:

One of the superlarge tank-carrying Hamilcar gliders had landed well near us but promptly ran into a large brick-built barn, which collapsed around it. There was silence for some minutes, and we assumed that all the occupants were dead, but suddenly there was the sound of a tank engine starting up, soon followed by an eruption of all the debris as the tank thrust its way out, accompanied by cheers from the troops nearby.

A C-47 followed this almost immediately:

[It came down] in a shallow crash dive after being hit, but dropping its paratroops as it did so. Ironically, most of them landed safely but fell directly in front of a German machine gun, leaving only five survivors out of thirty men. They joined us for the next ten days and were great guys who took part enthusiastically in everything we did.

But it wasn't only men from his own side who worked alongside Tibbs:

A tall, distinguished-looking German officer [came] striding through all the shot and shell, with several men following him. As they approached, I could see that this was a medical officer with his medics making for the Red Crosses. He saluted me smartly and wished me, "Good morning," and said, "Vy have you been so long? Ve have been up all night vaiting for you!" He went on to explain that they were expecting us to come during the night, but just as they were about to stand down, this extraordinary air armada appeared. (Several Germans expressed surprise that we had not used the unique skill shown in Normandy of landing at night and greatly admired by them.) He shared the house with me for a while, but as there were few Germans casualties coming in moved off.

The aircraft of Lt. Dixie Dean, Machine Gun Platoon, was fast approaching the zone:

On we flew, with quite a wide river passing below. Surely that's not the Rhine, I thought. It's wider than that, and besides, there were no signs of life of any sort around it. A burning farmhouse came in sight; then it was the Rhine after all, I realized. "Look at that," was the cry from behind. I turned my head. No. 2 was pointing to the starboard windows. A large group of Dakotas, lower than us, flew past in the opposite direction, and from one a long tongue of orange flame streamed from one engine.

I didn't want to be reminded that such things could happen, so I turned to look out of the door again, and what an impressive sight it was, and one which I will never forget. The airmanship of the American pilots was absolutely superb, as we flew in a tight box nine abreast in three vics of three. Our aircraft was the left-hand one of the right-hand vic of the second flight of nine. Back and front, left and right, Dakotas gently rose and fell as the pilots expertly kept formation. But my eyes were on one plane only—the one in the center of the leading vic, because I knew that when bodies started falling from it, it would not be long before I, too, would be taking that one inevitable step forward.

"Surely it's time the planes descended to the dropping height of 500 feet" (we were flying somewhere near 1,000) I was thinking, when the ground below was covered with abandoned parachutes as we passed over 3rd Brigade's DZ. They must all have reached their RVs in good time—there wasn't a soul in sight—but I knew now we were on our correct course, and there were only two miles to go, and the drop was but a minute away.

I would be dependent on the red and green light signals, since our jumpmaster and his communications with the pilot were not available to us. We were still flying high, and faster than normal dropping speed too. Standing in the door, you could watch as the undercarriage was lowered and half flap applied to reduce the flying speed, but this wasn't happening as we ran in to the DZ. Now we were over the woods, and ahead I could see the open farmland on which we were to drop. It couldn't be long, and my eyes were riveted on that lead aircraft. A blob appeared underneath it, and then another and another, and soon all the planes in the leading flight were disgorging their human cargoes. On came the red. A last look down to make certain we were clear of the trees, and I was tensed ready to jump "green on go." Whether [Sgt.] Frank Kenny [the stick commander] gave the order or not, I don't know, but I am sure the Dakotas were nowhere near stalling speed, and flying nearer 1,000 than 500 feet.

The impact of the former, was immediately apparent once my chute had developed, and I had released the kit bag, and lowered it to the end of the recovery rope. Instead of dropping below me, it swung upwards level with my head, before running backwards, as my chute oscillated wildly. I didn't look down or around; my efforts were concentrated on curbing the pendulum effect of the swinging parachute. I realized the ground was coming up fast, and I was in for a backward landing. My feet didn't touch—at least, not to begin with. Only feet from the earth, something caught my legs at ankle height, and I was thrown over onto my right shoulder. There was no wind, and my chute collapsed slowly around me.

All was quiet, apart from the departing planes—seemingly the "apple pie" treatment applied to the Boche guns had been successful. I tried to get to my feet, and there was a sharp jab of pain in my right shoulder. The arm was useless and just hung at my side. Using the left arm and hand only I got out of my harness but couldn't unpack the kit bag, so I hid it under a bush at the side of the track adjacent to which I had landed. In order to do this simple task, I first of all had to negotiate a post-and-wire fence. This type of fence crisscrossed the part of the DZ [where] I had landed, and was responsible for the bad landing I had made. Coming in backwards, my heels had caught the top strand of wire, pitching me onto my shoulder. These fences can't have shown up on the air photos, and we had not been warned of their existence. Fortunately, I only had to cross one such obstacle—once over the track, I was on open fields.

Facing the line of fly-in, and looking half left, I tried to locate the tower of an electricity substation, which was the landmark to guide us towards the rendezvous. I couldn't make it out, nor could I find any other distinguishing features, since the area was covered in a cloud of smoke or possibly mist. Whatever it was, visibility was limited to a couple of hundred yards. Before leaving Larkhill, our jumping jackets (a discardable overgarment) had been painted on the back with a 12-by-18-inch black rectangle, surrounded by a one-inch white border, and this played a big part in movement off the DZ. We started to move back along the line of fly-in, and I collected those who had dropped nearby. The 12th Battalion were now landing, and as one figure came trotting up, I called, "Good morning, sir, enjoy the jump?" to their CO.

"Yes, yes," he replied. "Have you seen my battalion?" which I thought a pretty silly question, since they were landing all around us.

At last the Boche came to life, and Spandaus opened up from our right, and bullets started to fly, but not too close to our little group. The visibility was so poor, I don't think we made a clear target, but the men with me must have been some of the reinforcements going into action for the first time, since they all dived to the ground. A couple of calls, "On your feet, let's get off this DZ," and we were moving again.

The battalion was funneling to woods, where a road made a dogleg turn. Some must have dropped quite close and had already flushed out parties of Boche. Arthur Higgins was in charge of one such party and was busy disarming and searching a sizable group of the enemy. As I approached and greeted him, he asked me whether I would like a Schmeisser or a Luger. Since I was already carrying a Sten and 9-millimeter pistol, to say nothing of several grenades and a fighting knife, I settled for a very fine pair of artillery binoculars, with a magnification of 10x50, far superior to the army-issue ones.

The scene was rather chaotic, with 100 or more men milling around, and officers and NCOs trying to sort out companies and platoons, but the Boche gave up and showed no fight at all. Men continued to arrive from all directions. Someone must have kept a lookout and called, "There's a jeep coming." It had to be enemy, so we all took up positions covering the road and prepared to open fire. Then another shout, "Don't shoot—it's Sergeant Webster," and indeed it was. Somehow or other he had convinced the German medical officer driving the vehicle to hand it over.

Order was gradually being restored, and the RSM [regimental sergeant major] was left to do the tidying up, as the colonel took his O Group across to a nearby cottage. It was unoccupied, and the colonel gave out orders for the move from the impromptu RV and the seizing of the objective. When he had finished, and we were about to rejoin the main body, I asked David Tibbs to have a look at my useless right shoulder. "You've dislocated it," he said.

Pvt. Bert Roe MM (one of our conscientious objector medical orderlies) was there, and he cut me out of my smock, removed my battle dress blouse and shirt, before resetting the shoulder joint. It was then strapped in position with Elastoplast, and my arm put in a sling. They then redressed me, fastened my equipment about me, slung the Sten over my shoulder, and we moved back towards the woods.

Orders had been given, and the battalion was on the road heading towards our designated objective, and I joined up with the gunners. Sergeant Egleton reported on the strength of the platoon. Nine men were missing, and two guns and tripods, but strangely, we had the condenser cans. Again two senior NCOs weren't present, namely Sergeants Drew and Kenny, so John Surgey was temporarily acting as section commander.

As the party reached the rendezvous, it met up with one of the missing gun teams. The two men had landed right on target and had their gun assembled and firing in no time. But as the gliders were now arriving, Jack Carr and Tommy Howell were in for a close call, as Lt. Dixie Dean explains:

A Hamilcar glider came diving straight for them, and they had to get out of the way PDQ (pretty damned quick). The glider caught the gun, knocked it over, breaking the traversing handles, and then smashed into a large wooden farm building to the rear.

Carr and Howell, shaken but otherwise fine, joined Dean and others in running to the building to see what assistance they could give to the glider's pilots and passengers. They need not have worried:

> Even before the roof tiles had stopped falling, an engine could be heard running, and then a Bren carrier drove out as if nothing untoward had happened. The two glider pilots were unharmed, and they disappeared with the carrier to their own RV.

Maj. Jack Watson, Company A's CO, was standing in the doorway of his C-47. He describes his jump and landing in Harclerode's history of the 6th Airborne:

> "Red on! Green on! Go!" Private Henry Gospel, my batman was behind me shouting, "I am right behind you, sir!" and out we went.
>
> It did not seem very long before I was on the ground and out of my harness. I threw away my helmet, put on my red beret and grabbed my Sten gun. The Commanding Officer had told us to put on our berets as soon as we landed in order to "put the fear of God" into the Germans.
>
> Like the Commanding Officer and all the company commanders in the Battalion, I had a hunting horn. We each had our different calls to muster our men. I blew mine as we went for the objective [a farm]. My batman was still with me saying "Right behind you, Sir!" as we took the farm with no problems.

Later that afternoon, the battalion and divisional COs arrived at the farm. The faithful Private Gospel served them a meal of bacon and eggs.

Pvt. William "Paddy" O'Rourke, in 2nd Platoon of Company A, had slept on the flight. He was in the middle of his stick, so had a few moments to get himself organized before jumping:

> Now it was my turn, and I took a giant step through the door. For a moment I was held up in the slipstream, but then began to drop. A lot of fire was coming up from the ground.

I landed at the side of the road, and as we got rid of our parachutes and prepared to move to our rendezvous, there was a shout of "Down, down! Get your heads down!" Along the road came a motorcycle combination, with two men on the bike and one in the sidecar with a machine gun. We all began firing at the motorcycle, but it just sailed past. We then got up and headed off to the rendezvous, where we dug in.

The other two companies fared similarly, and the battalion was dug in on its objectives by 1300. As Dean recalls:

While the position was being dug, I took the opportunity to ask around for information about the missing members of the platoon, and learnt that three had definitely been killed, attacking an ack-ack gun site at the bottom end of the DZ. Others had been involved in this little action and were able to confirm the report. Sergeant Drew and the youngster Private Colquohon, whom I had asked the NCO to look after, were two of the killed. "Taffy" Price, who until now had fought in all our battles completely unscathed, was the third. Armed with this information, I walked across to the second section digging in 100 yards away, and told John Surgey that he was now officially section commander. He, like myself, had started his army service in a Young Soldiers Battalion, and on D-Day was not even acting as a gun number, so he had come a long way in nine months. In fact, now all the NCOs, apart from Arthur Higgins, who was a lance corporal when he joined the gunners, were either privates on my posting in January '44 or when they joined as reinforcements. Yet the platoon functioned, tactically and administratively, as well as ever—clear evidence of the quality of the wartime volunteers the regiment attracted.

Digging in, though essential, was always a bit of a bind, but not on Operation Varsity. To begin with, it was an ideal site— the earth was sandy and free from stones and tree roots, but most important of all were the local volunteer diggers. Well, I think they volunteered their services, because they reckon a volunteer is worth ten pressed men, and nobody who didn't want the work could have produced such excellent weapon slits. We marked out what was to be dug, and then handed picks and shovels to our prisoners of war.

Once the drop was over and the objectives consolidated, Operation Varsity was very much a non-event—the aim of overwhelming the Boche defenses with a devastating display of airpower, rendering him incapable of any counterresponse, achieved 100 percent success. If there were any counterattacks, they never penetrated the defenses through to our positions, and once our prisoners had dug the slits, we stood to and waited.

Evidence of the violent reaction by some ack-ack guns lay all around. In the next field to us, an American Curtiss Commando had force-landed on its belly. The GIs were uninjured and for a time stiffened our defenses, until secure communications with their own unit were established. Broken gliders littered all the surrounding fields, and an inspection of the Hamilcar to our rear revealed a trailer loaded with spare Brens and boxes of already filled magazines for the same.

Of the four Vickers dropped, one gun and tripod were missing, two were complete, while the fourth was capable of firing, though damaged. To boost the firepower of the platoon, all except the gun teams acquired a Bren and a couple of boxes of magazines. Had a counterattack developed, we would have had a rare old shoot-out, but as I said before, nothing happened. We can't have been the only ones who raided the resupply gliders, because next morning Harry Watkins (CQMS [Company Quartermaster Sergeant] of A Company) came round with orders to confiscate such acquisitions, since there was a genuine need for them elsewhere in the division. But that didn't stop me from accusing him of being a spoilsport. Later, I was pleased he had, since for several days we marched, carrying everything on our backs.

A sizable body of troops was approaching along the road. They had already cleared an A Company outpost, so I knew they were friendly. I recognized the leading officer as Basil

Disley. All his party had been dropped in the woods, short of the dropping zone [as witnessed by Tibbs and Webster], so clearly some of the pilots had given the green jump too early, resulting in many men making tree landings, and some were shot still in their harness. There were none of the missing gunners in the party.

The arrival of this party coincided with a visit from the CO [Lieutenant Colonel Luard], who, on seeing me with my arm in a sling, wanted to know the reason, and I explained why. I have to admit that by now, I was feeling distinctly rough, and it must have shown, since the colonel called for my batman and instructed him to put me to bed. Jock Sloane retrieved one of the resupply parachutes, laid it in the bottom of our slit trench, and wrapped in that, I was glad to settle down. Before I did so, I asked Frank Egleton to arouse me at "stand-to." He deliberately misunderstood me, and it wasn't until dawn next morning that I was woken. It had clearly been an uneventful night.

Pvt. Paddy O'Rourke remembers the bodies in the trees:

Luard came down the line and said, "Get a patrol out to get those men out of the trees." I was chosen, and we set off for the woods. When we got there, Luard looked up into the trees and said, "Christ, no, it can't be. No, it can't be!" Then he said, "Cut those men down! Cut them down!" We did this quickly, and then I saw him looking at one of the bodies. It was that of a chap named Morrison. He wasn't nineteen, so he wasn't allowed to jump. He'd been to see Luard to ask permission. Luard had said, "It's the end of the war. There won't be much resistance, so I'll grant you permission." Morrison came back "cock-a-hoop." I remember Luard's face in the woods. I'd never seen tears in a man's eyes before. He said, "If I hadn't given him permission to jump, he'd still be alive."

12TH PARACHUTE BATTALION
The 12th Parachute Battalion constituted the majority of the first serial, B5, flown by the 315th TCG, and was to secure an area between the

woodland and two road junctions. The 12th's CO, Lt. Col. Ken Darling, had ensured that his men would jump as light as possible. So every other man carried a toggle rope, no one had any entrenching tools or grenades and the only spare clothing taken was socks. In addition, platoons were allocated to aircraft so that members would land on their intended part of the drop zone.

The 315th's CO, Col. Howard Lyon flew the lead aircraft in a formation from the 43rd Squadron. His aircraft carried Darling, his headquarters, and two navigators. One was Capt. Bernard Coggins, who recalls in *Airborne Troop Carrier Three One Five Group*, by George Cholewczynski: "Since we were only going four or five miles into enemy territory, this particular mission was considered to be a milk run. This was a terrible mistake."

Despite the reception from the Germans, Lyon took his aircraft down to about 450 feet before the green light was lit. The rest of the serial followed suit. Consequently, the battalion spent little time in the descent and landed close together on the zone.

Disaster struck as Lyon turned for the run back to the river. A shell entered the cockpit, went through his foot, and exited through his knee. Instinctively, he pushed everything that would make the aircraft climb, which she did. Coggins helped Lyon out of his seat just as another shell came into the cockpit. Lyon took another wound in the leg, as did Coggins, while the copilot, Capt. Carl Persson, had part of his hand taken off. All the crewmen managed to bail out and were captured by the Germans. The medical aid station where they were taken was overrun, however, and they were released.

Pvt. Bob Butcher's flight had been somewhat uneventful:

> The order came to stand in the door—this was it! Looking down, we could see the Rhine, but it looked quite insignificant from our height. The 3rd Brigade's DZ came into sight with the parachutes lying all over the place. There was no time to dwell on that spectacle, for then we heard flak bursting and our plane started to buck. The pilot held a steady course though. The plan was that the American crew chief would act as dispatcher and throw the switches to release the jettison containers. Our platoon commander, Sgt. Norman Walker, was jumping No. 1. As the switches were thrown, he

would throw out a kit bag containing a hand trolley, then jump.

Unfortunately, the crew chief's intercom became unplugged at the crucial moment, so that Sergeant Walker had to operate the switches, throw out the trolley kit bag, then jump with his own kit bag. The plane was jumping up and down as flak burst nearby, and when I got to the exit, I swear that I jumped, but the plane bucked up and I found myself sitting on the floor of the doorway. Nothing daunted, Jim Hanfey called out, "Come on, Butch!" and gave me a hearty kick. So I think that I can claim to have jumped over the Rhine twice.

My immediate troubles were not over. After my unorthodox exit, it took a little longer than usual to get sorted out. Then I pulled the kit bag quick-release tape. It released the upper buckle, but the others remained obstinately in place and in my tugging at it, the tape slipped out of my hands and fluttered just out of reach. I was getting nearer the ground now, so I just resigned myself to landing with the kit bag still on, which would almost certainly result in at least a fractured leg. Then I saw a copse of tall trees coming up and towards me at an alarming rate. Now, the approved drill for such an event was to hold the hands up to protect the face and pull up the knees to protect one's vital parts. With the kit bag still on my leg, I could only manage three-quarters of that procedure, but it was enough as I crashed into the branches with quite some force.

I was finally able to release the wretched kit bag, get out of my harness, and hanging on to it to shorten the fall, drop safely to the ground. My feet were on enemy soil—then, clumsy as ever, I lost my balance and sat heavily on the protruding sight pillar of the bipod in my kit bag. The height from which I dropped from the tree tends to get higher every time I tell the story, but I reckon that it would have been from 6 to 10 feet from my feet to the ground.

Our RV was a wood to the right of the line of flight, and sure enough there were some trees in the right place. It didn't look much like the wood we had seen in aerial photographs during briefing but it was in the right place and obviously in the right direction, so I joined the stream of paras heading in that direction. Some of them belonged to the 12th, as evidenced by the light blue DZ patch on their sleeves, so I was in good company. At this stage the enemy fire was, I would say, moderate, and I didn't see anyone hesitating to go forward.

Butcher was correct in his thinking that the wood didn't look like the one in the photographs. Poor visibility had confused the paratroopers, and they had assembled at the wrong piece of woodland.

As I neared the trees, Maj. Frank Bucher, the dour, strict, regular battalion second in command, could be seen standing at the edge of the wood. Despite the fire, he was quite unperturbed, as if on an exercise. I almost expected to be checked for being improperly dressed. In fact, he had recognized that the drop, though accurate, was slightly to the left of the real zone, possibly as a result of the area being covered with haze. He directed us on to the real RV, which we could now see over several hundred yards of field. We were beginning to become a battalion again instead of hundreds of individuals making their own ways.

Close to the real RV, our signals officer, Lt. Jim Absalom, with pistol in hand, was ordering groups to lie down and to proceed at irregular intervals. This was in accordance with the drill for moving across gaps in cover, but unfortunately, there was no cover for there to be gaps in. Still, it was encouraging to see that someone seemed to be in charge. As I approached him, we heard the noise of a tank approaching, and turning towards it, we could see an unusual shape coming towards us out of the haze. Remembering the damage that the Panzers had wreaked at Arnhem, it was disconcerting, but Jim had a VC [Victoria Cross] look on his face and an apparent confidence in the tank stopping ability of his 9-millimeter Browning pistol, which was not justified. Fortunately, as it got nearer, we could see that it was a Locust light tank of our Divisional Armoured Reconnaissance Regiment that had a piece of a glider resting on it. The tank went purposefully on its way, so I assumed, perhaps mistakenly, that the crew knew where they were going, and it was comforting to think that we had some armor on our side.

After a brief pause, I was waved on, and just on the other side of the wood, the rest of the Mortar Platoon was busy setting up and digging in. With my arrival, we now had three out of our four mortars in action, ready to support the rifle companies if required. Pvt. Robbie Anderson, who was carrying a part of the fourth mortar, was missing, and we later learned that he had been killed.

The position was under fire for some time, but then the shelling ceased. In accordance with the CO's orders to take risks early, Lt. Phil Burkinshaw had not waited for his platoon to be complete, but grabbed the first twenty men and made a textbook attack on the guns that had been causing us so much trouble. All three rifle companies had to fight to gain their objectives, which were farm buildings occupied by the enemy, but had succeeded in doing so within an hour or two, although not without suffering further casualties.

Private Butcher's account provides a clear summary of the work of his battalion to secure its objectives. His description of Lieutenant Burkinshaw's scratch platoon "textbook attack" warrants further explanation. Dispatched to the various company rendezvous, Company A was the first to take its objective. Burkinshaw's small force not only attacked the battery of 88s that was zeroed in on the rendezvous, with its guns firing at close range, but also captured the battery and its crews.

Company B had a real fight to gain possession of several farm buildings. Each was strongly defended and therefore had to be taken one at a time. Lt. Peter Cattell, although slightly wounded, led the assault. He suffered a further wound, as did his fellow officer, Lt. Ginger Delaney. Then the 4th Platoon, under the command of Sergeant Dobson, raced to the rescue and was able to take the remainder of the company's objectives. The rest of the company joined them and began to dig in.

Lieutenant Reed and Sergeant Wilson, from Company C, led an assault group on their company's objective—a group of farm buildings. These were cleared with little resistance and, with the help of the rest of the company, made secure. Soon after, a patrol made contact with a company from the Devons.

Shortly after this, the gliders came into the zones as Butcher was heading toward a slit trench:

> I saw two mortarmen crouching down, and one of them, George Presson, shouted to me to look behind—they had seen that we were in the path of a glider coming in to land. The warning almost certainly saved my life, for the glider pilot would not have been able to miss me if I had not moved out of the way.

Butcher returned unscathed to his position, as the general situation continued to be fairly quiet. The battalion established itself in various positions and settled in to await any counterattack.

Ken Darling reflects on the day in Harclerode's history of the 6th Airborne:

> An eerie silence fell over the DZ, which had been such a noisy battleground. Enemy resistance had been completely flattened and I was able to ride a horse around the battalion area.

7TH PARACHUTE BATTALION

While the 12th and 13th Parachute Battalions concentrated on capturing the brigade objectives, the 7th Parachute Battalion, in Serial B6, was to land at the northern edge of the zone. Its main tasks were to defend the zone and prevent enemy troops from reaching the brigade's objectives, until the other two battalions had consolidated themselves. At such time, the 7th would move into a reserve position.

Lt. Col. Geoffrey Pine-Coffin, the battalion CO, recalls in *BAOR Battlefield Tour*:

> My Battalion came down looking for a fight. The German flak gunners weren't getting much success in shooting down the Dakotas so a lot of them switched and burst their shells amongst the parachutists instead; this was most unpleasant and

we suffered a number of casualties before we even reached the ground. There was mortar bombing and shelling on the ground but it was a great relief to get there all the same.

Thanks to a well-considered drop plan, the battalion landed in companies. Companies B and C established themselves in their defensive areas and began digging in. Initially things were quiet. Over the next few hours, concerted enemy probing attacks kept both units busy. Company B contended with attacks of platoon size or slightly larger, while Company C fought off one attack, which was at full company strength.

Company A had been dropped some way from the zone. One of its members, a sergeant, saw that he was going to land beside a German soldier armed with a machine pistol. The sergeant made a good landing and closed his eyes, waiting for the German to fire. After several seconds, he realized that nothing appeared to be happening quickly, so he looked up. To his amazement, the German was folding up his parachute. Having finished this, he helped the sergeant out of his harness, unpacked his Bren gun from its valise, handed over his own gun and put up his hands. The two men were quickly joined by about twenty other Germans, who also surrendered.

As with the other companies, A's organization for the drop meant that it landed virtually complete and quickly made its way to its intended objective. Here things were somewhat different. The area was being shelled by the guns that Lieutenant Burkinshaw's group, from the 12th Battalion, finally captured. Company A should have taken this battery, but its late arrival prevented this. Consequently, while it was digging in, and the guns were still undisturbed, they sustained high casualties.

The battalion also had been given an independent task of taking and holding a road and rail junction that lay between the two parachute brigades. The problem was that the junction was some three miles from the zone and located in an area likely to be well defended. Pine-Coffin had allocated a platoon to undertake the task, and in the interests of knowing what faced its members, he had decided to send a reconnaissance party, with a radio, to spy out the land before committing the entire platoon. But the officer who was to lead the party was killed on the drop. Since he had lost more men than he could afford, Pine-Coffin abandoned the reconnaissance and sent Lieutenant Patterson with the platoon.

After some close shaves, Patterson and his men reached the junction. They dug in and held on for twenty-two hours before being relieved. During this time, the platoon sustained several attacks, most of which they fought off from their slit trenches. Occasionally the "Patterson Method" was put to use, however, as Pine-Coffin explains in *BAOR Battlefield Tour:*

> Whenever an attack developed [Patterson] sized it up as quickly as he could, and if he decided . . . it seemed stronger than he could hold off [he] would leave his position entirely and move his platoon round to one of the flanks; then, when the enemy had struck their blow at nothing and were wondering what to do next, he would rush them from the flank. In this way he killed a great number of Germans and captured many more.

Pine-Coffin was among his battalion's casualties when he was shot in the nose. Although in extreme discomfort, he maintained his command, and the battalion was well dug in by nightfall.

The brigade's objective was secured by 1500 hours, and the 7th Battalion was ordered into reserve. This was not an easy task, as Companies B and C were still fighting. With some careful maneuvering, all three companies withdrew in good order and without further loss. Casualty figures for the 7th were high. Initial losses had been caused by ground fire during the landing, as described by Pine-Coffin, and the requirement for the battalion to remain in the vicinity of the drop zone meant that it was easily targeted by artillery and mortar fire.

225TH PARACHUTE FIELD AMBULANCE

As with their counterparts in the 224th, the 225th Parachute Field Ambulance's medics also kept busy with the numerous casualties. The unit contingent had been similarly divided among the three parachute battalions. Headquarters and 4th Section were responsible for the medical dressing stations, while the remaining sections worked under command of the parachute battalions. Clearing posts and regimental aid posts were set up, and the medical dressing station was functioning by 1200 hours. Pvt. Bob Butcher, 12th Battalion, recalls:

Our medics had just finished clearing the DZ of our wounded, and I shall always remember one stretcher party, exhausted and bloodstained, bringing in one casualty. Some of the medics were conscientious objectors whose personal conduct and the manner in which they carried out their duties earned them our respect. One, who was not a conscientious objector, was Cpl. Harry Houghton, who gained a well-deserved Military Medal for his work that day. Padre Joe Jenkins [was also] busy supervising German prisoners of war taking the wounded to the regimental aid post and burying the dead. They were using farm carts.

The 12th's CO, Ken Darling, also paid his compliments:

Special mention must be made of the sterling work of our medical staff: Captain Wilson, who was our medical officer, Corporal Houghton and the stretcher bearers, and our most respected padre, the Reverend Joe Jenkins, all of whom tended our casualties under fire.

591ST PARACHUTE SQUADRON ROYAL ENGINEERS

There was no main engineer task within the brigade area, but the 591st Parachute Squadron Royal Engineers dropped to deal with any immediate tasks that might arise and to complete reconnoiters of the road that linked the brigade to the Airlanding Brigade and divisional headquarters. The troop was scattered on the drop and had four members wounded on the way to the rendezvous and one killed during the time there. All members were present within the hour.

A detachment "spiked" a battery of 88-millimeter guns at the eastern end of the drop zone. These had caused much disruption and destruction during the landing.

Maj. Gen. Matthew B. Ridgway.

Right: *Maj. Gen. William M. Miley.*

Medal of Honor recipient
Pvt. George J. Peters, 507th PIR.

17TH AIRBORNE DIVISION ASSOCIATION

Medal of Honor recipient
PFC Stewart S. Stryker, 513th PIR.

17TH AIRBORNE DIVISION ASSOCIATION

Cpl. Frederick G. Topham, VC,
1st Canadian Parachute Battalion,
in Ottawa, Canada, August 2, 1945.

LIBRARY AND ARCHIVES OF CANADA

PFC Curtis Edwards,
Battery B, 681st GFAB.

RHONDA EDWARDS

Above, left to right:
Cpl. John Cooper, Pvt. F. Heaton, and Pvt. "Geordie" Smith.

J. COOPER

Flight Officer George Theis, 98th TCS, 440th TCG.

GEORGE THEIS

Above:
*Lt. John W. Heffner and
Lt. Bruce C. Merryman,
62nd TCS, 314th TCG.*

17TH AIRBORNE DIVISION

ASSOCIATION

*Sgt. Fred Waggett (right),
796th MP Battalion,
and fellow MP Joe Leahy.*

FRED WAGGETT

Above:
*PFC Louis J.
Zoghby,
194th GIR,
studying a map of
the drop zone.*
LOUIS J. ZOGHBY

*Curtiss C-46
Commando.*
AFHRA

Douglas C-47 Dakota. AFHRA

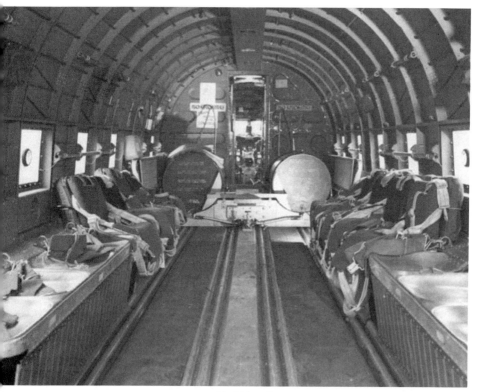

C-47 interior. AFHRA

Above:
*Consolidated B-24
Liberator.* AFHRA

*Lt. Col.
S. T. B. Johnson,
commanding officer,
139th Engineer
Battalion, briefs
the 440th TCG at
the Royal Theater,
Orleans.*
RANDOLPH HILS

Above:
RAF glider pilots.
CY HENSON

*Lt. Arthur Cox,
Maj. John Kippen,
and Second Lieu-
tenant Dudley,
B Company,
8th Parachute
Battalion.*
TONY LEAKE

Lt. Arthur Cox (back row center) with his "stick": half of his No. 4 Platoon.

TONY LEAKE

194th GIR troopers at Coulommiers gather equipment prior to loading their CG-4As.

AIRBORNE AND SPECIAL OPERATIONS MUSUEM

Hamilcar on Landing Zone P.
MUSEUM OF ARMY FLYING

Right:
Parapacks being fitted on a 440th TCG C-47.
RANDOLPH HILS

194th GIR troopers wait to board their glider. 17TH AIRBORNE DIVISION ASSOCIATION

MKII Horsa Chalk 356 on Landing Zone P, one of thirty B Squadron Horsas allocated to the 53rd (WY) Light Regiment. MUSEUM OF ARMY FLYING

513th PIR troopers wait to board C-46s of 48th TCS 313th.
AIRBORNE AND SPECIAL OPERATIONS MUSEUM

Below: *Hamminkeln Station.* MUSEUM OF ARMY FLYING

Troopers wait in pensive mood for takeoff. AIRBORNE AND SPECIAL OPERATIONS MUSEUM

Below: *440th TCG C-47s and CG-4As at Orléans/Bricy.* RANDOLPH HILS

Below: *Two Company B 139th AEB gliders.* RANDOLPH HILS

S.Sgt. Maj. L.W.
"Buck" Turnbull, CGM.
MUSEUM OF ARMY FLYING

680th howitzer being hitched to its jeep. 17TH AIRBORNE DIVISION ASSOCIATION

Above:
155th AAB 6-pounder antitank gun being towed off Landinz Zone N. 17TH AIRBORNE DIVISION ASSOCIATION

George Theis's prisoners.
GEORGE THEIS

A Bren section from 12th Battalion, the Devonshire Regiment, poses for a photo during a quiet moment. ALEX DALLEY

507th PIR troopers advance through woodland toward Diersfordt. AIRBORNE AND SPECIAL OPERATIONS MUSEUM

German paratroop prisoners taken during early morning landing, Xanten, Germany, March 24, 1945. LIBRARY AND ARCHIVES OF CANADA

Personnel of the 8th Royal Scots linking up with personnel of the 1st Canadian Parachute Battalion after crossing the Rhine River. Bergerfurth, Germany, March 25, 1945. LIBRARY AND ARCHIVES OF CANADA

CHAPTER 7

Securing the British Sector

6TH AIRLANDING BRIGADE

It had been a peaceful three-hour flight as the gliders and their tugs settled into the final approach. BBC war correspondents Richard Dimbleby and Stanley Maxted were passengers, Dimbleby in a Halifax and Maxted in a Hamilcar. Their eyewitness reports were broadcast on the BBC that evening. Dimbleby was watching the fly-in from the Halifax's astrodome, and he describes it in *War Report*:

> The Rhine lies left and right across our path below us, shining in the sunlight wide and with sweeping curves; and the whole of this mighty airborne army is now crossing and filling the whole sky . . . on our right-hand side a Dakota has just gone down in flames. We watched it go to the ground, and I've just seen the parachutes of it blossoming and floating down towards the river.
>
> Down there is the smoke screen laid by the army lying right across the far bank of the river. Ahead of us, another pillar of black smoke marks the spot where an aircraft has gone down, and yet another one; it's a Stirling; it's going down with flames coming out from under its belly—four parachutes are coming out—one, two, three, four parachutes have come out. . . .
>
> We haven't got time to watch it further because we're coming up now to the exact chosen landing-ground where

our airborne forces have to be put down; and no matter what the opposition may be, we have got to keep straight on, dead on the exact position. There's only a minute or two to go; we cross the Rhine—we're on the east bank of the river. We're passing now over the army smoke-cloud. The glider has gone. We've let her go. There she goes down behind us. We've turned hard away in a tight circle to port to get out of this area. I'm sorry if I'm shouting this is a very tremendous sight.

Stanley Maxted's glider, Chalk 277, was one of twelve assigned to the 716th Company Royal Army Service Corps (see the section on the 716th later in this chapter for information on the other eleven). Stanley Maxted continues the story in *War Report*:

There was just a minute or two of quiet as the great Hamilcar ran in with the sound of the rushing wind in her wings. Then, when just a few feet off the ground, pandemonium broke loose—the wicked snap of Spandau machine guns, mixed with the slower bong of 20-mm. incendiaries for just a fraction of a second before they started pricking out their trademark in the thin skin of the glider.

Things seemed to happen too quickly for me to take them all in at once. There was an explosion that appeared to be inside my head, the smell of burnt cordite. I went down on one knee. Something hot and sickly was dripping over my right eye and off my chin and all over my clothes. There was a doom-like lurch and a great rending as smoke, dust, and daylight came from nowhere. I saw the Bren carrier go inexorably out of the nose of the glider, carrying the whole works ahead of it, and wiping two signallers off the top of it like flies. Even then the bullets kept crashing through the wreckage. It didn't seem fair; but then there is no "fair" or "unfair" in airborne fighting.

At the moment of impact a trailer that was chained just behind me came forward about six inches and caught me in the small of the back. Mercifully the chains held on. Somehow Captain Peter Cattle and I hurled ourselves out of the

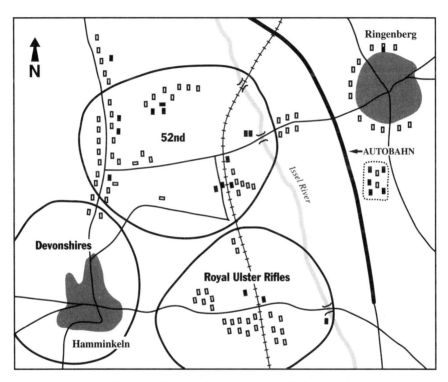

6th Airlanding Brigade Area of Operations

mess into a shallow ditch by a hedge. Looking up, and clearing my eyes with the back of my hand, I saw a man pinned across the chest by wreckage. One of the glider pilots was getting him out. How those glider pilots and the two signallers on top of the carrier escaped the mass of that hurtling iron carrier I'll never know, but they did.

A doctor came along and dressed Peter and me, and helped us to a dressing station. On the way I saw burning gliders, crashed gliders, and the great courage of men going in to fight almost before they had finished touching down. It was the old story of the men with the maroon berets who never worry about odds.

Also on that glider were Lance Cpl. Michael Ham, two fellow wireless operators, and Major Oliver, a public-relations officer. The trailer that hit Maxted in the back carried a wireless station. Mike Ham explains:

Our task on Varsity was to provide public-relations communications for Maxted to broadcast from 6th Airborne Division HQ, via Brussels, to the BBC in London. Prior to takeoff, I remember chatting to Dimbleby and Maxted on the runway. The glider crash-landed by Hamminkeln railway station, and the wireless station was "brewed up." So, sadly, there was no "live" broadcast by Maxted.

Apart from some minor bruising, Ham was otherwise uninjured and made his way with others to divisional headquarters at Kopenhof Farm.

2ND BATTALION OXFORDSHIRE AND BUCKINGHAMSHIRE LIGHT INFANTRY COUP DE MAIN

Lt. Hugh Clark, who was in glider No. 3, explains the plan for a coup de main by the 2nd Battalion Oxfordshire and Buckinghamshire Light Infantry (OBLI):

The detailed plan for the first three gliders was to secure the east bank of the river around the road bridge. No. 1 glider, due to land first, was to take the bridge and support No. 2

glider as they took an adjacent house, while No. 2 glider was to support No. 3 glider as they took a neighbouring house—all seemingly straightforward!

The official history of the British airborne divisions states that the assault was a particularly successful part of the operation, which it was, considering the reception met by the gliders' occupants. L.Cpl. Godfrey Yardley was in glider No. 2:

At last the River Rhine came into view and as we approached it at about 3,000 feet, the order was given to open the doors. As I sat on the starboard side forward, I watched [Pvt.] Ginger Belsham pull the forward door upwards and at that precise moment flak burst under the port wing, banking the aircraft over to starboard, almost throwing Ginger out of the door—only to be pulled back by the platoon commander [Lt. Bob Preston] and sergeant. This took perhaps two seconds and allowed this man to live for another few minutes—for he and 60 percent of the platoon were soon to die.

The dropping and landing zones were shrouded in smoke, which must have made target identification very difficult for the pilots. The gentle jerk of the towline being cast off was felt as the nose went down and the landing procedure began. Arms linked in each other's and a silent prayer.

The enemy was waiting for us with a prepared concentration of ack-ack guns, and being the first gliders in our regiment we took the full weight of the defenses, as historical records were later to show. We descended through the heavy barrage of flak, many lives being lost during those first few minutes, including one of the pilots, Geoff Collins, while S.Sgt. Bill Rowland was wounded. One chap by the name of Shrewsbury who sat opposite me got a burst of machine-gun fire through the neck—the bullets then passing between the heads of myself and Ted Tamplin, who sat on my right; a gap of about eight to ten inches (luck number one).

With some of the controls damaged and no compressed air to operate the landing flaps, we flew across the landing zone, over the railway and the River Issel, to crash head-on into a wood at ground level. At a speed of over 70 knots, a fully loaded glider—the size of a heavy bomber—becomes a pile of matchwood in about one second flat.

While all this was going on, No. 1 glider—17 Platoon—had also been badly hit by flak and was breaking up, spilling men and equipment out, finally to crash as we had done—except there were no survivors. I was one of the lucky ones (luck number two), being the center one of five men still sitting on one piece of seat with harness on. With the exception of a few cuts and bruises, we five were OK. I remember going over to Staff Sergeant Rowland, wounded by the flak, and asking him silly questions like what speed we had been doing and what had happened to the brake parachutes. Several other chaps were alive but wounded, but most were dead including the platoon commander, sergeant, and two corporals, leaving a corporal, myself, and another lance corporal and seven others unhurt.

The wounded were attended to by the platoon medic, Lance Corporal Greenwood, and Ted Noble, who did sterling work during the following few hours. During this time, a recce [reconnaissance] patrol reported a tank at the west end of the next wood and large enemy concentrations in the area.

I took a compass bearing on artillery fire, assuming it was our own firing according to plan, and established our position on the map (which I still have). From the information we had of the enemy strength and positions, it was agreed that the best plan would be to try to link up with the nearest Allied unit, which was the Royal Ulster Rifles at their objective on one of the two bridges over the River Issel. As the shortest distance between two points is a straight line, this meant we had to run like hell over some 1,000 yards of open ground to reach it.

There were about eight of us capable of doing this, but one man, Ted Tamplin, had an injured ankle and offered to stay behind with the wounded, knowing he would be taken prisoner or maybe shot. He was taken but did, however, escape some days later and rejoined the regiment.

Bill Rowland recalls coming round and finding himself looking up at a German officer demanding whether they were English or American. Bill was convinced that had they been American, they would have been shot—I wonder why? By the grace of God they were allowed to live and were told they would be left to their devices, as they would probably be picked up by our own side. They were—some forty-eight hours later.

The moment of our hasty departure was indicated by the sound of the enemy sweeping the wood from the other end, and so with the old saying "he who fights and runs away (may) live to fight another day," we ran like bats out of hell. A line of bobbing red berets weaving across a large open field must have appeared easy targets to the enemy, who promptly opened up on us from all angles. Either we had been very well trained or a lot of Germans were bad shots as no one was hit . . . or maybe we were very lucky (luck number three).

Fortunately, the Royal Ulster Rifles had taken the bridge, and the sound of a rich Irish voice shouting, "Halt, who goes there?" was a most welcome sound. We crossed the bridge between bursts of machine-gun fire and reported to an officer with a request for stretcher bearers and some help to go back for our wounded. This request was denied, coupled with an order to stay put.

Forty years later, I found that an artillery "stonk" [British military slang for a heavy bombardment] was coming down on the spot where we had left our wounded. An artillery shell landed by Bill Rowland, taking off an arm and leg . . . how many of our wounded died as a result of that shell?

We rejoined our regiment the next day—25 March 1945, my twentieth birthday.

S.Sgt. Norman Elton and Sgt. Des Page were piloting Lt. Hugh Clark's glider, and all three give their recollections. Elton's appeared in the August 2002 issue of *The Eagle*. Des Page:

It was now 11 miles to the Rhine and a further 7 more to our target at the farthest point beyond the river. Our tug crew

obligingly assisted our navigation by reporting over the intercom each mile. Very soon we reported to them that we could
see the Rhine below. Then came the unexpected. Across the
river was a pall of black smoke and dust stretching on either
side, as far as the eye could see and rising up to our flying
height of 2,500 feet. Paratroop planes having dropped their
troops, some 3 miles beyond the river, were now returning
towards and below us, some of them on fire. Flak was bursting
above the smoke and fire flashes could be seen within it. We
had 7 miles still to go. For the first 3 of those, heavy flak was
bursting all round, several shells exploding between the tug
and the glider. During the next 3 miles the smoke began to
thin. We could now see the ground, but equally, the German
gunners could see us and began firing over open sights. The
flak was continuous and heavy.

Hugh Clark:

To ensure we could make a quick exit from the glider when
we landed, we opened the forward and rear exit doors while
still flying. As we were flying at about 120 mph, we were met
with a rush of cold air through the glider. As we looked down,
we could see the assault boats of the ground troops crossing
the river.

It was at this point that Norman Elton told me to take my
seat and strap myself in.

Des Page:

I began to swing the glider from side to side on its towline
hoping to confuse the German gunners. A shell exploded
under our tail and threw Norman onto the Perspex in front
of me as he returned to the flight cabin.

Norman Elton:

I cast off and pulled in behind No. 1 who was already in free
flight. Almost at once, No.1 blew up in mid-air, portions of

his fuselage coming back to break through the Perspex of our cabin. I immediately turned on to No. 2 who was by now well below us. We had, as it were, a grandstand view of one wing crumpling and falling off while the glider spiralled slowly towards the ground.

We now started to feel our own glider shudder from the impact of what later turned out to be 20mm cannon shells. Obviously there was no future in hanging around so I went into a vertical dive. I feel sure that our airspeed indicator went around twice and maybe started a third circuit when I had to take my eyes away as the ground was alarmingly close. I glimpsed the canal and some open space alongside. I immediately pulled hard back on the controls, put on full flaps, and popped the arrestor gear.

Des Page:

We lost about 2,000 feet in the initial dive, turned to port and leveled out at 300 feet, and were now seconds away from our final turn to port and landing. Guns within yards of the bridge were now recovering from our surprise dive. We could see one of the guns and its crew, and it was clear that if we turned to port now, we would present them with a huge target and at touchdown we would be looking down a gun barrel.

Hugh Clark:

We in the back of the glider felt the pull of gravity as we headed for the ground. We thought that Norman and Des were dead and that we soon would be.

Norman Elton:

Although the arrestor gear slowed us up with quite a jolt, what stopped us in time were about six fences we ploughed through and being able to snaggle the edge of one wing on a tree. With our tail half off, and our undercarriage gone, we were able to step straight out onto the ground. We took up defensive positions around the glider and I remember looking up and seeing a row of bullet holes appear in the fuselage just above our heads.

Des Page:

A burst from my Bren gun gave a respite, and now under the command of Hugh Clark, we dashed for the canal. A man died as we reached it. Behind us, our glider was on fire and enemy mortar was raining down.

Hugh Clark:

As I looked at the glider, both wings had been clipped, the undercarriage had started to come up through the floor of the glider, and the arrestor parachute had started to pull the tail off.

The enemy were peppering the top of the glider with machine-gun fire. I was unable to pick out any landmarks to pinpoint our position. I saw there was a bank some hundred yards to our right, and I gave the order to make a dash there a section at a time. We had left the glider with just our weapons and wearing skeleton webbing, with the intention of going back to collect our packs later.

One man, Lance Corporal Graham, had badly injured his shoulder in the landing and had to be helped along. We all got safely to the far side of the bank, only to find it was the bank of a not very wide river, which I felt could not be the River Issel.

We waded the river with the water only coming up to our thighs, again a section at a time, and slid down the far bank, where we rested to take stock. In fact, I realized later that it was the River Issel. Each of us in the platoon had an antitank mine tied to our entrenching tool and hanging down our backsides. I decided we should get rid of these, which was a great relief. We also took off our steel helmets and put on our red berets which were a recognition sign, particularly with the U.S. airborne troops of the 17th U.S. Airborne Division, who were landing alongside our division.

While looking over the river, I saw the glider hit by a number of mortar bombs and catch fire. I was still unable to pinpoint our position, so I decided we should move away from the river and head for some trees a few hundred yards away, as they would offer better cover.

As we were ready to move off, word came to me that Corporal Durbidge, one of my section commanders, had been shot through the head and was killed. As there was nothing we could do for him, we had to leave him there and headed for the wooded cover. All this time we could see other gliders coming down through the haze and A/A [antiaircraft] fire.

A Hamilcar glider made a very heavy landing close to us, and we saw men thrown out as it came to a halt. It was at this point that our two pilots left us and went to the help of their glider pilot colleagues in the Hamilcar.

As we approached the wood I was relieved to meet Capt. Tod Sweeney, commander of the Mortar Group of the regiment. He had had to abandon his jeep on the wrong side of the river and had with him as well as his own men a number of men from other units. Tod knew just where we were and arranged that he would lead the way back to our position with my leading section. The remainder of the men with him would move in the middle of my platoon, who would provide protection.

We passed through the wood and reached the railway line and headed north. We passed on our left an area where a lot of American WACO gliders were landing and saw a number crash to the ground. Tod found that the Americans had established a first-aid post nearby, so he dispatched the wounded who were with us to be attended to. All this time there was a lot of small-arms fire going off all around, but none seemed to be aimed at us specifically. However, one of my platoon headquarters group was hit in the leg. We applied a field dressing and assured him that we would send stretcher bearers to pick him up.

Des Page:

We didn't go to the bridge but waded the river at a point closer to the Royal Ulster Rifles' bridge. We crawled to the railway, and as I popped my head up to look over the line, an American officer's head appeared on the other side. We quickly worked out that we were friendlies, and we continued on our way towards our RV at the station.

Norman Elton:

As we waded the river a Hamilcar made a perfect approach alongside the canal, but for no apparent reason failed to straighten out and hit the ground at an acute angle. A large pick-up truck with a seventeen-pounder gun attached shot out the front with bodies flying in all directions. We found out later that her controls had been shot away. Des and I managed to have a chat with the pilots before being gathered up by our Squadron Major.

En route to Hamminkeln we came across the Oerlikon battery, which had done so much damage. The Major sent myself and another bren gunner to rout them out whilst the others were prepared to give us covering fire from behind a hedge. I will always remember walking forward, a cigarette hanging from the corner of my mouth and a machine gun in the crook of my arm—the epitome of a Chicago gangster! A white handkerchief on the end of a bayonet poked itself from one of the dugouts and out came, not the arrogant Nazi type one might expect, but a rather timid bank clerk type. We searched the prisoners, one of whom had a beautiful jewelled gold watch tucked away in an inner pocket. The look on his face when I took it was inexpressible, even more so when I handed it back. I thought, "You'll be lucky mate if you get away with that." Later on it struck me— where did he get it? Anyway, we did get in a plug for British probity.

Flight Lt. J. Courtnay P. Thomas was piloting the Dakota towing glider No. 4. As he recalls in the December 2004 issue of *The Eagle*:

> Soon the Rhine could be recognised and the anti-aircraft fire ahead of us looked foreboding and having to fly directly into that "net curtain" of dense black gunfire was intimidating. Suddenly, there was an unexpected shudder. Causing the Dakota to lose height. Realising that the last burst of gunfire must have been close, my wireless operator went to look through the astrodome to see what had happened. He yelled in my ear that the glider had been severely damaged having "lost its nose" and looked like an open matchbox! The motionless legs of the pilot could be seen dangling in his seat. The Dakota was certainly behaving in an erratic manner, due to the glider's constant change in altitude.

The glider was carrying the 16th Platoon and the quartermaster, Major Aldworth. The shell, which had hit the glider, had slightly wounded him and killed both pilots. Aldworth managed to get one of them out of his seat and took control of the aircraft. He had no flying experience, except as a passenger, but during exercises had seen how pilots landed a glider. He had no idea about brakes, flaps, and so forth, but he knew that as the ground came closer, he needed to pull back on the column.

Flight Lieutenant Thomas called up the glider, and after several minutes, the faint voice of Aldworth answered him and explained the situation. Thomas continues:

> My co-pilot hastily explained the use of the controls, but by now we were drawing closer to the landing zone. Wishing him the best of luck, I reminded him to pull into the high position before releasing.

There then followed a most bizarre few minutes, as both aircraft appeared to be working against one another. With all the stress and strain, the towrope snapped and the glider headed toward the ground. Aldworth managed to straighten up for a landing, and the glider came to earth. It careened through a ditch and hedge before coming to a stop. No further injuries except bumps and bruises appear to have occurred, and Aldworth and the platoon made their way to the railway station.

1ST BATTALION ROYAL ULSTER RIFLES COUP DE MAIN

The 1st Battalion Royal Ulster Rifles (RUR) also came down hard in its coup de main. Major Dyball, the Company Commander, was in the first glider. As planned, it landed 150 yards from the bridge. The pilots and front passengers went through the glider's nose. Passengers farther back exited through the door and came under intense machine-gun fire. A burst killed the radio operator and put the radio out of action. Dyball, for the moment, was out of contact with his front platoons.

Fortunately, the angle of the glider's landing had caused one of the wings to dig a trench in the ground. Seven of Dyball's party managed to scramble into this, and they set up a Bren gun to attack the German machine-gun position. They silenced the Germans, but almost immediately came under fire from another position.

There being no other sign of the remaining platoons, Dyball decided to dash across the open ground to a small wood, where he hoped to be able to contact more of his men. The Bren gun covered him, and he made it to the wood and managed to contact two glider pilots, two men from the OBLI, and a few Royal Engineers. These men had established a good, reasonably well-protected firing position, which happened to be covering the house Dyball wanted as his headquarters.

As luck would have it, the 21st Platoon had landed on the other side of the house. Being in good order, despite a fiery welcome, the platoon had assembled quickly and attacked the house, taking twenty-five prisoners as a result. Meanwhile, Dyball had moved his party into the wood and positioned the men so that they had a view of a trench, which ran up to the house and bridge. They allowed a small group of Germans, escaping from the house, to approach to within 20 yards, then threw a grenade at them, which missed the trench but exploded alongside it. The Germans quickly surrendered. Dyball went across the bridge to see how the 21st Platoon was faring. He reports in *The Royal Ulster Rifles*, by Charles Graves:

[I] found that [they] had done their job in clearing the houses. Although the platoon commander had been killed, the platoon sergeant, although wounded in the head, arm, leg and thigh led the platoon against strong opposition, which was dug in. The bridge was in our hands, and an all-round defence was quickly organized, consisting of four groups made up of the two platoons, Company H.Q., some glider pilots, anti-tank gunners without their guns, and a few men from the Oxfordshire & Buckinghamshire Light Infantry. Although it was originally planned to capture the bridge with four platoons, this was the force, which actually did so—some fifty men in total.

The RUR bridge party had done sterling work against strong opposition. As well as some fifty prisoners, a damaged German self-propelled gun was also accounted for. One of a group of five that attacked down the road, it was hit at short range by a PIAT (projector infantry anti tank), a crude British invention, the effectiveness of which was more by luck than judgment. The German gun was only damaged, but this was enough to make the vehicles retreat in swift order.

2ND BATTALION OXFORDSHIRE AND BUCKINGHAMSHIRE LIGHT INFANTRY MAIN PARTY

The gliders carrying the remaining 2nd Battalion OBLI approached their release point over Hamminkeln. Captains Everett, Godsal, and Gerharty describe the approach and landing in *OBLI Chronicles*:

We caught a glimpse of Hamminkeln church ahead, but our landing zone was obscured by a thick haze of smoke and dust drifting down from Wesel. Gliders were crashing down, gliders were on fire, the sky was full of airbursts and ribbons of tracer, but our pilots carried on. They were wonderful. We cast off and slowly circled round looking for the field in which we had to land, and were followed all the way down by flak. There were four enemy anti-aircraft gun-pits near the station, each having four multiple two or four-barrelled 20mm. anti-aircraft guns. Some of these were deliberately run down by landing gliders.

During the landing, which took only ten minutes to complete, we lost about half our total strength. The casualties were awful. Gliders circling in through the gloom of the smoke and flak piled into woods, into buildings, collided with the ground, crashed flaming from the sky, and some blew to smithereens as they came in. Captain Bousfield, of A Company, landed almost on a German half-track which he immediately commandeered. Despite the chaotic landing, a useful number of gliders landed correctly on the chosen objectives, but it was impossible to unload many of the gliders containing jeeps and heavy supporting weapons until after dark.

Captain Sweeney, whom Hugh Clark would later meet in the woods, was in Chalk 64 at the head of the serial second behind that of the coup de main. Captain McMillen and Sergeant Stevens were piloting the glider. McMillen's experience appears in the December 2004 issue of *The Eagle*:

We had a relatively safe run-in apart from the sight of four of the seven combinations, which we had seen in front of us going down in flames after we had crossed the Rhine. I released at 2,000 ft in the middle of a considerable amount of light flak and headed for our L Z at Hamminkeln Railway Station. I built up quite a lot of speed in order to get below the flak when a very near burst went off under the starboard wing. I called for full flap when we were in the right position for landing. Nothing happened. Sgt. Stevens reported that our starboard undercarriage had been hit and the compressed air required for the flap operation had leaked out. This left me going at 90 mph and without any means of slowing down. I headed for open country between the railway line and the autobahn and found myself faced by a large wood. With fingers crossed I lifted the glider over the treetops and fortunately found a clearing. I put her down hard and dug the starboard wing in to slew me around and slow us down. We eventually stopped and disembarked without casualties.

Strapped in my seat just behind the glider pilot I knew nothing until many years later. All I knew was that Capt. McMillen had suddenly dived down to earth and we landed. I leapt out of the glider, had the ramps placed by the nose and drove out the jeep. Then we found ourselves in a certain amount of trouble. From the autobahn, which was about a hundred yards away, came the sound of shooting. As I looked round I saw this half made-up autobahn was manned by a row of grey steel helmets. With the bullets pinging around us we then realised that we had landed between the autobahn and the River Issel.

I rapidly gave orders to leave the jeep and trailer where it was and to get on the other side of the Issel where we could get some protection from the high bank. We waded the Issel and got soaked up to our chests but at least reached the safety of the high bank. All my glider carried, apart from the two glider pilots, were four members of my headquarters so we were not a very strong fighting unit. With the help of Capt. McMillen we pinpointed where we were from the map and decided to go from the Issel through a thick wood to the railway line and then move up the railway line till we came to Hamminkeln railway station where we should have landed in the first place. However, in the meantime gliders were coming in from all angles crashing down on both sides of the Issel and hitting trees in the wood, many spilling out their casualties. Eventually we had about 30 or 40 injured soldiers. Another 30 or 40 were fit men from different units. Then fortunately an infantry platoon from my own battalion, a platoon of "B" Company [Hugh Clark's] landed intact nearby. So we picked up all the gunners and sappers and men from other units who had landed amongst us, and the able bodied men carried the wounded. With my intact platoon I had at least a proper fighting force and I led the way. We set off through the woods away from the river towards the railway line. As I called to everyone to fall in, Sgt. Stevens my glider pilot did not get up from where he had been behind the riverbank. I went over to him to find him dead. He had unfortunately been shot through the head.

Sgt. Pilot Brian Latham gives his recollections of the approach and landing:

We were in a very loose formation and left England over Selsey Bill. We had to go south of Dunkirk, as the Germans were still there. We then turned northeast when we were south of Brussels to take us up to the Rhine. Turning point was over the site of the battle of Waterloo.

The Dakotas, which were taking the paras, passed underneath us, and there were plenty of fighters milling around to discourage enemy aircraft approaching. The American Dakotas with their Hadrians joined us here, and they were to land south of our landing ground.

We fondly imagined that when we reached the Rhine, we would see Bailey bridges over it with armor streaming across. But no bridges were seen, just thick smoke from German smoke generators and from the artillery barrage, which the second army had put across.

Despite the barrage and the fighter sweeps, the flak was very heavy, and a lot of the paras' Dakotas had been hit. Now it was our turn. We were so low that we were sitting ducks. We lost a lot of gliders on the way down, and it looked a shambles. We were hit in the right wing and in the cockpit, which blew our air bottle, which operated the flaps and brakes. We also lost our right wheel, so the brakes did not matter. We were going very fast when we landed. It tore off our nose wheel and smashed the cockpit, so we could not unload through the front and had to unscrew the tail to get out our load.

There were a lot of wrecked gliders around, and burning Dakotas, but our job was to unload and get to our rendezvous at the farm. We were pinned down by a German machine gun, so two of the men took the PIAT gun and took it out. The tail was held on by four bolts, each one with a ratchet wrench, so I was able to unscrew it and it fell off, allowing us to release the jeep and trailer. The mortar section moved off, and we made our way to the farm. It all seemed to be a complete shambles, but Germans were surrendering and glider pilots were being used to take them to a compound. We reached the farm, and the terrified occupants who were then taken out of harms way to Hamminkeln.

Because so many people had been lost in the landing, we were sent off to the perimeter by the station to dig in and await developments. This we did and realized that only an hour had passed since our landing.

The glider of the CO, Lt. Col. Mark Darrell-Brown DSO, became the target of a 20-millimeter antiaircraft battery near Hamminkeln. The first pilot, Squadron Leader V. H. Reynolds, CO of F Squadron, put the glider into a steep dive, as described in Chatterton's report:

> I ordered my second pilot to open up with the Sten through the front clear vision panel, when we came within range, and landed alongside the AA position, between it and the railway station. The port wheel having been shot off, the glider canted to port when it came to rest and the mainplane gave a certain amount of cover while we deplaned.
>
> After the AA position had been captured I went into the station and reported to the OC [officer commanding].

Squadron Sgt. Maj. Lawrence "Buck" Turnbull's glider had a platoon on board. He cast off from his tug and settled for the landing. At that moment, a C-47 cut in front of him, and its trailing towrope began to wreak havoc on the glider. It caught the starboard aileron and tore it off. It then wrapped itself around the lower part of the cockpit thus ripping out the air bottles, required for brakes and flaps, as well as most of the instrument panel and half the control column. As the rope came away, the Horsa was virtually flipped upside down. While all this was going on, antiaircraft batteries were targeting the glider. Turnbull, showing great calmness, managed to right the glider and then land with out crashing. For this action, he was awarded the Conspicuous Gallantry Medal, the only one to be awarded to a soldier during the war.

Lt. R. A. A. "Sandy" Smith MC had also been a platoon commander on the Pegasus Bridge coup de main. He details his experience in the December 1990 issue of *The Eagle*:

> I flew in a Regimental HQ glider, which also carried the signal section and medical sergeant, a jeep, trailer (with 3" mortar ammunition on board), motorcycle and assorted signals and medical equipment.
>
> We were hit after crossing the Rhine and the First Pilot and some of the signallers were slightly wounded. We then had to land pretty quickly as we were smouldering; though we were blazing on landing. We landed with our nose up to a road and a farmhouse on our immediate right. It was near the signal box, not far from the station.
>
> There were four 20mm gun emplacements in the field, which fired at us when we landed. The Signal Sgt and I got out on the side opposite to the farmhouse and found an empty German slit trench where we stayed put. The glider pilots and the medical sergeant got out the other side and disappeared into the farmhouse, where I eventually found them behind some potato sacks in the cellar.
>
> The glider was shot at by a tank from the road—about ten yards range! The signallers were all burnt alive.

Sgt. Pilot Stan Jarvis recalls:

> When we reached the Rhine, the strength of the flak became apparent. A few of the tug aircraft flew past us on their way home; some of them were on fire and others were bullet-ridden—not a welcome sight to us who were going in to stay. As we flew across the Rhine, to our dismay we found that the whole area was covered with gunsmoke and other smoke artificially created to conceal the ground troops who were going across the Rhine by boat and amphibious tanks, etc. It had not

been appreciated that the airborne troops would need to see the ground when they reached the landing zones. When we reached our release point, flak was coming in thick and fast, and some of the gliders went down in flames; others broke up in midair, which was a quite horrifying spectacle.

Upon being advised by Alex Blyth that we were over our landing zone, I had no alternative but to release the glider, and we slowly descended. At that point we could not see the ground at all, as we were technically in cloud—but it was smoke—and we were trying to avoid other aircraft flying in our direction. My copilot Peter Geddes was meanwhile desperately trying to identify anything through the smoke from which we could locate our position. The first landmark that we saw was an autobahn east of Hamminkeln, and at that moment a tremendous explosion occurred on the starboard side and about 4 feet of the wing tip was blown off, together with most of the aileron. I managed to regain control of the aircraft, with the assistance of my copilot, then I put on full flaps and went into a steep dive.

By this time the visibility was becoming clearer, and I could see the railway lines and our objective, Hamminkeln station, but enemy gunfire was becoming more accurate. I pulled out of the dive at about 50 feet above the ground, then descended to almost ground level. We flew low over three fields, hitting post-and-wire fencing, which we were not aware existed, and were followed down the fields by a stream of tracer and incendiary bullets before I put the glider down. Fortunately very little further damage was done until we slewed sideways close to the railway fence, when the tail unit was shot away. Miraculously, none of the airborne troops was injured, for which I was very relieved.

The troops quickly left the glider and took cover in a ditch while they oriented themselves prior to capturing the station. The gunfire was intense and coming in from all directions. Gliders were landing fast—some were crashing and others on fire. While lying in the ditch, one of the airborne troops turned to me and said: "When we left Birch, we asked you to land as

close as possible to the station—to avoid being exposed running over open ground—but if you had been any closer we
would have been in the booking office!" I replied that it was
compliments of the RAF, and we had a little laugh in the seri-
ousness of war.

Pvt. Denis Edwards was one of Jarvis's passengers:

I recall a glider coming in just above us. It was aflame
from end to end, and while still some way above, men, with
their clothing alight, were jumping from the stricken craft.
Although they were individually not recognizable, we knew
that they were our mates, men we knew well and with whom
we had shared barrack rooms. It was a truly terrible sight.

My own twenty-six-man platoon was relatively lucky and
every one of us got clear of our glider and reached the station
yard, where we took refuge from the murderous German fire.
The yard covered a considerable area, part of it being stacked
with neat piles of timber, each approximately the size of a
two-story house.

Unfortunately, it turned out that the Germans were using
these stacks of timber to cover their approach as they advanced
towards us. We spent the first few hours dodging the German
Mk IV tanks, which trundled up and down the rows of stacked
timber seeking us out.

We were not equipped to deal with German heavy tanks.
Indeed, the antitank guns that we did possess, 6-pounders
which could dispose of even a Tiger at close range, were
almost certainly still within the Hamilcar gliders used to
transport our heavier equipment. The concentration of enemy
fire over the landing zones would have made it virtually
impossible for such weapons to be removed. Most men were
just thankful if they were able to crawl away from their gliders and find some sort of shelter from the incoming German
fire.

Pvt. Harry "Nobby" Clarke was in Edwards's platoon:

As we took up our positions, two Horsa gliders appeared out of the cloud passing low overhead, and within a few seconds there came a fearful noise as they crashed. One of them hit the railway station and disintegrated. There were no survivors. The second passed further over and crashed between the railway and the road.

While we were within the cover of the stacked timbers, a lone figure suddenly appeared, hands above his head and repeating over and over the word "lightning." He was an American war correspondent, clearly in a state of shock, and whose aircraft had been shot down, forcing him to parachute to safety. While in flight, he had been busily typing out his story on a portable typewriter that he had borrowed from a friend. Regardless of the carnage and mayhem all around us, he was mainly concerned about how he would have to tell his friend that his typewriter had been lost! As he was unarmed we gave him a liberated German P38 pistol and told him to stay in hiding among the stacks of timber until the fighting was over

The platoon moved off in a westerly direction towards our D Company rendezvous point. At this stage, the company was in reserve with no objectives to capture. Arriving at the rendezvous point we were given the grim news that many of the company had become casualties during the actual landing. Our platoon was, in fact, one of the very few to be still completely intact. Unfortunately, because of damage to radios during the rough landings, we had no radio contact with our battalion HQ, and I was handed a written message from our company commander, Major Tillett. I was instructed to deliver it with all haste to our battalion commander, Lieutenant Colonel Darrell-Brown, at his HQ at Hamminkeln railway station.

I began my return journey back towards the station by crossing the glider landing zone, which was by now mainly clear of the smoke. With enemy snipers and tanks still around the area, I dodged from one wrecked Horsa glider to another, while many of them were still burning.

I edged carefully towards my destination. The many dead, injured, and seriously wounded in and around the gliders were a horrific sight. At the front of one burning aircraft was its glider pilot, still wearing his headphones, arms outstretched and forming the shape of a crucifix in the flames. Fifty-three years later, that sight still haunts me.

There were also a number of bodies of paratroops, all close together and covered by white parachutes. They were Americans from the 17th U.S. Airborne Division, who should have landed to our south but had been dropped into our area.

Arriving at Hamminkeln railway station, I had no difficulty in locating our battalion commander. He was riding towards me on one of our small and flimsy folding airborne pedal cycles. I passed my written message to him, which he read swiftly, and then told me that he had been in contact with D Company. It seemed that my highly dangerous journey had probably been unnecessary!

I learned from our battalion commander that C Company was under considerable pressure at the railway bridge, and it had been decided that D Company should be sent to reinforce them. I asked him what the casualty situation was within our battalion, and he told me that about 62 percent had been killed, wounded, or were missing. That left about 250 men to capture and hold all of our predetermined objectives, compared to our original force of around 650. Telling me to hurry and rejoin D Company, he wished me good luck, and to my complete surprise, he shook my hand!

Following the railway track along its western side was the quickest, but not necessarily the safest, route back to the company, but I could not face the prospect of recrossing the landing zone and seeing all that carnage again. Apart from that consideration, exploding ammunition, shells, and mortar bombs were creating a deadly danger around the burning gliders.

As I hurried towards D Company's positions, I could see a number of enemy tanks cruising around and setting fire to those gliders that were not yet burning. They faced little opposition, since most of our antitank guns and mortars were destroyed during the landings, and presumably the Tempest and Typhoon tank busters were still busy supporting the land-based forces crossing the Rhine.

Arriving at the company, I found most of them grouped around a deep bomb crater. Cpl. "Bill" Bailey, a Normandy veteran, came over to tell me that an enemy sniper had just killed Denny White, one of my best mates. I was then told that another of my close friends, Don Fogaty, had been killed in one of the other Horsas that had crashed. Both were long-standing mates of mine. There was certainly not a lot of good news to be had on that fateful day.

Captain Sweeney describes the scene that met them:

Around the station, all was chaos. There were gliders in all conditions and positions: Some had crashed into buildings, had caught fire, and burnt out; others had spilt their contents on the area where they should have landed; many had blown up in the air. There was a casualty clearing station just beyond the railway station, and there were so many casualties that they were lying on stretchers outside the buildings.

I went into the railway station itself, where I reported to my commanding officer. On the way in, I went past the quarter-master, who was well over the age when he should have been fighting in an airborne unit. He was in a state of shock [and remained that way] for the rest of the day. The command-ing officer, who had a sense of humor, put him in for a DFC [Distinguished Flying Cross], but the higher authorities, who lacked any sense of humor, turned it down.

As the above descriptions show, confusion reigned from the outset. Denis Edwards and his pals were involved in just one of several private battles. The gliders were still being riddled with bullets, which set off the loads of ammunition and added to the smoke and haze already making it difficult to distinguish friend from foe.

The antiaircraft guns, which had caused so much damage during the landings, were overrun and their crews taken prisoner. Yet the fight was still on. From the direction of Ringenberg, machine guns and mortars sprayed and pounded the landing zone. Over by the RUR bridge, a small garrison added its fire and three German medium tanks drove through the area, firing tracer bullets into gliders, setting them alight and killing wounded still waiting to be evacuated. In the words of the afteraction report, the RUR "drummed up" one of the tanks before it managed to cross the bridge. In spite of the heavy casualties, all the OBLI's objectives were captured and secured shortly before 1100 hours.

Company B dug in by the road bridge, and Company C by the railway bridge. Company A took control of the road junction to the west. Denis Edwards's Company D was held back in reserve, to the west of the station. Occupation of the station buildings fell to the Reconnaissance Platoon.

When Hugh Clark reached the station, he reported to his company commander, Maj. Gilbert Rahr, who told him that of the three remaining platoons, only the 16th Platoon had arrived and was digging in on the riverbank. Nothing had been heard from the two parties of Royal Engineers.

S.Sgt. Joe Kitchener was carrying one of those parties:

> My glider was hit at about 2,000 feet by light ack-ack. There was an almighty "Bang!" and the instrument panel disintegrated. The air bottle was also hit, so the flaps came down, increasing my angle of descent.
>
> I then saw a row of trees with a large field beyond. In the row of trees was a small tree with larger trees either side of it. So I aimed to go over the small tree, hoping to take my wings off with the larger trees, which they did. The fuselage slid along the ground.
>
> The jeep, trailer, explosives, and six engineers all stayed intact, and once more I had survived. I was completely lost and slightly wounded, as were two of the six engineers. Then I heard English voices, and it was Captain McMillen and a party of soldiers. He knew the way to Hamminkeln, so we tagged along.
>
> When we got to Hamminkeln, I saw a glider with the nose rammed into a building. I climbed into the back of the

glider, and up front was Sergeant Love [RAF] and copilot Sergeant Skeldon, dead in their seat—as were others in the glider. Also in the wreckage was a dead horse and a dead German civilian with a cart. It seemed as if the glider had hit the cart, man, and horse and rammed them into the building.

I looked around at the dead GPs and smashed gliders and thanked Lady Luck for another op and hoped it would be the final one.

Nothing further is known about the engineer support parties, but help did arrive at the station, as Clark explains:

A group of engineers [from the 591st Parachute Squadron] from brigade arrived with a jeep and trailer load of explosives. Just as they arrived we had called for more fire from the artillery, and we all dived for cover. I arrived in the slit trench on top of one of the engineers and as we heard the first shells exploding, he said to me, "I hate to tell you, sir, but there is a trailer loaded with half a ton of explosives just a few yards from your head." When the shelling stopped, they placed the explosives under the bridge with a wire to a detonator at company HQ.

Squadron Leader Reynolds had been organizing the glider pilots as they arrived at the station. As he explains in Chatterton's report:

The Oxf and Bucks had suffered rather heavy casualties so their CO asked me to relieve C Company and hold the position. I formed the glider pilots into two sections, collected about thirty prisoners and took over the buildings. The buildings had been used as a Forced Labour Camp with high-netted surrounds, and very good defensive positions had been dug around the Northern and Eastern sides. The prisoners were housed in the buildings under guard.

Sgt. Pilot Stan Jarvis and Peter Geddes were involved in guarding the prisoners, as Jarvis explains:

The pilots' job was to guard and to search them for specified possessions, e.g., weapons, maps, money, and any intelligence material, etc. Personal items, such as photographs, letters, and nonmilitary items, were returned to the prisoners. I was personally directed to search prisoners in a large room, about 25 feet square. The German troops were facing the walls all the way around the room with their hands up. I started to search each prisoner while another pilot covered them with a Sten gun. After a time, I realized that an enormous amount of Dutch guilders were accumulating on a table which I had been given for the purpose. Bundles of bank notes were being removed from prisoners' pockets, amounting to thousands by value. After questioning a couple of prisoners who could speak English, they admitted sheepishly that their unit had been withdrawn across the Rhine a short time previously, and they had ransacked a bank before leaving and they still had the money with them! In a lighter vein, I searched a young prisoner—about my own age—and removed a handful of contraceptives from his tunic pocket. I requested his English-speaking comrades to tell him that it would be a long time before he would be able to use them, now that he was a prisoner of war. The other enemy troops roared with laughter when it was explained in German.

The glider pilot position began receiving sniper fire from antiaircraft positions. At 1400 hours, Darrell-Brown ordered Reynolds to lead a glider pilot assault on the antiaircraft pits, beginning at 1500. The party would receive covering fire from the station buildings. The sniping from one of the enemy positions, however, became so irritating that Reynolds ordered one of his officers, Flying Officer Bailey, to lob a few PIAT bombs onto it. After three close shots, Bailey scored a direct hit on the gun mounting, killing the crew. Meanwhile, Flight Lieutenant Ince and an NCO had worked their way around the back of a windmill, which gave them cover from another antiaircraft pit, and charged at the crew, killing all of them. The officer at the other gun hoisted a white flag.

Jarvis and Geddes and their fellow guards now had something in the region of 150 prisoners housed in the buildings, and they "marched them all to the village of Hamminkeln," says Jarvis, "which had been captured by the Devon Regiment, who landed next to the village."

The pilots would soon be back in the defense line, as Squadron Leader Reynolds details in Chatterton's report:

> At 1600 hrs we were ordered by OC 2nd Oxf & Bucks to take over a section of the line along the railway line between the Oxf & Bucks troops and the RURs.
>
> Accompanied by my 2nd i/c [second in command], Capt. T. D. B. McMillen MC, and the 2nd i/c [of] the Oxf & Bucks, I recce'd the posn and brought up the glider pilots, now about forty strong, at 1730 hrs.
>
> I deployed my glider pilots in position either side of the railway line, with one PIAT covering the road and another the railway track.

Stan Jarvis recalls:

> About 1800 hours, we were allocated defensive positions as part of the airborne perimeter. The German troops were approximately 250 yards away beyond the River Issel; therefore, we were instructed to dig slit trenches for protection.

Darrell-Brown had ordered Company D to move out of reserve and dig in between the glider pilots and the RUR, as Nobby Clarke describes:

> Our new position on the eastern (enemy) side of the River Issel was very exposed to German forces, who were now grouping along the partly built autobahn which ran along our front and was about 150 yards away. To our right front, and about half a mile distant, was the village of Ringenberg. We were told that around that area was a large enemy force with numerous tanks.

The sector was put on "stand-to" alert but all seemed quiet from the Germans. In fact, they were re-forming around Ringenberg in preparation for a counterattack. Col. William Faithfull, commander Royal Artillery, explains:

> The appreciation that Ringenberg would be a forming-up place proved right. In anticipation of this, the fire plan catered for a carefully spaced concentration by three medium regiments. This concentration was constantly called for and probably prevented the enemy from pressing home his attacks more than he did. A few shells from medium guns fell short, close in front of or among our own infantry, but considering the ranges involved and the closeness of the enemy, this was to be expected, and the few casualties caused thereby were not a serious matter.

Stan Jarvis remembers:

> Suddenly a vast series of whines were heard overhead followed by crashes; the noise was tremendous. The Second Army had started a bombardment beyond the autobahn to prevent the enemy bringing up reserves. Incandescent shells ceaselessly passed over for a couple of hours, which was very reassuring, as they were from our side! The bombardment suddenly stopped, and the silence was almost deafening!

Nobby Clarke's platoon was at the wrong end of the concentration:

> During the afternoon, some of No. 25 Platoon, including myself, moved into a small house close to where the railway bridge crossed the River Issel. Several counterattacks were launched against us during the fading hours of daylight. Although we received considerable support from our own heavy artillery, which was some miles away on the other side of the River Rhine, to our dismay some of their shells were exploding around our own positions!
>
> Every time that this occurred, we were forced to wade across the river and take shelter under the railway bridge, and then rush back to our defensive positions when the shelling

eased up. Much of the enemy counterfire at that time was from mortars and machine guns.

Denis Edwards and other members of 25th Platoon were outside, but in cover:

> A lot of heavy stuff was crashing in all around the place, and without well-dug trenches such as we had in Normandy, it was impossible to find anywhere that offered good protection. There were several of us crouched in the lee of the embankment, when apparently a large shell exploded on the top of the bank just above my head, killing many of those in the immediate area, as well as some others who were further away. I neither remember the shell burst nor anything more for a period of thirty-six hours or so.

His comrades thought Edwards had been killed and Major Rahr sent a signal reporting his death. After the bombardment stopped, Nobby Clarke was given another task:

> I was ordered by our platoon commander to accompany L.Cpl. "Swill" Balaam to go forward on a two-man standing patrol. Firstly we were to carry out a recce of the area around the autobahn, and then to lie up close to the road to detect possible enemy movements. We were both veterans of the coup-de-main force at Pegasus Bridge in Normandy, and so were all too well aware of the danger of the mission upon which we were now about to embark.
>
> Fortunately, the area was well covered by trees and bushes. Just before midnight, we moved out into no-man's-land, carrying only our small arms in order to avoid noise. We reached a point some twenty-five yards or so from the road and settled down behind a clump of bushes to listen and observe. Almost immediately, we became aware of movement beyond the autobahn. The rattling of equipment and low-pitched voices warned us that an enemy group was on the move and coming our way.

Throwing caution to the wind, we hurried back to our platoon, calling out the night's password as we approached our defensive positions. We gave our information to Lieutenant Shaw immediately, but before he was able to act upon it, an attack was launched against one of our other companies [B] over to our right.

Artillery fire from Ringenberg had been directed into the area, but it had proved very ineffective. It was then that the combined tank and infantry attack began. Hugh Clark describes the situation:

Late in the afternoon, one of the regimental 6-pounder anti-tank guns was brought into position near the level crossing in order to cover the road from the bridge. This was commanded by Lt. David Rice. David and I had been together for the previous fifteen months, having met at Dunbar early in 1944. The rest of the day until soon after dark remained reasonably quiet. Soon after dark, we heard tracked vehicles moving in the area beyond the autobahn and wondered what was in store. We were to find out when at about 2100 hours, a heavy German tank moved down the road towards the bridge. As it approached the bridge, David Rice and a member of his platoon manhandled the gun onto the road. The tank crept onto the other side of the bridge and stopped with only the upper part of the tank in view. The 6-pounder opened fire, but much to our dismay, we heard the shells bouncing off without any apparent damage. My platoon fired 2-inch mortar parachute flares to illuminate the tank, but still the shells had no effect. The tank then withdrew back the way it had come.

But the enemy was not quite finished:

Sometime soon after midnight, No. 16 Platoon [Company B], who had been in position on the bank beside the bridge, pulled back and reported that the enemy had crossed the river and were in the house beside the bridge. I was ordered to retake the position they had left. I ordered my platoon to fix bayonets, and as soon as we were in line, gave the order to charge. We moved forward at the trot, shouting and firing from the hip as we went. We only had to go about 150 yards to the riverbank, and about halfway there, a corporal beside me said, "Hold it a minute, sir, we are on our own," the rest of the line having fallen behind. With a lot of shouting, I told the platoon what I thought of them and got them back in line.

Fortunately, when we reached the river, any Germans who had been there had pulled back to their side of the river. The platoon stayed in position along the riverbank, and it was not long before we heard and then saw the outline of two heavy tanks moving forward towards the bridge. We could hear a number of infantry moving near the tanks, which came to a halt just short of the bridge and no more than 75 yards from our position. I called for the PIAT, our platoon antitank weapon and asked the man with the PIAT if he could guarantee to hit the tank first shot, as I was sure that once we had fired, they would direct their gun on our position. He replied that he was not sure that he could, so in a moment of bravado, I told him to give the weapon to me. I loaded and took aim, not easy in the dark, and scored a hit with the first shot. Fortunately, the tanks did not reply, and I think that we must have put the gun out of action. We heard the infantry scatter when the round hit. I continued firing and scored four more hits but much to our disappointment, the tanks did not blow up, but they both pulled back. It was not long before they began to creep forward again, and I reported to my company commander that if they rushed the bridge, there was no way we could stop them. Having obtained permission from brigade to blow the bridge, he ordered me to withdraw. To cover our withdrawal, we lobbed both smoke grenades and 36 grenades over the river and pulled back to the railway line before the bridge went up with a tremendous bang. [This was about 0230.] The remainder of the night was reasonably quiet on our company sector.

I learned later that a platoon from D Company, commanded by Lt. Chalky White, had been placed in position across the road on the riverbank to reinforce our position. They did not receive the order to withdraw, and when the bridge went, Chalky was hit on the head by a falling brick and was not a pretty sight when I saw him next morning. For years afterwards, he blamed me for what happened to him.

Hugh Clark was awarded the Military Cross for his leadership in this action. As he states, the remainder of the night was fairly quiet in the Company B sector. For Companies A and C, it was a different matter.

On the northern flank of the OBLI position, the defensive line was very thin. Through reconnaissance, the Germans had noted the situation, and at 0400, a small force of infantry began working its way around this flank and, finding a way through the line, organized for an assault. They attacked at 0445, and a Company C platoon position was overrun. The Germans captured a 6-pounder gun and its crew. Lieutenant Colonel Darrell-Brown ordered Company A to counterattack in an attempt to stabilize the situation. At the same time, two platoons from the Devons moved up to the road junction, which had been held by Company A, to fill the gap while the counterattack was carried out. Under the weight of Company A's advance, the Germans retreated and the defense line was secured.

1ST BATTALION ROYAL ULSTER RIFLES MAIN PARTY

As for the remainder of the 1st Battalion RUR, the gliders of Company A were to land on Landing Zone U2, and those of Companies B and C on Landing Zone U3.

Company A had Hamminkeln railway station and level crossing to secure. Only two of its platoons landed on the zone, so it fell to Lieutenants Laird and Stewart to lead their men in the planned seizure. As it happened, there was no organized resistance on the level crossing, although 20-millimeter guns were firing on the area from the direction of Hamminkeln.

Lieutenant Laird organized the defense, which included a platoon of the Devons dug in some 100 yards from the station. The RUR's Support Company headquarters and two machine guns arrived soon after, but there was still no sign of the missing platoons from Company A, or of the remainder of the battalion.

The small defense force received no direct counterattack, but one strange incident did occur. Less than half an hour after digging in, lookouts saw three self-propelled guns coming along the road from Hamminkeln. They drove over the level crossing and the Issel bridge without slowing. From accounts of those present, it would appear that the vehicles' occupants neither saw nor fired on the men, who were only a few feet away from them. It was assumed that the vehicles were escaping the cordon being set up by the Devons around Hamminkeln. The British had no hesitation. No antitank guns were available, but the Devons had a PIAT and took a shot at one of the vehicles as it crossed the river. It was damaged but kept on going.

Companies B and C landed under intense fire from surrounding houses. The glider of the CO, Lt. Col. Jack Carson, broke up on landing. His first pilot was S.Sgt. H. N. "Andy" Andrews DFM, a veteran of the three previous European operations, who describes their experience in the December 1988 issue of *The Eagle*:

> With some difficulty, due to a faulty tug engine, we struggled across the North Sea and got over the target. The element of surprise was gone and there was very active German ack ack to greet us.
>
> Smoke obliterated the LZ and I had to pull off blind. Eventually, I saw the canal running North to South and turned approximately in the right direction. We had lost valuable height in free flight and the ack ack had damaged something. In any case the descent and the gliding speed were too fast. Until we got to 500 feet we couldn't see the ground and there was no place to land. Flying straight ahead, I made for a small field but knew that, at 250 feet, I would have to go through some tall trees to get in. We got through the trees but the undercarriage was half off. The next thing we knew was that the Horsa II was disintegrating around us and the tail detached itself to fly over the nose and land facing us.

The RUR adjutant, Capt. Robert Rigby, also had his glider break up. Shaken up but otherwise all right, he took command of the battalion. His jeep was wedged in the remains of the glider, but he was able to get his fellow passengers into a nearby ditch.

Between them and the houses was a Company C glider, which was on fire with ammunition exploding from it. Some minutes later, about half of its occupants ran toward the ditch. They told Rigby that about two-thirds of the platoon had gotten out alive and worked their way toward the house, but they had to abandon the assault because of the fierce firing. Two further platoons from Company C arrived, along with one from Company B. They all brought in prisoners.

Assessing his current situation, Rigby decided to leave a small-fire group in the ditch and attack the houses, using an orchard to cover his approach. Lieutenant O'Hara-Murray from Company B obviously had the same idea, because his platoon was already in the orchard and making for the houses. Seeing this, Rigby had one of his men lay down some smoke and led his assault group at a right angle to O'Hara-Murray's platoon. The German put up a halfhearted defense, and as the RUR got within 40 or 50 yards, most of the enemy threw down their weapons and surrendered. Within twenty minutes, the houses and surrounding barns were in the hands of the RUR.

There were still men from the RUR out in the open. One of them, Rifleman Paddy Devlin, a Bren gunner in 18th Platoon, Company C, had taken cover under the tail of his glider while putting down suppressing fire on the houses.

> Then there was a shout that two German tanks were coming up the road, which ran north south and bounded the landing zone. It was about 70 yards away. I repositioned my gun so that I could fire as they came opposite the glider. I would only have fired if the tank commander had his head exposed from his turret. In the event, they weren't tanks but armoured personnel vehicles. As the first one came opposite I let them have a burst and all the occupants collapsed behind the armoured sides. I couldn't have hit them all, but there was an amount of shouting and screaming.

Two 6-pounders had taken up positions to cover the road along which the German vehicles were moving. Devlin may have caused some casualties, and certainly confusion, but the antitank guns made the difference. One shot from each knocked out the personnel carriers, and prisoners were taken.

With things much quieter, Rigby ordered Companies B and C to make their way to their original rallying point. As Devlin crossed the plowed field he dropped the empty magazines he was carrying. Stooping to pick them up, he realized he was the target of a German machine-gun crew. A burst from the gun broke his right arm, creased his side and ripped through his small pack. He fell forward and lay absolutely still.

> The pain wasn't too bad, like a nagging toothache, but I could feel what I thought was my blood pouring along my right thigh and I thought I would bleed to death. I discovered later that it was the two tins of Carnation evaporated milk I had in my side pack. I also had tea and sugar, which I had purloined with the aid of the cook.

Devlin was rescued by two of his mates from the platoon and, after a hairy session with another personnel carrier, eventually made it to the regimental aid post, where he was treated. His tea and sugar were also put to good use.

Rigby had heard from Company D of its success at the bridge, but he had not been able to raise Company A. By 1215, and satisfied that no further members of the RUR remained on U3, Rigby ordered an advance to the level crossing.

At the dispersal point, Companies B and C were to make their way to the positions selected in the original plan. In the absence of the Reconnaissance Platoon, one platoon from Company C would guard the left flank with the two antitank guns, and one platoon would cover the rear. The right flank was safe, as American troops were arriving by glider on Landing Zone N.

On the march to the station, two OBLI platoons joined the group. Arriving at the station, Rigby found Major Liddle, with a platoon from Company A and the Machine Gun Platoon, dug in at the level crossing.

The pilots who had flown the RUR's gliders relieved Company A of the protection of the station and level crossing area. Company A then moved to a position covering the exits from Hamminkeln. Companies B and C moved to their blocking positions and battalion headquarters was established in the wood southwest of the level crossing.

By 1430, the fighting had died down. Those who had landed outside the area, and fought their way to the station swelled the defense. Among the new arrivals was Maj. G. P. Rickcord, who assumed command of the battalion.

For the remainder of the day, there was little enemy artillery activity, but a group of three self-propelled guns made an attempt on the perimeter. They were swiftly dealt with by the Typhoons. The RUR could see activity in the houses on the east side of the bridge and troops and vehicles were moving in and around Ringenberg. Prisoners were being collected all the time, and by nightfall, there were 650 in the brigade cage. A large number were there through the actions of the RUR's patrols.

The members of the RUR witnessed the fighting at the OBLI bridge, and its subsequent demolition, but were not themselves tested by any German activity.

12TH BATTALION DEVONSHIRE REGIMENT

The 12th Battalion Devonshire Regiment's mission was to isolate Hamminkeln. Company C was given a task outside the specific battalion plan. With two of the Light Regiment's A Troop guns in support, it was to clear the divisional landing zone and concentration area and cover the forming up of divisional headquarters.

For the remainder of his battalion, Lieutenant Colonel Gleadell had a two-phase plan. In Phase One, Company A, with antitank support, was to land to the south and southwest and isolate the village from there. Company B and the Reconnaissance Platoon, with two 17-pounders, would isolate the village from the north and northwest. A particular role for this platoon was to make a link with the RUR and assist in preventing enemy infiltration into Hamminkeln. Company D, also supported by an antitank platoon and some Pioneers, would land in a coup-de-main role as close in to the village as possible, on the west side. Objectives were the crossroads and nearby road junctions. The three Mortar Platoons were to support the blocking positions set up by the three companies.

Phase Two would begin as soon as the situation allowed. Company D was to clear the village center, and take responsibility for the defense of the east and southeast sectors. Company A was to clear and hold the village on its south side, while Company B would do the same on the northeast and northwest sides. When it had completed its task on the landing zone, Company C was to move into a reserve role.

The 513th troopers of the 17th Airborne were dropped on the Devons' zone and eliminated the majority of the opposition. Nevertheless, there was still a heavy presence of machine-gun and infantry strong points.

From a total of sixty-five gliders, seven did not reach the Rhine, four having suffered broken towropes. One of them, Chalk 213, piloted by Flying Officer Percy Edwards and Sgt. Pilot Bill Fleming, came down in the Channel. On board were the Mortar Platoon commander, Lieutenant Ash, and five platoon members, as well as a jeep, trailer, and motorcycle. The flight had been a bumpy one, as the Stirling and Horsa combination flew into the slipstream of aircraft ahead. About halfway across the Channel, the glider began moving left and right, which finally led to the towrope breaking. The pilots and passengers prepared to ditch. The glider made a flaps-up landing, stalling onto the surface. The occupants climbed out onto the top of the fuselage as an Air Sea Rescue launch drew up alongside. The glider had been in the air less than an hour.

Lieutenant Colonel Gleadell was accompanied by Private Jolly, his batman; Lieutenant Brixey, the battalion intelligence officer; and Private Bray, Intelligence Section; and Private Tremeer, Regimental Police. The aircraft commander, Maj. Maurice Priest, released over the landing zone and pointed the glider's nose at the ground. Not far from landing, an antiaircraft shell burst close to the glider, its smoke obscuring the pilots' view. Priest, and his copilot, managed to keep the shuddering glider under control, and the passengers were warned to prepare for a hard landing. Two bursts of machine-gun fire ripped through the fuselage. Tremeer was hit in the back. Priest, still with no clear view, steadied the glider and tried another attempt to land. The next second, a huge crash shook the glider and the floor gave way. The Devons found their feet being dragged along the ground, and Tremeer was thrown forward against the cockpit bulkhead.

The glider had come to rest on the edge of a bomb crater in no-man's-land between the OBLI at Hamminkeln station and the Germans in Ringenberg. Gleadell's jeep was caught in the wrecked glider, so his party made a hasty exit on foot. Tremeer was left with OBLI medics, and Gleadell joined a platoon from his own Company D. As the lieutenant colonel reported in *BAOR Battlefield Tour*:

> After meeting some resistance, we eventually reached the northern edge of Hamminkeln. Touch was gained by wireless

with Battalion HQ and B Company, and so I gave the order for Phase II at 1135. Companies duly assaulted and the objective was taken by midday.

S.Sgt. Jack "Timo" Jenkins and Flight Sgt. Andy Anderson were carrying a platoon from Company A. To the surprise and delight of Jenkins, some of the platoon was from his old section, when he had been a Devons platoon sergeant. They had been greatly relieved to see their old Sarge. Now the glider was approaching the zone, as Jenkins describes in the December 1998 issue of *The Eagle*:

> We glided gently down, completely isolated, and only our compass reading told us we were heading in the right direction—due south. Then the fireworks started—a series of ominous thumps from all around us, a swishing sound nearby, as another glider plunged earthwards, with pieces falling from its burning fuselage.

The altimeter read a fraction under 2,000 feet, but the ground remained hidden by the smoke and haze. Taking a chance, Jenkins performed a three-leg turn—east, north, west—losing about 200 feet on each leg. If he had gotten it right, then Hamminkeln church, their "beacon" should be in front. Jenkins continues:

> Andy had discarded his safety belt and was coolly standing up in the cockpit peering down into the murk. Suddenly, he gave a great shout—"Church spire ahead, Skipper, ten degrees starboard." I saw, for the first time in my life, a miracle. The smoke was still a blanket, but just about half a mile ahead was a small circular opening in the haze, about the size of a dinner plate. Up through this hole that beautiful church spire was pointing triumphantly to the heavens.

Jenkins made a textbook landing, and he and Anderson gave the Devons covering fire from their Bren until the troops were in cover by a hedgerow. The two pilots then made their way to their rendezvous, a shop in the center of Hamminkeln.

One of the passengers in L.Cpl. Richard Dunkley's glider was the Devons' chaplain. Dunkley recalls:

> It was then, just before we were warned to be ready to land, that the padre suddenly decided to offer up a prayer on our behalf. I'm sure he meant well, but it made us all very nervous and made us think of our then fragile hold on life, which was truly in the hands of the gods.

Any prayers were rapidly curtailed as the order was given to take up landing positions:

> Not a sound from any of the passengers added to the notable lack of engine roar as our tow plane shot away into the distance and, hopefully, safely home. But not us. I distinctly remember the light fading, and it became quite dark inside the glider. In fact, this was our passing through artificial smoke drifting up from the battlefield, referred to by the ground troops as "Monty's fog." But also there was the distinct chemical smell from explosions. This was, of course, the flak, but I do not remember hearing or feeling any explosions. Then we went into a steep dive, and the passengers slid up against each other. This angle of attack only lasted a few seconds, when the glider pulled up sharply to level flight. At that moment, someone said, "I've been shot"; it was a soldier three down to the rear of me, who had been shot through the upper thigh, but that was all he said and no more was heard from him. My heart then missed a beat as we hit the ground and the pilot made a beautiful landing. We stopped quite quickly about 50 feet from a hedge on our port side; just in front and a little to the left was a large farmhouse.
>
> I cannot remember how I exited the aircraft, but I distinctly remember someone shouting about the copilot having been shot through the neck and two or three men struggling to help him out on a stretcher.
>
> From my experience in Normandy, I knew that some of the close-by bangs were mortar bombs, and as most of our

casualties in Normandy were from mortars, I decided to look after Number One and ran to the farmhouse past a deserted German slit trench with two rifles nearby and one of the potato masher grenades. I did not go into the farmhouse but found an unoccupied pigsty. It had nice thick brick walls, which were just fine, and my fear of the German mortars, and in particular, the scary multibarreled mortars, lessened somewhat. Soon others joined me in my sanctuary. We had only been there a short time when someone suggested that we had better make for our rendezvous at the church, but first let's check the farm out for snipers. After all, we did not want to get shot at from the rear, as we had to progress across open fields to the town of Hamminkeln and our rendezvous.

I distinctly remember that of the five or six in our group, I was the first through the farm door into a great barn of a room, with wide wooden steps from the center of the room leading up to a loft which made up half the roof area, and just that half was about 30 feet square.

The first Germans I met were two old ladies in their sixties, who just stood there holding each other's hands. I'm not sure what they wanted, but I could see that they were scared. I asked them in broken German were there any soldiers in the farm, and one of them pointed up the stairs. I thought they appeared somewhat reluctant about showing me, so I indicated for them to call out to whoever was up there to come down. I was sure they understood me, but they refused to call out so I pulled out my No. 36 grenade and pulled the pin. I remember this quickly quietened down my mates who were jabbering away at the old ladies, and scared the hell out of them. Of course, I had no intention of using the grenade, just wanted a little cooperation. Then one old lady shouted up through the trapdoor, and after a few seconds, the faces of two Jerries appeared. When they saw this Luft trooper with a hand gre-nade in the throwing stance, they very quickly tumbled down the stairs. It seems they were antiaircraft personnel being used as ground troops and only too pleased to surrender.

I removed their identification shoulder tabs, and at that moment, an officer arrived and told me to hand the prisoners over to the padre, who by now was just outside with some wounded waiting for a jeep. As I was the only NCO in the group, he told me to gather as many men as I could and make our way to the rendezvous. As a lance corporal, I quickly found a sergeant and told him the captain had instructed me to find a senior NCO to lead the boys to the rendezvous; as I expected, he said, "Right, Corporal, I'll do it." After only two years in the army, I had learned quickly.

I do not remember the march to the church, but I do remember pulling our handcarts across fields, so the whole mortar crew must have collected together. My position in the team as lance corporal was No. 1 of four, being responsible for laying [aiming] the mortar.

The British 3-inch mortar, crewed by four men, was in fact one of the infantry's most effective weapons, and the British mortar, when manned by a well-trained team, I think is second to none. This, along with British artillery, I am sure was the prime reason in breaking up so many enemy attacks while in Normandy; in the Rhine Crossing and the fighting to the Baltic, no German attack against the 6th Airborne Division ever succeeded.

Much to our surprise, we managed to cross the open country. I think it was because there was a terrific firefight going on to our right, which probably took the attention of any Germans in the area.

We were aware of some Yanks to our right, and it was common knowledge that they expended vast amounts of ammo when contacting the enemy. It should be remembered that they had a great number of automatic weapons in each platoon, but it helped us clear the open ground.

It seemed only about half an hour had passed when, sweating and puffing, we broke through a hedge onto a road just in front of the church, our rendezvous in Hamminkeln. To our surprise, we met a group of Glider Pilots who had occupied the farm beside the Church and were in the process of searching about 100 prisoners, I imagine for pistols and binoculars (another of our targets). The prisoners were a mixed bunch, most of them well dressed and from a mechanical unit, but all seemed quite resigned to their fate.

We then quickly set up our mortars after digging our 6-by-6-by-4-foot Mortar pit. It was prior to this that a strange thing happened. One of the Glider Pilots, who spoke excellent German (I later found out he was Jewish), came over to us and, tapping me on the arm, said, "Come with me and I'll get you some help." We then marched over to where the prisoners were held, there being about 300 by now. He told them to be quiet and asked for three volunteers to help dig trenches. I heard him mention cigarettes, so there was a little bribery involved. To my surprise, we had to turn away a small crowd, so I went back to the boys with three volunteers to do the digging for us, which they did quite happily.

I remember paying them off with cigarettes and some chocolate, and then, to our surprise, they shook hands and strolled back to the pen. Such a crazy situation, considering their comrades just about 200 yards away were planning to kill as many of us as possible.

Pvt. Leonard Waller, HQ Platoon, describes his experience:

Our pilots made a very accurate landing on our target. Compared to many others who went adrift, we were very fortunate. It was clear from the sound of gunfire and explosions of some very accurate defensive ground fire that the Germans did not welcome our arrival.

Our immediate concern was to get out from the glider safely and set up a ramp so that the driver could get the jeep out, followed by our wheeling out the motorcycle. This was where we benefited from the presence of the strongly built Captain Bowman to help place the ramp safely in position, so that the very anxious, fidgeting driver could drive away across the plowed field. We achieved this successfully in about five minutes, compared with twenty minutes in previous practice sessions.

Sixty years on, my memory of what happened next is somewhat hazy, but I do recall seeing two or three German servicemen hurriedly leaving the nearby farmhouse. This was quickly taken over by Captain Bowman, Sergeant Muffet and others, leaving Raeburn and me to stand guard in a nearby trench. In the rush, I dropped my rifle, but having been trained to always keep my rifle barrel clean and ready for action, I hastily used my "pull-through" (a piece of 4-by-2-inch oiled rag) to make it fit for inspection as on guard duty!

Raeburn and I continued on guard outside the house when, after a few minutes, we heard the clanking of a tank, which appeared around the corner of the farmhouse with its gun swiveled round pointing straight at me. Strangely enough, I felt no fear, but a distinct feeling of regret that, having arrived here safely with the end of the war possibly only a few weeks away, I was facing immediate death. The only avoiding action I could take was to keep quite still in the hope that the tank's vision was so limited that the driver had not noticed any movement. After perhaps ten seconds when my world stood still (while it seemed like ten minutes), the tank turned away from us and trundled off out of sight.

Raeburn and I congratulated ourselves on our lucky escape, the reason for which, we assumed, was that the tank had used up its ammunition or was scared of our presence. Then our group received orders to move forward to Hamminkeln, where 6th Airlanding Brigade units were taking over from some German resistance.

Flight Lt. Ken Scolding was carrying a gun and crew from the Anti-Tank Platoon. His experience appears in the December 1985 issue of *The Eagle*:

> The smoke haze made it very difficult to judge distance. Landmarks that should have been sighted early were hidden from view until, for some, it was too late.
>
> That I had never flown a fully laden glider before has to be put down to one of those gaps in the training schedule that could be called criminal. One trip with 300 pounds of

concrete blocks was the heaviest load carried during my training. My load of a 6-pounder anti-tank gun, a jeep and three men weighed twice this. That we should arrive safely to form part of the defence of the village against a counter-attack by tanks was essential.

I came in over the village at about 500 feet, instead of 150, not daring to use full flap as the glider would, I assumed, drop like a stone when I took it off. There seemed only one course open to me and I said to my second pilot, Nick Nicholson, a man of infinite humour, "I am going around again." I heard him say, "For what we are about to receive," as we crossed the road for the second time, tearing through telephone and power lines to a landing, which I still believe was reasonably adjacent. I landed about 150 yards from a trench manned by the enemy. This fact, together with the loss of one landing leg, causing the glider to come to rest on one wing tip, meant that without covering help we could not unload.

Sgt. Pilot Alan Stredwick and Flying Officer "Tiny" Ledbrook, who had flown on Exercise Token, were carrying a full platoon. Stredwick recalls:

After releasing from the Stirling at 2,500 feet, I was able, with the help of the detailed photographs with which we had been provided, to shout directions to Tiny Ledbrook. The heavy smokescreen was much in evidence, but it was not obscuring the area of our own LZ. At this time, we came under fire with a great deal of green tracer coming towards us from mobile quadruple 20-millimeter cannon units, known as "flak vier-ling," and heavier-caliber guns. I remember little after this, and we must have been hit by cannon fire at this time. I then found myself lying in the grass beneath the wing of a damaged glider, where I had been placed for safety. I had a bullet (or shrapnel) wound to my left hand; my face was a mess and cov-ered in blood. I thought I could move my left leg, but then realized that when I moved it, the boot did not respond in the same direction. After attempting to move, but finding that I was unable to, an airborne medic noticed me and came over to attend to me, cutting my clothing away and giving me a shot. I was taken, eventually, on the hood of a jeep to a cowshed, where I joined other wounded, including German casualties. I recollect an ambulance journey past some damaged trees and resting in some sort of a school on a stretcher. At some point, I was treated in tented field hospital and recall crossing to the west bank of the Rhine in a DUKW [pronounded "duck," a type of amphibious vehicle]. I arrived home in England quite naked except for two blankets covering me, but in the little "personal effects" bag which accompanied each stretcher— containing odd coins, penknife, etc.—was included a piece of khaki which someone had cut from my uniform and to which was still sewn my pilot's wings. I still have these wings with the khaki material backing them.

It was at Wroughton that I first learned that "Tiny" Led- brook had been killed and I received a letter from his mother and two from his wife (a WAAF [Women's Auxiliary Air Force] corporal) asking about details of which I knew little myself but replied as best I could.

Flying Officer Gordon Procter and Sergeant Reed had on board Captain Bailey and eight other ranks. Procter describes what they went through:

Our tug came through telling us that we had twenty seconds to our designated pull-off point and wished us good luck and said they would count us down from ten seconds. We were the fourth glider of a group of six and I remember being very concerned as, when the first two pulled off, they were almost immediately hit by antiaircraft fire, one going into a near- vertical dive and the other seemed to lose a large part of its port wing.

As we pulled off, we were quite close to the third Horsa, and we both put on full flaps and started our steep descent. We were probably still at 4,000 feet, when the third glider was hit, and I said to Sergeant Reed, "Christ Almighty, we're next." I pulled up the flaps and banked heavily to the right and dived, hoping that I would get out of range of the guns, which had clearly fixed in on our position. What happened to the two Horsas behind I do not know.

Our speed, with our 3,000-pound overload, built up rapidly, and although we were redlined at 150, we were close to 200 mph, and both Sergeant Reed and I had to work very hard to pull the Horsa out of its rapid descent, which we did at about 300 feet, where we did a 180-degree turn, hoping it was back in the direction of Kopenhof farm. The smoke over our landing zone made it extremely difficult to pinpoint Kopenhof farm, and when we landed fairly close, we had not made our designated field.

Having put down full flaps, we landed intact, and I hope it doesn't sound boastful, but we were the only Horsa from A Squadron to do so; in fact, one of only a few to be completely undamaged, out of the 400 Horsas which landed across the Rhine that morning.

As we rolled to a halt, I opened the plywood door, mightily concerned when everybody seemed to be slumped forward, as they had all blacked out in the descent. I am sure we spoke to all the soldiers, but I remember Captain Bailey expressing delight and surprise that we had all made it.

We rapidly unloaded the jeep and trailer and took cover in a ditch while we endeavored to pinpoint our position, and I remember saying to Captain Bailey that I was sorry that we hadn't put down in exactly the right spot, and he quipped that they could hear and smell the antiaircraft fire and never expected to land safely and all in one piece.

I don't think he realized how hazardous our descent had been, what with the extra height which made us vulnerable for so much longer, the fact that it was almost impossible to see the ground due to the smoke, and importantly, our heavy overload. I remember thinking how composed he was and how embarrassed I felt to be thanked for landing his troops safely. It was my job.

We took cover in a ditch and compared notes to establish our exact location, and as we appeared to be no longer under direct fire, we bid Captain Bailey and his men, "Good luck," and they set off in what they thought was the route to their arranged map reference.

We decided to have a cigarette, and suddenly we saw what appeared to be a Japanese in an airborne smock and as an indication of how confused we must have been, as he got closer, I challenged him for the password as Sergeant Reed took aim with his cumbersome rifle. He turned out to be a Mexican-American paratrooper who was highly amused when we told him we thought he was a Japanese. He joined us in the ditch and swapped two Lucky Strikes for two of my Capstan Full Strength.

All three of us compared notes on our likely position, and we certainly helped him, as he appeared to be completely lost. We then set off to make our way to Kopenhof farm. Suddenly we were terrified to hear a tank approaching, me with my Smith and Wesson revolver, and it stopped behind the hedge and fired above us, and then, thank goodness, backed away. Once again I thought, weren't we so lucky?

As we continued in the direction of the farm, we met some Americans who were under fire from a farm some 200 to 300 yards away, and I took aim with my 2-inch airborne mortar. The shell exploded to the left as far away from us as the target! I said to Sergeant Reed, "I'll load, you aim," and he nearly hit the target. Although I had inadvertently selected a smoke shell much to the amusement of the Americans, all the Germans came tumbling out with their hands up. My mistake is another example of my military inexperience.

The two pilots then continued their journey to Kopenhof.

In the assault on Hamminkeln's southern side, Maj. John Rogers, CO of Company A, his batman, and company sergeant major took on two tanks and two half-tracks. They put one of the tanks and both half-tracks out of action and managed to drive away the second tank.

The glider of Lieutenant Allanson, Company B, encountered the first flak as it crossed the Rhine.

> On our left, a glider went down in flames and the tug, out of control, crashed onto a glider and tug below. All three went down together. At this moment, our glider received a direct hit on the left wing, and 3 feet of the end was knocked away. Small pieces of shrapnel penetrated the fuselage, but there were no casualties. The next few minutes were very confused. We cast off from the tug and went into a steep dive to port, missing another glider, which collided with one below it. It was impossible to identify the LZ, and we banked to starboard through the wreckage of a Stirling shot down above us. We dived steeply to port, just cleared telephone wires, and made a very bumpy landing in a plowed field.

Allanson's platoon met up with that of Lt. Eric Nuttall, whose glider had broken its towrope shortly after takeoff but had been quickly linked up to a reserve tug. The smoke and dust did not help with navigation on the ground, and a German civilian put them on the right track. They arrived on the outskirts of Hamminkeln and took up their allotted positions.

The glider of the Company B CO, Maj. Wallie Barrow, landed near Ringenberg after taking several hits from antiaircraft fire. He was the only survivor and, although wounded, managed to hold out against the enemy for twenty minutes before being taken prisoner.

Company C, commanded by Maj. John Haythornthwaite, had landed off-target, and he had only two platoons to complete his task. Lieutenant Slade, along with his platoon and pilots, had all died when their glider was destroyed by antiaircraft fire. The fourth platoon had landed alongside Company B and stayed under its command. The work of the 513th made the job of the two remaining Company C platoons much easier, but they still suffered casualties from snipers and mortar fire.

Battalion headquarters was established in Hamminkeln School. Gleadell's pilots had stayed with him, and after settling in the school, he ordered Maurice Priest, according to the commander glider pilots' report, "to take over duties of guarding prisoners, rounding up civilians and to provide a small fighting reserve as soon as sufficient glider pilots became available. By 1400 hrs more glider pilots had arrived and our strength was in the region of 20 all ranks." The report continues: "All civilians were rounded up and women and children were separated from the male population. Two churches and a large hall were set aside for the housing of the civilians about 800 in all. Enemy food stocks were centralised and the village baker was ordered to produce bread."

S.Sgt. Timo Jenkins had the job of guarding the access to the wine cellar of the shop, "a job which, unbeknown to me at the time, was to start me off on the road to being a real wine lover, and eventually something of a connoisseur," he says in the December 1998 issue of *The Eagle* But liquid of another sort was also in demand: "Some of the locals, under escort, were detailed to milk the cows, in order to provide relief for the animals and sustenance for the children."

Another A Squadron pilot, S.Sgt. Ron Bartley, noticed a young mother and her baby among the crowd of women and children standing outside the hall. The mother caught his eye and held up a can. Through gestures, she indicated that she wanted to get some milk for her baby. Bartley relates:

> I beckoned her over, and she handed the baby to another woman. Her English was good enough to explain that there was a cowshed nearby. Two German 88s and some mortars were firing on the village, and some shells were getting very close. We got down on our hands and knees and crawled to the shed. She milked a cow and we crawled back. It was a most extraordinary experience.

Each woman was also allowed to go home, again under escort, to bring back a suitcase of essentials. Jenkins accompanied one of these women. "I well remember how my protégé, with her small child, ran the whole way back to her cottage, with repeated fearful glances over her shoulder at the 'awful Red Devil' accompanying her," he recalls in *The Eagle*. "When we arrived at her home, she found that she had mislaid the key and I had to restrain her from scrambling in through a window of broken glass in her terror." Jenkins went in through the window and opened the door. The woman grabbed a prepacked suitcase and was on her way back to the church before Jenkins barely had time to catch his breath. "'But for the grace of God, these might have been our own womenfolk,' I thought and, as graciously as I could, took the heavy bag from her trembling fingers and carried it the rest of the way."

On the outskirts, Companies A and B spent what remained of the daylight digging more defensive positions and improving those already begun. Members from all companies continued to drift into the village, many having had to fight their way through determined resistance.

Throughout the late afternoon and evening, the German forces made little effort to infiltrate the defenses, content with shelling the village center. During the night, the enemy was more active, and Company A was moved to the northeast of the village in support of its counterpart in OBLI, which was much depleted.

ROYAL ARTILLERY

2ND AIRLANDING ANTI-TANK REGIMENT

The 3rd Battery of the 2nd Airlanding Anti-Tank Regiment was split between Landing Zones A, B, P, and R, while the 4th was assigned to B only. Both batteries were to give supporting fire for their parachute brigades, airlanding brigade, and divisional headquarters. Six of the fifty-four gliders did not reach Germany.

Lt. John Slater was in a battery headquarters glider of the 3rd Airlanding Anti-Tank Battery:

> We saw how bad the visibility was as we crossed the Rhine, but we soon cast off, and for a few minutes all was quiet and peaceful. Then we were hit by light flak—twice, I think, once in the starboard wing just behind me and also in the undercarriage. I clearly remember the pilot saying, "Christ, I'm getting down out of this," and get down he did—I'm sure we came down almost vertically! When we landed, it was quite a heavy one; the undercarriage came off, and the nose wheel shot up through the floor.
>
> Immediately after we landed, we found we were trapped inside the glider, as the nose was firmly embedded in the field

and the quick-release bolts holding the tail on were so corroded that we just couldn't get them off. It seemed hard to believe that only three hours earlier, we were being given cups of NAAFI [Navy, Army, and Air Force Institutes] tea in England, and now here we were in Germany, trapped in a glider in the middle of the German gun area! We finally got the side door open, with a certain amount of chopping with an axe and an incredible amount of bad language!

We soon pinpointed our position and tried to salvage the load from the glider, but soon came under mortar fire, so we went over to a nearby farmhouse. Here we found two American pilots who had been shot down—one was badly wounded—and two Germans who surrendered without delay. There was an incredible armory of weapons in the farm, machine guns and mortars in particular, and we gathered that the platoon that owned them was down in Hamminkeln on a bath parade. How lucky we were!

After this, we made our way to battery HQ, and we were soon joined by the battery second in command, Maj. John Maddocks, and later by the battery commander, who had gone on ahead while we were trying to unload the glider. He had been briefly captured by some German paratroops. As far as I can remember, they relieved him of his pistol, binoculars, and watch, and after giving him a cup of coffee, let him go!

S.Sgt. Arthur Shackleton and Sgt. John "Willy" Williamson were carrying a jeep, trailer, and 6-pounder gun. Shackleton recalls:

The flight across the North Sea was relatively uneventful, except for the telephone cable snapping as the towrope stretched. This meant we had to communicate with the tug by Morse code using a torch. The tug's tail gunner was a wireless operator/air gunner, so was proficient in the code. He flashed a message to us on his lamp. I turned to Willy and said, "What did he say?" "Buggered if I know," he replied. So we had to carry on without being able to communicate.

We released from our tug and prepared to land. As I turned to starboard to prepare for the final approach, I found that I could not move the rudders. They were jammed solid. I had no option other than to fly straight ahead. Luckily, I found a field fairly reasonable in length. The flaps were still working, so it was full flap, dive approach. We went through a wire fence and stopped without any serious hurt to our passengers or ourselves. Later inspection showed that a burst of antiaircraft fire had blown away part of our starboard tailplane and shredded the rudder.

Our Horsa was a Mark II, which meant the nose swung open to allow cargo to be taken in and out. Unfortunately, the quick-release mechanism, which secured the jeep and trailer, had become fused through antiaircraft fire and was inoperable. Fortunately, a REME [Royal Electrical and Mechanical Engineers] unit came to the rescue and soon our passengers and their jeep and gun were off to engage the enemy.

While all this was going on, Willy and I had joined Arnold Baldwin and Jock Glover, who had taken up defensive positions with some Canadian paratroopers. The Canadians had captured a young Italian, Luigi Marco Antonio, who had been conscripted into the German Army. Luigi was extremely grateful that his life had been spared and performed various domestic duties for us, including making a "brew." We were sorry to say good-bye to him when we left on the twenty-seventh.

Approximately two hours after landing, the Canadians wanted to attack a large house from where there was sniper and mortar fire. They asked me to give covering fire with my Bren gun. This I did, emptying six magazines into the front of the house and shattering all the windows. Whether I killed any of the enemy or not I shall never know, since the Canadians didn't return to let me know. In the evening, two Germans ran along a hedge about 300 yards to our right front. Arnold Baldwin, looking through his binoculars, thought they were setting up a mortar, so I gave them a burst. They were indistinct through the hedge, but we saw no more movement, and

as there was a German minefield between them and us, we did
not investigate.

Flight Lt. David Marande and Sergeant Brown, both RAF glider
pilots, were carrying a 4th Airlanding Anti-Tank Battery jeep, trailer, and
gun. Marande recounts their experiences in a letter to their former head-
master at Lewes County School:

> We had a very good trip over, doing a young "Cook's tour" of
> the continent to arrive at our destination.
> We had talked very optimistically about the terrific force
> of UK troops which would be crossing the Rhine when we
> arrived, and you can imagine our horror when, as we flew
> over that stretch of water, search as we might we could see no
> boat, no pontoon, and not even a single swimmer. Had the
> offensive gone as scheduled or had something gone wrong?
> Was this operation to be another Arnhem? However, it was
> too late to turn back now. There was the release point coming
> up straight ahead and the captain of the tug was saying: "This
> is where you get off, chum." We exchanged wishes of good
> luck and we released the rope. We were at last on our own. We
> had to go down, and what awaited us below?
> Over our whole landing zone floated a blanket of smoke,
> and we loudly cursed Montgomery for his smoke screen. Later,
> we found out that it was nothing to do with Monty but was a
> Jerry effort.
> My co-pilot was wriggling about in his seat, photographs
> and maps in hand trying to pierce the smoke to find some
> landmark, which he could recognise. Suddenly, he gave a yell:
> "There is the railway and the wood, turn right 45 degrees." I
> did as he had said. I had to rely entirely on him, as I was busy
> watching and avoiding other gliders, which were obviously as
> uncertain as we where the landing zone was. All this time flak
> was bursting all over the place, but apart from the occasional
> bump as a burst came close to us we suffered no harm from
> that quarter. My co-pilot had got accustomed to picking out
> reference points and he told me that we were just going over

the far boundary of our area. I took time out for a quick glance downwards and caught sight of a point, which I easily recognised. I knew then just where to make my approach for landing.

I was about to make a wide circuit losing height as I went—I was still very high—when I caught sight of a Halifax with one engine on fire still towing its glider to its release point. Just as the glider pulled off another burst of flak hit it and with two engines blazing it lazily rolled over and went into a steep spiral. We stayed just long enough to see the crew bail out and although the whole thing had seemed very unreal I realised it wasn't healthy to stay upstairs any longer so we put our flaps down and our nose and dived to earth as fast as the old crate could go. I pulled out at about 20 feet above the deck peering ahead for a row of high tension pylons and cables which I knew were there somewhere but the first thing that loomed out of the fog was a farmhouse and its outbuildings. Thanks to the excess speed, which we had gained in our desire to get down to earth in our own manner, we were able to pull up over these obstructions only to find that 30 yards ahead were the high-tension cables. So we dived again and happily got under them.

By now we had slowed up considerably and avoiding a large tree we touched down in a small field separated from the next one by a barbed wire fence which failed to stop our rush forward. Our brakes, too, let us down and we finally pulled up with five young trees in one wing and two in the other. Fortunately we had been able to steer the nose between two of them so quickly out of our seats and swung open the nose and proceeded to get our load out of the glider.

It was hard work getting the jeep, trailer and gun out. But we were spurred on by the whine of bullets and the thud of mortar and shellfire so that we had the job finished in about 15 minutes, which is quite fast for such a job. We were really very fortunate as the paratroops had dropped half an hour before us and had cleared the local farmhouses etc. of Jerries and were proceeding to fan out into the surrounding countryside so that within two hours or so things in the locality were quietening down, and from then on we were only worried by the odd snipers and the mortar and shellfire which, in its turn, finished about the end of the second day. A few days more and our slit trenches and field rations were left behind as we flew back to England, our first engagement with the enemy finished.

Tom Wallis, 4th Airlanding Anti-Tank Battery, relates his experience:

Sudden quietness as the glider detached and the noise from the bomber disappeared. I struggled to get back to my seat, my fingers incapable of fixing my safety belt. I just grabbed the guys each side of me. Then we were down—a perfect landing. I could not believe it; we had landed without a scratch.

The jeep and trailer were unloaded into a landscape thick with smoke and shadowy groups of troops moving in all directions to find their meeting points. As I made my way to the road, a para handed me a PIAT bomb, minus its safety cap, saying, "You better have this, mate," and disappeared into the fog. Two minutes later, I tapped another solder on the back and handed him the live antitank bomb mumbling, "You better have this, mate," before I slipped back into the fog. Gliders were still landing, with the vast shape of a Horsa suddenly passing overhead in total silence, everyone needing four pairs of eyes. The sound of small-arms fire was intermittent, but German antiaircraft fire seemed to be all around us.

Having reached the road, we seemed to be very much on our own. The colonel walked down the center of the road with his side arm drawn. I ran alongside in a ditch with Pat driving the jeep in a somewhat exposed position; at that time, coming up the road behind came a tank—one of ours.

The tank took the lead, and it was most reassuring as we approached any potential danger spots, the tank turret swung round giving us cover. A little later, we came across an American paratrooper riding a donkey. "Hi bud," said the Yank with thumb extended. "Are you going to Salisbury?" He then asked, looking at the tank, "Did that come across the river?" "No mate," I said with enormous pride. "That came by air."

For Bob Mortimer, 2nd Forward Observation Unit (2FOU), and his comrades it was a different matter:

> We had sustained flak damage during the descent, and a 20-millimeter shell had exploded in the cockpit area. The first pilot sustained a broken ankle, and the second pilot a buttock flesh wound. The captain was seriously wounded but fortunately survived. We landed near Hamminkeln and found ourselves "in the bag" [prisoners of war].

The men remained "guests" of the Germans until released during the Allied advance.

Antiaircraft fire accounted for many of the gliders as they crossed the Rhine or arrived over the landing zones. Eight officers and 154 other ranks of the 3rd Battery had taken off for Germany. Casualty figures stood at one officer and twenty men dead, one officer and seventeen men wounded, and ten men missing. Similar casualties had occurred in the 4th Battery. The CO, Maj. Peter Dixon MC, was killed soon after landing.

The situation with the guns was also desperate. Thirty-two guns had set out on the flight, but only half arrived in a fireable condition. After the first hour on the ground, only three were in action. By 1700, some five and a half hours later, only another nine had been salvaged.

A decision was made to temporarily amalgamate the batteries, and Maj. Joe Woodrow took command.

53RD (WORCESTERSHIRE YEOMANRY) AIRBORNE LIGHT REGIMENT

The men and equipment of the 53rd (Worcestershire Yeomanry) Airborne Light Regiment were carried to Germany in seventy-eight gliders, both Horsas and Hamilcars, which were to land on Landing Zones B, P, and R. Of these, seven failed to reach the landing area. Of those that did, thirty-five landed on, or very close to, their intended landing zones. Another fourteen landed close enough to allow the men and equipment to join the regiment within a few hours. Seven more landed to the west of the Rhine, and their loads made contact with the regiment by the twenty-sixth.

S.Sgt. Eddie Raspison and Sgt. Pilot Sid Edwards carried a forward observation team. The glider was to land one and a half miles to the east of the main part of the 53rd Light Regiment, which would be coming in on Landing Zone P. The pilots' CO, Maj. Ian Toler had warned them at the briefing that their isolated landing area contained several 88-millimeter guns. Raspison recalls in the December 1997 issue of *The Eagle*:

> Shortly after take-off, the Artillery Captain came into the cockpit and proffered a full bottle of whiskey. We both took a good slug and the Captain returned to the fuselage presumably to treat his men in a like manner.
>
> The flight was uneventful and after crossing the Rhine the main force began casting off. Our tug crew warned that we would have about a further ten minutes on tow. We came to a position where we could pinpoint the landing area and said our "Cheerios" and thanks to the tug crew. I had to turn to port to bring us in line with the approach and straighten out before applying full flap.
>
> As we glided in, I felt two impacts on the glider, though everything was responding normally, and I assumed that any hits had been indecisive. I noticed however that Sid was not only slumped in his seat but there was smoke coming from one of his ammunition pouches, one of which I knew contained two phosphorous grenades.
>
> I could do nothing other than control the landing but in putting the glider down it sank lower into the ground than normal. I thought that maybe the undercarriage had been shattered by one of the hits and this proved to be the case.
>
> After coming to rest, I unstrapped Sid as carefully as possible and managed to get him into the fuselage where everything was in disarray and a hole had been blasted in the port side where the entrance door had originally been.
>
> The jeep driver assisted me in getting Sid out through the hole and into the shelter of the furrow, dug by the glider in

landing, which offered some protection from the small arms fire we were encountering.

We returned to the fuselage where we found that the driver and I were the only ones who had escaped injury, though none was in a critical condition. We got them all out into the shelter and beside Sid and had a look at their general condition.

My first action was to relieve Sid of his webbing, throwing it as far as I could in case either of the grenades had been triggered. I assessed the situation and told the driver that, in view of the overall position, I was in charge.

We got the jeep and trailer out through the nose with little difficulty and then put the men on the jeep. I ordered the driver to take them as carefully, but as quickly, as possible back to the main force where they would get the necessary medical attention.

I waved them off and started walking back to the main force. I met no opposition on the way and saw nothing of the jeep and trailer or those who were aboard.

WO Len Macdonald gives his account in the April 1995 issue of *The Eagle*:

Eventually with the flooded Rhine in sight I gave the RSM permission to awaken the Staff Sergeant. On emerging from under his blanket the Staff Sergeant took one look forward and said, "Ah . . . coming up to the Channel are we?" We were soon across the Rhine and on being given the pre-arranged signal for the moment to part company with our tug . . . a steady green Aldis . . . I pulled off and with the assistance of Staff Sergeant Penketh made an excellent landing only a couple of fields away from our chosen landing spot. The aircraft was absolutely intact except for a few bullet holes in the flaps. I hopped out to open up the nose of 397 and commence unloading and immediately came under pretty heavy fire. Here, and as he did throughout our time in and near Hamminkeln, Staff Sergeant Penketh showed what a splendid soldier he was.

He was in action straight away with his Bren gun and as a result I was able to complete the unloading in relative comfort. On the way to our appointed place of meeting we were involved in a number of skirmishes, which resulted in our accumulating a number of prisoners and being somewhat behind our estimated time of arrival.

We were greeted by a military gentleman of considerable rank who it seemed was in need of the communications unit that I had loaded into 397 at Great Dunmow with such care a few days earlier. He looked at his watch, looked at us with what I thought was a twinkle in his eye and said, "You're late . . . what kept you?" Needless to say, we took this to be a form of congratulations for a job that I think was quite well done.

During the past fifty years I have often thought about Staff Sergeant Penketh and sought for an explanation for his conduct on our trip to Germany. If he felt unwell he certainly was not the least bit bothered about what might lie ahead and, due to his experience, he had a pretty good idea of what we could expect on touch down. He DID know that VARSITY was my first operational sortie and I am convinced that he decided that if I was kept busy I would not have time to worry about what our reception might be.

Despite many enquiries at reunions and elsewhere I have not been able to find any trace of this remarkable man who in my opinion was a credit to that happy and remarkable band of brothers, the men of the Glider Pilot Regiment, with whom it was a pleasure to serve.

The 53rd Light Regiment was responsible for two 25-pounder guns, to be used for marking targets with smoke. The guns, with modified carriages, were carried in Horsas Chalks 305 and 364. Chalk 305, carrying Battery Sgt. Maj. Frank Bentley, Sergeant Nicholds, and four gunners, landed nearly 2 miles away to the northwest. All on board were wounded, two of the gunners, Hare and Lawson, fatally. Nicholds was shot in the leg and Bentley through the wrist. Bentley was captured and held prisoner for six days. Interestingly, the German doctor who first treated him after his capture had studied for his medical degree at Manchester University before the war and stayed in lodgings about 200 yards from Bentley's house.

The glider of Capt. D. K. Thomas, B Troop, 210th Battery, and two others landed close together 3 miles east of the zone. Thomas gathered all three parties together and began a march toward the intended rendezvous. The group was met by machine-gun fire and sustained several casualties. Thomas crawled back twice to collect wounded and stragglers. Eventually he realized further progress was impossible without increasing the casualty level and established his men in a farmhouse. The citation for his Military Medal takes up the account:

> Meanwhile the house had been surrounded by much greater numbers of enemy and from 12.00 hours to 18.00 hours was subjected to continuous small arms and mortar fire. Nevertheless the little force held out and even broke up an infantry assault on the house with heavy losses to the enemy largely owing to Capt Thomas's courage and leadership. He himself killed seven enemy for certain. It was only when all their ammunition was exhausted that Capt Thomas was compelled to surrender his force.

Lt. D. F. Hurndall, the regimental survey officer, was in the glider carrying his survey party of five gunners, along with a wireless-equipped jeep, a trailer, and two motorcycles. The glider came under machine-gun fire, which wounded Gunner Rowlands in the shoulder. An antiaircraft shell then smashed through the fuselage, killing Gunner Adams, who was sitting next to Hurndall, and setting the glider on fire.

The glider crash-landed some 2 miles from its landing zone, killing one of the pilots and Gunner Diggory, and rendering the remaining survivors temporarily unconscious. Gunner Baines rescued Hurndall, and they were joined by Gunners Hooper and Rowlands, who had managed to get a field dressing on his wound. Lieutenant Hurndall recalls in *The Queen's Own Worcestershire Hussars, 1922–1956*, by David Guttery:

> I had no maps left and my compass was broken and there was no landmark in sight. I decided to join a "stick" of one of the

para Battalions which was passing and, assisted by Baines and
Hooper, I made my way to a building which was held by the
RUR. Baines and Hooper then went back, found the second
pilot and brought him in. They were both awarded the Military Medal.

Sgt. Sam Groom was in a 211th Battery glider, which landed on its
nose. It took Groom and his detachment about an hour to hack their way
through the fuselage. When they finally got outside, Groom says in *The
Queen's Own Worcestershire Hussars*:

> I got my detachment together and we tried to pull down the
> glider tail so that we could get the gun out. We were unsuc-
> cessful in this and it looked as if we should have to chop a
> hole in the glider big enough to get the jeep through it. Then
> I saw Sergeant Thomas of 211 Battery with his gun moving
> off. I stopped him and we put a towrope round the tail of the
> glider and hooked it to a jeep; that did the trick and we got
> the gun out without any more trouble.

The glider was where it should have been, and Groom had no prob-
lem getting his bearings. He and his crew set off for the rendezvous,
where they found Maj. Charles Russell, the 53rd Light Regiment's CO.
Russell showed Groom where to position his gun, and digging in began.
Sgt. "Sam" Hardy was only one of two sergeants in F Troop, 212th
Battery, to reach the ground alive. He describes his experience:

> Our glider hit the ground with a terrific bang and then did
> the same again. The noise of tearing plywood was frighten-
> ing. We hit a post-and-wire fence, and the first pilot discarded
> the undercarriage. We tilted to the left, and that wing buried
> into the ground, swung us round, and brought us to an abrupt
> stop.
> Sudden peace and silence and I shouted, "Hurrah!" I opened
> my door and stepped out. Ahead of me I saw a bunch of
> about twenty German soldiers. They just stared at me, and as I
> looked around, I saw the adjoining field had a scattering of

parachutes and that an American soldier was covering the Germans with his gun.

A glider landed about 500 yards away. The occupants unloaded and made haste to join us. They turned out to be the second half of a gun crew from my troop and were led by Sgt. "Stan" Matthews, a good friend. We embraced, and he said, "My God, Sam, I am pleased to see you!"

Our glider had been badly damaged, and the pilots' cabin, which was hinged to allow easy loading and unloading, would not function. So the next thing was to unbolt the tail section, but this had also been damaged, and the bolts could not be released. So I gave the order to axe the tail off.

Eventually, with the help of Stan's lot, we managed to get everything out undamaged. We gathered into a group, and glider pilot Staff Sergeant Hall said to me, "You're in charge. What do you want us to do?" I can still remember my exact words: "Right, there is a farmhouse over there. It's the only building to be seen, and we're going to take it. If it's a farm, there will be a road nearby."

I spread them all out, with the jeeps in the rear, and off we went. We came to the near end of the slope when, as if by magic, from behind a clump of trees came a jeep and trailer with a motorbike following. I could tell from the way the rider sat that it was our troop sergeant major.

The jeep contained our troop command post officer, Lieutenant Farrer. I asked him where we were going, and he replied, "Nowhere. This is to be our troop gun position."

My driver, Frank Halford, was killed in the afternoon, and the rest of my crew did not appear until 5:00 P.M. the next day.

S.Sgt. John Perfect was first pilot of one of the ammunition-carrying Hamilcars. His story appears in the August 2006 issue of *The Eagle*:

Fortunately a soldier from the unit flew with us down below with our weapons and kit etc. I say fortunately because as soon as we were landed he discovered the position of his troops, took us there and our mission was completed.

For this operation, I was issued with a Bren gun to take instead of my rifle. We were able to fire on a range at Wood-bridge but I did not look forward to the prospect of blazing away at uncertain targets. So I told the QM that I must have field glasses. He retorted that binoculars were "only on issue" to officers. However he reluctantly agreed to my request on two conditions. I was to have the glasses, but not the case in which they were kept; I must promise to return them.

When I emerged from the Hamilcar on landing, with my Bren and binoculars at the ready, I could see in the middle distance hedges and crouching figures moving among them. How relieved I was that I could confirm that these were our men.

The other ammunition carrier was among those gliders that landed away from the zone. The situation was too dangerous to attempt retrieving the load in daylight, so it wasn't until shortly before midnight that a party of the 53rd, with infantry support, made its way to the glider. Over the next three hours, the men brought all the ammunition back to the guns.

By evening, with all the division's objectives secured, the 53rd Light Regiment was able to settle into its positions and take stock of its losses. There were ninety-two casualties, of which twenty-one had been killed and two mortally wounded. Seventeen men were missing in action. It was later ascertained that all but three had been taken prisoner.

The comparative peace of the night was broken only once. In the very early part of the twenty-fifth, a group of about 100 German troops attempted to return to their own lines. In doing so they stumbled into the headquarters area. Major Russell came out to see what was going on and found the Germans covered by the Brens of the Glider Pilot Regiment defense force. Russell walked toward the Germans and called forward an officer, who did not hesitate to offer his surrender.

ARMOURED RECONNAISSANCE REGIMENT
Tom Wallis's tank was one of four in the Armoured Reconnaissance Regiment (ARR) that eventually reached the rendezvous. Flight Lt. Patrick Edmonds and Lt. John D'Arcy-Clark were just two of the many witnesses of the fate of one of those that did not. Edmonds recalls: "We

watched in horror as a Hamilcar glider above and to our right disintegrated without obvious cause, its load, a Locust tank [commanded by Sergeant Dawson], and crew falling like puppets to their death." The Hamilcar was Chalk 262, piloted by Staff Sergeant James and Lieutenant Graefe, and towed by a Halifax of 298th Squadron. Its fate is recorded in Chatterton's report as "disintegration."

In the Hamilcar carrying Lieutenant Kenward's tank, driver Sgt. Colin Peckham had spent most of the flight lying on his stomach, observing the scene through the Perspex nose panels. As the glider was on its final approach, Peckham got back into the tank and, like the rest of the crew, braced for the landing. The Hamilcar hit the ground hard, coming to a halt close to a farm. The heavy landing caused the nose mechanism to jam, but Kenward hardly drew a breath as he ordered Peckham to drive through the door, which the sergeant did.

A Panther tank was in the farmyard, and the Locust fired about six rounds from its 37-millimeter gun, all to no effect. The Panther returned fire from its 88-millimeter, scoring a devastating direct hit. Kenward was wounded in the thigh, and Peckham was badly burned on his left leg. The sergeant managed to open the driver's hatch and roll into a ditch. The men were treated by American medics before being moved into an aid station in a farm. They were evacuated back over the Rhine in a DUKW late on the twenty-fourth.

Trooper K. W. Dowsett and his two crewmates had a very lucky escape. As they were preparing to land, their pilot told them that he was on the final approach to the field when everything, literally, turned upside down. Dowsett explains in Harclerode's history of the 6th Airborne: "With an almighty crash, we came to a halt upside down, suspended in our safety harnesses. We had glided down very close to a light flak position, which took part of the Hamilcar's wing off." Both pilots were killed, and the tank tore loose from its moorings and flipped onto its turret. Dowsett continues: "We eventually were able to crawl out from under the tank. We were a pretty sore and sorry crew."

Keeping their heads down, the men assessed their position. They heard tank tracks approaching and feared the worst. All fear subsided as they saw it was another Locust, with their CO, Lt. Col. Godfrey Stewart, standing up in the turret blowing his hunting horn. Stewart and his crew helped them clamber up and the tank continued on its way to the rendezvous.

On the way, they came across another tank, which on landing had gone through a house. Although it was running, its guns were out of action.

The fourth Locust, which did not reach the rendezvous, was reported as being damaged but remained in action, protecting the 12th Parachute Battalion. S.Sgt. Harry Dent and S.Sgt. Derek Rodgers piloted the Hamilcar that carried it. Dent relates in the August 2003 issue of *The Eagle*:

> Our flight was uneventful until we reached the Rhine. When we were approximately half way across the river we ran into heavy flak. A shell must have pierced one of the fuel tanks of the Halifax and a huge ball of flame suddenly enveloped the front of the aircraft.
>
> Although my attention was riveted on the fire, I was also considering the best evasive action to take, but fortunately managed to remember to release the towrope in the very short time before the blazing tug fell like a stone into the river.
>
> Meanwhile the rudder of our glider was damaged. We continued on a straight course to the other side of the Rhine where the area ahead was fairly heavily wooded. Fortunately there was a field ahead, which was within our limited gliding distance, and I was able to make a safe landing.

The tank and its crew made a rapid exit and headed for the rendezvous, but sadly, Dent and Rodgers were taken prisoner.

The four successful tanks occupied high ground and a railway embankment in the vicinity of the Devons' positions, on the edge of Hamminkeln. A platoon of the Devons was detailed to support the tanks, as they came under increasing fire from German artillery and machine guns. As the fighting intensified, the platoon commander was killed and a troop sergeant wounded. During the night, the tanks withdrew into section areas, which were reinforced by glider pilots.

Most of the gliders carrying the Mortar Troop landed beyond the zone and close to the outskirts of Hamminkeln. They came under intense artillery and small-arms fire but were gathered together by Captain d'Hulon and fought their way back to the gun area, with the loss of one jeep. The mortars were dug in and gave supporting fire over the next few hours.

195TH AIRLANDING FIELD AMBULANCE

The 195th Airlanding Field Ambulance was carried to Germany in thirteen gliders. S.Sgt. George Nye and Sergeant Gough were carrying medics, with their jeep and trailer. Nye recalls:

> We had a trouble-free flight but problems arose as we approached the LZ. It was obscured by smoke. Sergeant Gough and I decided to reduce speed as much as possible to allow us time to recognize any salient features. This decision actually created further problems, since we were then over-taken, at high speed, by gliders on all sides. We managed to avoid an accident and completed a safe landing. The jeep and trailer were unloaded quickly, and the detachment sped off to its RV.
>
> We made our way to our own RV that was a farmhouse. Sad news greeted us when we were told that a mortar bomb had killed our flight commander, Capt. Rex Norton, and his second pilot, S.Sgt. Doug Harris, also from 19 Flight.
>
> I took it upon myself to gather together Captain Norton's personal effects and wrapped them in his airborne scarf. Among these items was a rabbit's foot, which Captain Norton had carried with him throughout the war. I asked Major Toler, B Squadron's CO, if I might keep the foot in memory of such a fine officer and soldier. Major Toler agreed. I kept the foot until the fiftieth anniversary of Varsity. I then buried it in my garden—a final resting place.
>
> With the "help" of some prisoners, who dug trenches, we established a defended area around the farm buildings. We were then largely concerned with guarding prisoners. When we were withdrawn on the twenty-sixth, we left behind quite an elaborate trench system.

Cpl. John Cooper gives a full and clear account of his own and his unit's experiences on the first day:

> My first sight on disembarking was an 88-millimeter self-propelled gun, fortunately pointing away from us. It was not

fortunate for a Hamilcar glider, which was larger than our Horsa, which landed and proceeded to unload its cargo of two armored cars laden with ammunition. The first had just reached the foot of the ramp when the 88 gun scored a direct hit, sending the whole assembly into the air in a terrible explosion.

Despite the warnings received at the briefing, the undercarriage of our glider did catch the power lines and we nose-dived into a plowed field. The "skid," a landing device in addition to the tricycle wheels, was forced through the floor of our glider later, leading to difficulties in getting the jeep out.

My instructions were to be first out of the rear section and to receive the packs of the remaining occupants. This I did, and my first sight on disembarking was a 88-millimeter self-propelled gun, fortunately pointing away from us. It was not fortunate for a Hamilcar glider, which was larger than our Horsa, which landed and proceeded to unload its cargo of two armored cars laden with ammunition. The first had just reached the foot of the ramp when the 88 gun scored a direct hit, sending the whole assembly into the air in a terrible explosion.

Having put all our packs on the ground, I noticed a hole some 24 inches in diameter through the tail of the glider and not very far from the place I had been sitting. We had been told at the briefing to be careful not to cause any unnecessary damage to the gliders, as it might be wise to recover them for us. In Normandy, fighting had taken place over a period of two or three weeks over the landing zone, and a great deal of damage had occurred to the gliders.

Bearing in mind, we set about disconnecting the tail section of the glider, which, according to the drill which we had performed on many occasions, was accomplished by unscrewing eight quick-release bolts, being careful to release the last two simultaneously, when the tail would fall away from the fuselage. This was done most meticulously, but nothing happened. Again dismounting, we swung on the tail in an effort to dislodge it, but without success. All that happened was that the glider rocked onto its belly!

We then discovered that the platform upon which the pilots rested their feet had been forced up around their waists, and despite the instructions regarding unnecessary damage, we decided that the only course of action was to chop away the nose of the glider. This we did, and we had an aperture large enough for the jeep to be driven out, the driver started up the engine and released the clutch, but due to the damage to the floor of the glider, the wheels of the jeep were resting on the plowed earth and simply just spun. Pieces of the glider that had been chopped off to release the pilots were pushed under the wheels and when the driver tried again, the jeep shot out like a champagne cork from a bottle and traveled 100 yards before the driver could stop it and return to us. We loaded the equipment onto the jeep, and after a discussion to determine the direction of the assembly point, we were persuaded by rifle fire to take refuge in a nearby farmhouse. This we found was already occupied by a glider party from brigade headquarters, and two men were resting on a vegetable clamp ready to return fire. Unfortunately, some of the firing was coming from behind them, and they were told to retreat to the safety of the farmhouse. As they got up from their positions, one was hit in the leg, and two of our party dashed out and brought him in. The officer in charge, seeing that I had a revolver, detailed me to guard one side of the farmhouse. So there I was at an open window and protected by a mattress, on guard armed with a pistol, with which I doubted I could hit a barn door at six paces, which, fortunately, I was not called upon to prove!

The initial casualties had been fairly heavy, first count revealed a loss of 40 percent of the brigade, but a number had been taken prisoner, only to be released after a brief period and able to rejoin their units. Of the thirteen gliders, one came down in Holland; one with fifteen personnel was captured as it landed, but were released by the Americans a few hours later; and a third carrying twenty-five personnel was also captured, and they remained as prisoners of war till the end of the hostilities.

The work on the main dressing station was hectic, and by midnight a 700-bed hospital was fully operative. In addition to the blankets carried by the unit, additional supplies were scrounged from the locals. Apart from these duties I had been occupied as a stretcher bearer, and as the wards were on the upper floors, this was heavy work. At midnight, half the unit was stood down and I was able to get some sleep till 06:00; at this time, I had to complete a state-of-unit report for divisional headquarters. After seeing that off by dispatch rider, and a wash and shave at the cattle trough in the yard, we finally had some breakfast, this being the first meal since leaving England over twenty-four hours earlier. Incidentally, while washing and shaving, I met one of my colleagues from the office. He was in the light artillery that was supporting our division. Although, as mentioned, we had not eaten for over twenty-four hours, we were sustained during that time by cigarettes.

716TH COMPANY ROYAL ARMY SERVICE CORPS

The 716th Company RASC was carried in twelve Hamilcars, which were to land on Landing Zone P. The fate of the one carrying Stanley Maxted and his PR team was described at the beginning of this chapter. Of the remainder, seven made it to the landing area, but were hit by anti-aircraft fire, one was found on the twenty-ninth, and three have never been traced.

The one that was found, Chalk 273, had landed at Margraten, about 100 miles from Wesel. The bodies of the pilots, Staff Sergeant Spowart and Flying Officer Ankers, who had been shot in the head, were found propped up by one of the main wheels. The body of one other passenger, Driver Baker RASC, was close by. The load, consisting of a Bren carrier and associated equipment, was never found.

S.Sgt. Denis Cason, Chalk 271, describes his experience:

The flight was uneventful, but it was a different situation when we reached the LZ that was covered with smoke and dust. Monty had put down one of his barrages and more or less obliterated the small town of Wesel, which was upwind of the landing area. We released from our tug and went down through the smoke. The lower we got, visibility improved. Coming in to land, we took down some power cables, lost our undercarriage, hit a ditch, and slid to a halt. Ray tapped me on the shoulder and indicated the cigarette he was smoking. A bullet had gone through the cockpit and taken the end off the cigarette. All was well down below, apart from a track that had come off. This was soon replaced, and the vehicle and its crew were soon heading off for their RV.

After our passengers left, Ray and I went into a farmhouse, whose occupants were down in the cellar. On the kitchen table was a meal, still warm. We decided not to waste the opportunity and polished it off. Having eaten, we made our way to our HQ at another farmhouse. U.S. Liberator bombers were dropping large wicker supply baskets, and for a few minutes it became quite dicey on the ground. One plane was fired on by a German machine gun. We saw the tracer going into the bomb bay. The plane suddenly went straight up, stalled, nose-dived into the ground, and blew up. Arriving at HQ, we found it had been the Jerry HQ. Some American paratroops had been dropped right across the buildings and were still hanging in their chutes; all were dead. We dug a slit trench and the order was for one of us to be on watch while the other slept. We both fell asleep.

In the morning, we were woken by the noises from the next trench as the body of a colleague was taken away. He had been killed during the night when a Jerry patrol had stumbled on our position.

Pilot Officer John Love and Sgt. Pilot William "Mac" McEwan were flying Chalk 275. Things had been great during the flight, but then, as Love explains:

As Burns would say, "The best-laid schemes o' mice an' men gang aft agley [often go awry]," and so it proved, for just across the Rhine, the landing zone was covered by smoke. Suffice it to say that when we reached the point where we released from the tug, and started gliding to our landing zone, we found ourselves flying on instruments and flying through antiaircraft fire, which was pretty heavy. Our glider was hit several times, and I myself was hit by shrapnel in the legs.

The hydraulic system was damaged, but mercifully the controls still worked, so that by the time we broke into the clear at about 200 feet, we were able to attempt some sort of a landing. With no brakes, we careered across a field at about 80 mph through some trees, which slowed us considerably, and finished nose-down in a ditch. The normal landing procedure was for the copilot to nip out and turn the hydraulic tap on the landing wheels so that the glider rested on its belly; he then had to open the door at the front, and the tank and the accompanying soldiers went into action. There was no need for him to do this on this occasion, because the impact of the crash into the ditch tore the carrier from its moorings, and it shot through the front of the glider with the army lads hanging on for dear life.

Lieutenant Starkey, who was wearing a pair of earphones so that, according to the textbook, he could be kept informed of all stages in the landing procedure, had his ear nearly torn off. He was able to apply a field dressing and bandage and keep it in place. One or two of the army lads were badly bruised, but nothing serious.

When everyone had got over the shock of the crash, they gathered in the ditch and started digging in. My legs were a mess and my foot was trapped by the control pedals, so I shouted to Mac that I would have to stay put, but at the moment, some Germans opened with a machine gun and the bullets were flying around. Somehow or other I got my foot out without my boot and was in the ditch in five seconds flat. From then on, we were pinned down for what seemed an eternity, before we were relieved by some Americans from 17th Division, complete with a bazooka. Lieutenant Starkey and I were taken to a first-aid station and, as the senior NCO,

Mac took charge of the soldiers and succeeded in joining up with their unit.

Perhaps I should elaborate on Sergeant McEwan's exploits, because it says a lot for his leadership qualities that he should take charge of a squad of soldiers, some of whom had seen action in Normandy. In trying to get them back to their unit, they came across a house full of German prisoners, and the officer in charge ordered Mac and his lads to guard the Germans so that he could get his men back to their unit. Within an hour, some Americans came along and started to knock hell out of their farmhouse with mortars, and it was only after some frantic waving of their yellow identification scarves that they finally got things sorted out and could proceed to their unit.

The 716th's War Diary entry for the twenty-sixth completes the story:

> At approx 1700 hrs 6 ORs [other ranks] from Glider No 275 previously missing reported in. Glider set on fire on 25th by shell fire and it is believed Bren Carrier was destroyed at the same time.

The War Diary also explains in some detail the role played by the 716th's members:

> Glider landings were very widespread and all personnel were under sniper fire when making for the RV. At approximately 1330 hours all available personnel moved forward to RV which had then been cleared of the enemy as far as possible. At 1400 hours collection of containers and panniers was started using 3 Bren Carriers and 1 Trailer also 1 3-ton captured enemy vehicle [thanks to the 8th Parachute Battalion] which was repaired under sniper fire by unit fitter and which had to be unloaded of enemy ammunition. Dumps were set up and issues were being made by 1600 hours, also direct from the

DZ. To save time, owing to shortages of transport, containers and panniers were unpacked on the spot and ammunition and supplies brought to the dump loose. While unloading glider 1 OR was shot through the back by sniper and killed outright.

3 ORs with a captured enemy vehicle were detailed to remove casualties from Div HQ to a Field Ambulance. On returning from completion of detail they ran into an enemy patrol and were taken prisoner. During the night they were utilised as stretcher-bearers by the enemy.

Lieutenant J B Roberts and 1 OR were detailed to take ammunition to 5 Para Bde. On completion of detail they ran into the same patrol as the other 3 ORs and were taken prisoner. Lieutenant Roberts informed the Offr i/c Enemy Troops that the War was over and it was no use carrying on any longer. The enemy officer was quite prepared to give in if he could be assured that he and his men would not be shot on capture. After much talk on both sides it was decided that Lt Roberts and 1 of the enemy should pass over to the British lines leaving our 4 Ors in the enemy's hands as hostages. The German OR was given assurance in our lines that they would not be shot if they gave themselves up as prisoners. Lt Roberts then returned to the German lines with the enemy OR and without any further trouble was able to take the lot prisoner amounting to sixty odd prisoners.

At nightfall collection of further ammunition and guns was suspended and personnel dug in for the night. A stand to was carried out during the night. Suspension of collection during the night was only stopped because of very active sniping on most of the outlying DZs.

DIVISIONAL HQ

Three gliders, including that of Eric Bols (Chalk 135), went in Serial B11. The bulk of the headquarters contingent followed in Serial B18.

The fate of the Devons' Company C, whose members were tasked to clear the landing zone and help in the establishment of headquarters, has been described above, as has that of the 513th Parachute Infantry

Regiment, which was "fortuitously" dropped on Landing Zone P. Nevertheless, Bols and his group still had a fight on their hands to make Kopenhof farm theirs.

Lt. P. E. M. Bradley, CO of Royal Signals, recalls:

> Our glider was Chalk 320, the sixth of the divisional headquarters and Signals' gliders. There was a crack as the pilot cast off. It was then that we realized more and more the presence of those other, less pleasant noises, the crack of AA fire, the automatic and mortar fire on the ground. There was a bump and we were down, bumping along the ground.
>
> Within five minutes, we were moving in open order across the LZ with jeep and trailer behind. We met little parties doing the same. It was all very strange, almost like a dream, this sudden change from the quiet Essex countryside to a battle in the middle of Germany. My OC, O Section, relates how he met a lone American on the LZ and said, "Good morning." "Good morning," said the American and passed on, much as if they had met on a stroll in the country.

The party soon arrived at Kopenhof farm:

> The A Command set was brought in and opened at 1100 hours. Immediate contact was made with 3 and 5 Para Brigades, who reported all well. The commander was there at the time, and I don't know which of us was the more excited and pleased.

Rear headquarters was set up at another farm, Oly-Hollshof, and a wireless link was established. Bradley learned from the divisional adjutant of his experiences after landing, as detailed in Chatterton's report:

> His glider was briefed to land very close to an enemy "strong point." This was marked as such on the defence overlays and photo interpretation successfully showed it as steadily growing in size. He was naturally a little apprehensive. The glider landed

exactly as briefed, almost on top of the "strong point"; at that moment it went on fire. He hurled himself out right into the defences prepared for untold glories! Imagine his slight embarrassment and even perhaps relief in discovering that the "strong point" was nothing more than an enormous heap of mangles that the local farmer had daily been piling up and increasing in size!

Maj. Hugh Bartlett, CO of A Squadron, relates in *BAOR Battlefield Tour*:

Eventually, all Divisional HQ personnel gathered together by the farm and orchard. A skeleton HQ had commenced work together with a wireless set within 40 minutes of landing. American parachutists dropped two miles north of their DZ assisted in clearing LZ P. They were of very great use in winkling out very small bodies of the enemy from the various farms in the area. They were particularly useful in the initial period of the operation when, due to the haze, a certain amount of disorganisation existed.

As pilots of A and C Squadrons arrived, they came under the command of Major Bartlett and took up an all-around close defensive position. A Squadron was dug in with the Defence Company around the majority of the perimeter, while C Squadron was given the southeastern sector. Pilots from both squadrons were checking in until around 1630. Eventually, three flights were formed under Flight Lieutenant Lodge and Captains Aston and Urquhart.

According to Gordon Procter:

When we arrived at Kopenhof farm, it turned out to be closer than we had thought. There were only a few glider pilots there to protect it, and my vivid memory was of American paratroops hanging dead from the trees. They had obviously dropped in the wrong landing zone and been shot to pieces. We tried to climb the trees to cut them down, but sniper fire

carne immediately, and it was two days before we got them all
down. In the next hour, we were joined by a substantial number of glider pilots and started to dig a trench.

Most of us anticipated a German counterattack, but I suppose, on reflection, the whole airborne landing was so substantial that we and the Americans had virtually destroyed all
German resistance, thereby achieving our objective of establishing a bridgehead over which the main British and American forces could proceed into Germany on the way to Berlin
without consolidation. Without doubt, this was crucial in the
final stages of the Second World War, which ended twelve
weeks later.

That night we were alerted as a convoy of German troops
marched past Kopenhof farm, and all of us were sorely tempted
to cut them down, but we were instructed not to open fire as
an ambush was being arranged, where, we were later told, very
heavy casualties were inflicted.

CHAPTER 8

The 17th Airborne Lands

507TH COMBAT TEAM

The 507th Combat Team (CT) was to land in an area south of the Dierfordter. Its objective was to clear the area, including the castle in Diersfordt, of enemy and provide a defensive screen to assist the British 15th Division, as it crossed the river and established itself on the east bank. The 507th's final position would be the eastern edge of the forest.

507TH PARACHUTE INFANTRY REGIMENT

Col. Joel Crouch from the Pathfinder Group piloted the lead aircraft of the 507th Parachute Infantry Regiment (PIR). The serial lost its way in the smokescreen, which led to the 1st Battalion being dropped in the vicinity of Diersfordt, about two and a half miles from where it should have been.

Col. Edson Raff had actually bet Crouch that he would not be dropped in the right place. Crouch accepted the wager, having no doubt that he would place Raff right in the center of the drop zone. He said that he would give Raff a crate of champagne if he missed. With the operation his focus, Crouch put the bet to the back of his mind. I have not been able to find out whether Raff ever got his champagne.

As he jumped, at about 0955 hours, Raff noticed Germans on the ground preparing to fire on him and his men. Then an equipment bundle came into view, and the Germans, probably thinking it was a bomb, ran for cover in nearby houses. Raff landed alone in the chicken yard of one of the houses. There were no other members of his regiment in sight.

Soon they came from various directions, and getting his bearings, Raff quickly realized that the woods were east and southeast, not north and northwest. Machine-gun and artillery fire was coming from Diersfordt and the nearby woods, as well as a battery of five 150-millimeter guns. Raff detailed a party to capture the guns, while he and the remaining troopers engaged in clearing the woods and taking the village.

At about 1100, Raff and his men were close to the castle when they met up with another group from the 1st Battalion, led by Maj. Paul Smith, which had landed closer to the village. The majority of the 1st Battalion now assembled, they made an immediate assault on the castle. Company A led the attack, but just as the remaining companies were about to commit, Company I from the 3rd Battalion arrived. Since the castle was an objective of this battalion, Raff withdrew the 1st Battalion, minus its lead company, and ordered it to proceed to its primary role as regimental reserve.

The 2nd Battalion, traveling in the second serial and carried by the 438th Troop Carrier Group (TCG), was dropped squarely on Drop Zone W and assembled quickly against heavy machine-gun, small-arms, and light artillery fire from in the woods north and east of the zone. They worked their way southwest to a position where they could set up a blocking position to protect the 15th (Scottish) Division. Sgt. Irvin Holtan recalls:

> I landed in a field near a house. A C-47 came down in flames. I don't know if it had unloaded its paratroopers or crashed with them. Before I could join my squad, an officer said, "You are going with me on patrol."
>
> I was in the lead when I first saw a German helmet moving above a bush. I gave the signal of "an enemy in sight" with my rifle over my head held with both hands. I also motioned for all behind me to get down. I then sat down on the German's side of a large tree and waited for him to cross a clearing. When he came by me, I knocked him out.

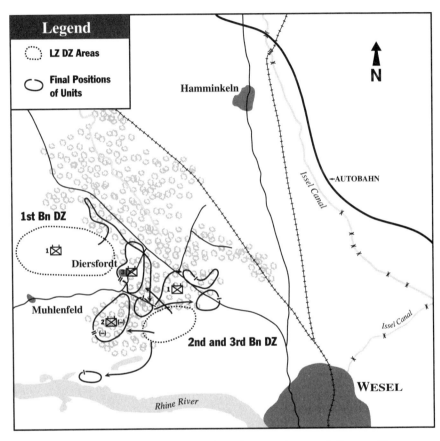

Legend

LZ DZ Areas

Final Positions
of Units

Hamminkeln

AUTOBAHN

Issel Canal

Issel Canal

N

1st Bn DZ

Diersfordt

Muhlenfeld

2nd and 3rd Bn DZ

WESEL

Rhine River

507th Parachute Infantry Regiment Area of Operations

The patrol gathered around the German, and the officer said, "Let's get him back for questioning." Now he tells me! I didn't want to carry the German, so I kicked his foot and told him to get up. Germans follow orders, so he stood up. But that was all he could do, as he promptly fell down again.

When we got back to where our patrol started, I helped a buddy to dig a foxhole. He said that there should be holes all around. He looked under a pine tree and found the entrance to a dugout. He yelled and two Germans answered, "I surrender, I surrender!" They were glad the war was over for them.

The position was secured by 1100. The best prize of the overall action was a battery of 81-millimeter mortars, which had been zeroed in on the drop zone. Patrols from Company F were sent out toward the river. At 1434, one of these made contact with 15th (Scottish) Division troops. This meeting meant that the first phase of the 507th CT's mission had been accomplished.

In the 3rd Battalion, which also landed on the right zone, eleven members of Company G came down in a field about 75 yards from a German machine-gun position. The men struggled to get out of their parachutes and reach their equipment bundles, which were a few yards away. They were prevented from the second by heavy, direct fire. In the group was Pvt. George J. Peters, a radio operator. His Medal of Honor citation explains what happened next:

> He stood up without orders and began a one-man charge against the hostile emplacement armed only with a rifle and grenades. His single-handed assault immediately drew the enemy fire away from his comrades. He had run halfway to his objective, pitting rifle fire against that of the machinegun, when he was struck and knocked to the ground by a burst. Heroically, he regained his feet and struggled onward. Once more he was torn by bullets, and this time he was unable to rise. With gallant devotion to his self-imposed mission, he crawled directly into the fire that had mortally wounded him until close enough to hurl grenades which knocked out the

machinegun, killed 2 of its operators, and drove protecting riflemen from their positions into the safety of a woods. By his intrepidity and supreme sacrifice, Pvt. Peters saved the lives of many of his fellow soldiers and made it possible for them to reach their equipment, organize, and seize their first objective.

Within forty-five minutes, about 75 percent of the battalion had assembled, and it continued to clear the woods as it headed for the Diersfordt castle. Company I took over the assault on the castle. Further troopers from the 3rd arrived, and the men reduced the castle's complex of buildings room by room. Within an hour, they had occupied the largest part. The only remaining resistance consisted of a large group of officers who were holding out in an isolated turret. In the ensuing assault on this strong point, the men took 500 prisoners.

Raff set up his headquarters on Drop Zone W, and at 1600 hours, he gave orders for Company B to clear the woods northeast of the 464th's batteries and for Company A to protect the guns and crews.

Further work was done to complete the linkup network. Raff's men met elements of the 194th east of Drop Zone W early in the afternoon. At 1803, they encountered British airborne troops on the 507th CT's northern perimeter. A march toward Wesel to meet up with the Commando Brigade led to some stiff fighting with Germans entrenched on the city's western edge. Artillery support helped overcome this threat, and the two groups of Allies met up at 0200. After that, there was little more to do except "mop up."

464TH PARACHUTE FIELD ARTILLERY BATTALION

The 464th Parachute Field Artillery Battalion (PFAB) began landing on Drop Zone W at 1008 hours and immediately set up three .50-caliber machine guns in an attempt to suppress enemy fire from the woods. Twelve 75-millimeter howitzers were also delivered to the drop zone, but three arrived damaged. Within a few minutes of landing, three howitzers were in position and firing in support of the 507th CT's 2nd and 3rd Battalions. By 1200, nine guns were in action, and an hour later, using parts salvaged from two of the damaged howitzers, the gunners got the tenth one in firing order.

PFC Robert F. Nicholls, Battery C, recalls his experience:

The flight to the Rhine was uneventful, but as we got close to the river, we began to catch flak, and the smell of smoke began to fill the plane. I guess the smoke was from screen that had been laid down earlier. We had not been told what the situation at the jump zone was going to be, so I was surprised after my chute opened to hear gunfire, lots of it, as I was coming down.

As soon as I hit the ground, things started to go bad. We had been issued a new release system for our chutes whereby the straps hooked up to a device at the chest, which when turned and hit would release all the straps that connected to the body. We had only been given a dry run on this a few days before the jump, and in my state of mind I forgot to twist it before I hit, and I was unable to get out of my chute until I recalled the whole procedure and got out.

When I exited the chute, I looked around for other people in my battery, and the pack for the howitzer that was supposed to be nearby. I could see neither, and there was a lot of bullets flying by, so I decided to look for some cover. Nearby was a hole that looked like it was the result of previous artillery fire, and I jumped into it. It had another occupant who was face-down, and I said, "Are you 464?" and received no answer. He hadn't moved, so I touched his shoulder and got no response. I rolled him over and saw that he had been shot and was dead. I could also see a glider not too far from the hole, and I ran to it. Just outside the glider were three men in British uniforms and red berets who were looking at a map spread out on their vehicle, and I recall one of them pointing to the map and saying, "Here's where we are and here's where we are supposed to be." They loaded up and took off. I later found out that they were with the British 6th Airborne Gliders and that their glider had been cut loose in the wrong area, and that the trooper I had joined in the shell hole was also with them.

I found another hole and tried to find my gun crew but could not, and there was still a lot of direct firing going, so I waited for some time there until one of our sergeants found me and told me where our 75 was, still in its pack from the jump, and told me to help assemble it as soon as it could be reached, which I did. I later found out we had been jumped almost on top of a German 88 antiaircraft battery that had been moved in because they knew when and where we were coming.

The thing that I recall that seemed so out of synch was that it was such a sunny and warm day and it was ten o'clock and we came down in what seemed to be a farmer's field. It didn't take long to dispel that notion. By midafternoon, the jump zone had been secured, and my piece joined the rest of the battery to give support to the infantry.

The 17th Airborne Divisional Report states that "the artillery fires on the DZ were a large factor in neutralizing the enemy fires and demoralising their forces."

The 507th CT's command post was set up in a preselected area, and by 1500, the regiment had established contact with British troops who had crossed the river. During the afternoon, it continued to clear out the enemy and strengthen its position. In all, by the end of the day, the 507th CT had taken some 1,000 prisoners, destroyed five tanks (one with a Gammon bomb and two with 57-millimeter recoilless rifles) and several artillery batteries and commandeered two personnel carriers, an armored car and a light car.

513TH COMBAT TEAM

The drop zone for the 513th Combat Team was bounded by two railway lines east of the Diersfordter. While the 1st and 2nd Battalions were to secure the area and move into a blocking position to assist the work of the 507th CT, the 3rd Battalion was to work its way toward the Issel and prevent the enemy from crossing the river.

513TH PARACHUTE INFANTRY REGIMENT

Two serials from the 313th TCG, led by an aircraft piloted by its CO, Lt. Col. William L. Filer, carried the 513th Parachute Infantry Regiment

(PIR). As the serials approached the Rhine and the pilots prepared for their run-in to the drop zone, there appears to have been some jockeying for position, which may have caused the adjustment to the course flown and the subsequent events explained below. Pilots reported that they believed they crossed the river at the right location. Identification panels that had been laid out at the correct point appear to have been seen by only one crew. The smokescreen also made it extremely difficult to identify landmarks. Antiaircraft and small-arms fire was light and largely inaccurate, although accurate enough to hit Lieutenant Filer's aircraft and set it on fire. It kept flying.

The antiaircraft fire that erupted as the serials crossed the Diersfortder was a different matter, however. From the west bank of the Issel, intense and accurate fire began to break up the formations. C-46s began to tumble from the sky, and the pilots of those still flying weaved to avoid collisions or become further targets of the German gunners. Some aircraft slowed down to as little as 80 miles per hour, making them even easier targets. Troopers exited at heights between 600 and 1,000 feet. In the turn after the drop, the aircraft took more hits. Nineteen of the seventy-two were shot down, and of the remainder, thirty-eight were severely damaged. Ground crew counting the holes in one gave up at 200.

The 513th PIR began its drop at 1010. Bud Hutton, a staff writer with *Stars and Stripes*, traveled in the aircraft of the 513th's executive officer, Lt. Col. Ward Ryan. Hutton writes in the 26 March 1945 issue:

> The C-46 was burning when we hooked up and shoved for the door. Bob Reeder and the rest of the carrier's crew never said a word. They stayed in there and kept us level and we went over the side into a weird sky of bursting flak, lazy tracers and colored silk.
>
> Flak hit the next man in the air and he blew up. Troopers touched the ground and started fighting, but some of them died in their shroud lines.
>
> Col Jim Coutts slipped out of his harness, walked through the burp-gun fire and began to attack before he had a battalion.
>
> Lt Col Ward Ryan, and the rest of our stick, landed square in the middle of a German artillery CP [command post]. Some of the stick died where it hit and some closed on the burp gun.

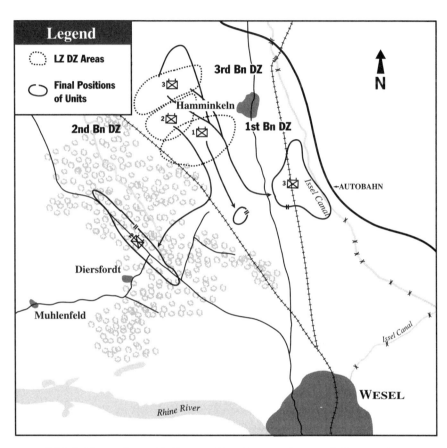

Legend

⬚ LZ DZ Areas

◯ Final Positions of Units

N

3rd Bn DZ

3 ⊠

Hamminkeln

2 ⊠

2nd Bn DZ

1 ⊠

1st Bn DZ

3 ⊠

Issel Canal

←AUTOBAHN

2 ⊠

Diersfordt

Muhlenfeld

Issel Canal

Rhine River

WESEL

513th Parachute Infantry Regiment Area of Operations

Pvt. Robert Vannatter, HQ, 1st Battalion, had a hard landing as he jerked to a stop about 20 feet above the ground in the tops of two tall trees. As he took stock of his situation and got his breath back, he was horrified to see a German soldier about 30 feet away. The soldier had his back to Vannatter and seemed totally oblivious to the fact that an enemy paratrooper was hanging only a few feet behind him. Vannatter could only surmise that the noise from the battle had drowned out his journey through the trees. As he was thanking his lucky stars, there was a ripping sound, the result of his canopy tearing. This time he was not so lucky, and the German spun around. Vannatter had managed to release his carbine from its holster and pointed it at the German. He then realized that there was no magazine fitted. Still threatening the German with his useless carbine, he got a magazine from his pouch, inserted it into the gun, and chambered a round. He still had the problem of being hung up in the tree. Motioning to the German, now technically his prisoner, he covered the man with his gun while the German worked to free Vannatter from his harness. Vannatter then delivered his prisoner to a prisoner-of-war detention area.

S.Sgt. "Lendy" McDonald, Company A, had a close call during his flight:

> As we had no navigator, I sat in the metal bucket seat that he would usually occupy. There was a large observation bubble above me. I could see the whole show outside. In every direction, except to the front, there was a continuous convoy of planes and gliders as far as one could see. The largest airborne invasion the world has ever known was finally in full flight.
>
> At about 0945, we got the red light to stand up and hook up. As I stood up and hooked up, the whole area was splattered with Perspex. I thought we had been hit with fighter fire and all the side windows had been shot out. But checking around, I could find no one hit. Bill Trigg was the only trooper behind me. I turned to see if he was OK. As I turned, I saw the navigator bubble was gone, with only jagged Perspex projectiles probing the sky. My eyes dropped to the bucket seat I had just vacated. And there was no seat left, just a mass of jagged metal fingers looking for a body to pierce. We had taken

a ground ack-ack round straight through the C-46. Now the port engine was on fire.

It was time to leave:

> The jump started about 600 feet in the air, and by the time the two sticks were out, we couldn't have been over 300 feet off the ground. The few moments I was in the air after my opening shock, I watched our plane crash with its precious crew. None got out after Trigg. They completed their mission and forfeited their lives. All the crew was lost.
>
> I hit the ground hard, but in a soft plowed field; got my carbine out at the ready as soon as I hit the quick-release from my chute. I then began to cut a big piece from my chute with my jump knife. Remember the cold in Belgium? Well, this was going to be my warm nylon battle blanket!
>
> As I finished cutting my chute suspension lines, I heard a muffled swishing sound. My God! I thought, a mortar shell is coming in right on me. Then, a sickening thud. Some poor trooper's chute had failed. He landed square on his left side. I ran to him, but he had paid the supreme price. With a perfect median line of demarcation, the left side of his face was purple-black and the right side was absolute white. It was as if he were painted for a carnival, but there was no carnival. Some mother had just earned her Gold Star.

S.Sgt. Jake Dalton, 1st Battalion, was in the right-hand stick in his C-46:

> I mentioned before about the difference between jumping from a C-47 and a C-46. I was on the right (not correct) side of the plane, so had to remember to do things different. In all of our unit practice jumps, I was always No. 2 man, and the battalion S-2 [intelligence] officer was No. 1. In Varsity, we kept the same order.
>
> As we stood up and hooked up, I could see the Rhine River below us and the puffs of flak that seemed below and

all around the plane. As we stood in the door, the plane was literally bouncing and bucking from flak and other antiaircraft weaponry.

The two of us landed in a corral about 15 feet apart. While lying on the ground, getting out of my chute, I could see 20-millimeter shells hitting the dirt a foot or so from me. It's amazing what you can see out of the corner of your eye, though 20-millimeter is ¾ inch.

Guess what? We were dropped about a mile northwest of our drop zone, so the sand table didn't help much. Besides that, the flak and anti-aircraft fire made getting on the ground in any condition, anywhere, the number-one priority!

I could see my lieutenant lying on the ground about 20 feet from me. I got out of my chute and crawled over to him. He was lying on his back, not moving, and covered with blood. I zigzagged out of that corral under fire, and when I spotted a medic, sent him in the right direction toward the lieutenant. The lieutenant didn't make it.

Since we were not in our drop zone, we had to fight to get back to where we were supposed to be. Needless to say, some of the glider units had a rough time of it. The smell of burning flesh as we neared some of the downed gliders is one that I'll never forget.

Like Robert Vannatter, Pvt. Thomas Hashway also came down in a tree, as he describes on the Drop Zone Virtual Museum website:

I had a quick descent with a low branch landing. While releasing the harness, I looked up around and saw flaming planes and crashing gliders, wondering if those troops got out alive. Gunfire brought me back to reality. I crawled towards a few troopers, saw Colonel Coutts, and joined him in the move to the assembly area. We had missed the drop zone by a few miles.

The whole of the 513th PIR had come down on an area straddling Landing Zones P and R, where the 6th Airborne HQ and Devons' gliders were due to land within the next ninety minutes. As Jake Dalton said, this was about a mile and a half from the 513th's designated zone.

Much conjecture has arisen about the reasons for the misdrop. The pilots had been given plenty of flying time to become familiar with the C-46, but the opportunities to fly in tight formation were somewhat lacking. This may well have been one of the reasons for the milling about as the aircraft approached the Rhine. The shape and width of the section of the Diersfordter that the aircraft crossed, was not dissimilar to the section they had planned to cross. With the haze being thicker on the east side of the woodland, any brief openings in it only would have given the pilots more confirmation that they were on the right track.

The 1st Battalion was missing several senior officers and it fell to Lieutenant Cosner, the HQ Company CO, to organize a move toward the assembly point. After about a third of a mile, more men joined the assembly, and Cosner decided to stop and set up a perimeter defense. Not long after this, the battalion executive officer, the 2nd Battalion's CO, and the regiment's CO, Colonel Coutts, arrived, each leading a group of men. Coutts took command and put Captain Ivy, the 513th PIR's intelligence officer, in charge of the battalion.

S.Sgt. Lendy McDonald tells of his experience:

> I gathered four or five troopers and we ran and scrambled to a ditch about 20 yards and suddenly drew machine-gun fire from a house about 75 yards away. We slithered on our bellies down the ditch, trying to flank the house and get close enough to throw grenades. Suddenly a British or Canadian officer came running and dove into the ditch from the other side whence we had come, with a couple of his men. He asked who was in charge and what was the problem. My staff sergeant stripes made me it. I told him of the fire we were drawing and what we were trying to do. With that, he abruptly stood up and said, "Let's go get 'em, blokes." He never said another word. He fell back into the ditch, almost cut in two by machine-gun fire. We continued on down the ditch and got within about 10 yards of the house. Our only chance of knocking out that machine gun was with grenades. We threw fragmentation and Gammon grenades through the windows.

When the dust and debris settled, all was quiet from the house.

McDonald and his group joined up with the main party, which headed off for the battalion's assigned area about 1330. McDonald searched for the rest of his company:

It was early afternoon before I finally found Captain Anderson with a small part of A Company. He had a badly injured leg from the jump but was able enough to still be up and moving around, trying to get his men assembled to move and take our company objective, which was supposed to be a nearby T-shaped woods. Too bad, but we had missed our drop zone by a couple of miles. We knew of a train track that ran near our objective from our orientation in the war tent during the days in the marshaling area.

We were finally getting a good number of men together. Captain Anderson ordered us to move out. We had to find that track. After moving with little resistance for about an hour, sure enough, we came upon the train track. It was not long until we could hear a firefight up the track a ways. By now we had picked up more men, among them 2nd Platoon leader Lieutenant Beckett. Captain Anderson couldn't keep up with us, so he put Lieutenant Beckett in charge and ordered us to the firefight and said he would get to us as soon as and as best he could. Poor guy couldn't hobble, much less walk or run.

We took off up the track as ordered and soon came to the action. About thirty troopers were pinned down on our side of the tracks. They said they had crossed the tracks and got about 50 yards into a plowed field; suddenly they drew machine-gun fire from an attic window of a house about 200 yards in front of us. They had all made it back across the track and had taken cover behind the railroad bed. He was gut shot and leg shot, lying a few yards out in the field. We laid down a heavy barrage of rifle and carbine fire right on that attic window. Under this fire cover, Graan and I ran to the downed man, dragged and carried him back across the tracks. The medics took over and got him out of there. Graan and I both dropped in exhaustion. As we lay on the ground, Captain Anderson, using a rifle for a crutch, hobbled over to me. He looked down at me and said, "McDonald, I saw that and I'm turning you and Graan in for Silver Stars." The words had hardly cleared his lips, and before I could reply, these same medics grabbed him and hustled him away. Never saw or heard from him again.

A bazooka team finally fired a perfect round. It must have hit right at the bottom ledge of that attic window, and we never heard from them again, either.

As the hours passed and the day wore on, we encountered less armed resistance and met with more and more unarmed "soldatens." They had given up the fight at that point. By early evening, it became apparent that we had more prisoners than we had troopers in the regiment. We rounded them all up in a very large walled courtyard, appointed some guards over them, and set out in search of more of the same, because we were still surrounded.

Bob Patterson, Company E, 2nd Battalion, recalls:

They knew we were coming, and as soon as we crossed the Rhine, we were receiving antiaircraft fire. Quite a few planes were hit, some shot down. We were dropped quite low, so you really didn't have time to get oriented on the way down. As soon as I hit the ground, I looked back up at our planes, because they had given us their azimuth, which would help us to determine our destination on the map. I took off my helmet, got out my map, and studied it, but nothing looked right. We later learned that they had dropped us over a mile from our designated area. It was then that somebody going by, with a voice of authority, said, "Patterson, let's get the men off the drop zone."

The 2nd Battalion cleared its drop zone of enemy and marched toward its assembly point. During this advance, they encountered further resistance, which required considerable maneuvering to overcome, as Patterson explains:

We were organized to move up the railroad. I was given responsibility for one flank. I had only two men from my squad, but I did have an experienced scout, one of our original company. We soon joined with the rest of Company E. Just off the tracks, the company [was given the task of clearing] a very large, solid-looking house, which could have passed for a fortress and from which was coming considerable small-arms fire.

I now had my squad and a mortar tube, but no bipod or base plate. As the company organized for the attack, I placed the tube on the ground in front of me and had one of my men drop in a round. It fired and cleared the house, and probably was effective on anyone leaving the rear of the house. But I will never try that stunt again, because I almost had the shell in my hands as the tube sunk almost a foot into the ground.

Across open ground, the company charged directly at the house. One of our original mortar squad members, Stewart Stryker, led the charge, was killed, and for his actions was posthumously awarded the Medal of Honor.

At the same time, some of us executed a flanking maneuver through the woods. We arrived at the side of the house with the loss of only one man. I had a bazooka man fire a rocket right through a window, and considering the explosion, it must have had an effect. By this time, the company had the house surrounded and took quite a few Germans prisoner.

The citation for Private First Class Stryker's gallantry adds more detail:

Attacking along a railroad, Company E reached a point about 250 yards from a large building used as an enemy headquarters and manned by a powerful force of Germans with rifles, machineguns, and 4 field pieces. One platoon made a frontal assault but was pinned down by intense fire from the house after advancing only 50 yards. So badly stricken that it could not return the raking fire, the platoon was at the mercy of German machine gunners when Pfc. Stryker voluntarily left a place of comparative safety, and, armed with a carbine, ran to the head of the unit. In full view of the enemy and under constant fire, he exhorted the men to get to their feet and follow him. Inspired by his fearlessness, they rushed after him in a desperate charge through an increased hail of bullets. Twenty-five yards from the objective the heroic soldier was killed by the enemy fusillades. His gallant and wholly voluntary action in the face of overwhelming firepower, however, so encouraged his comrades and diverted the enemy's attention that other elements of the company were able to surround the house, capturing more than 200 hostile soldiers and much equipment, besides freeing 3 members of an American bomber crew held prisoner there. The intrepidity and unhesitating self-sacrifice of Pfc. Stryker were in keeping with the highest traditions of the military service.

Bob Patterson continues:

The company reorganized and moved on through the woods. It was getting late in the day, and soon we were in line with flanking units and dug in for the night. Fortunately, there were many German entrenchments, so my squad settled into a small bunker. I posted a guard, and we broke out rations and tried to get some sleep. About midnight, I was called to platoon HQ and told to take a couple of my men and man an outpost where a guard had just been killed. It was a bit scary, especially for my men, as this was their first day in combat.

The 2nd Battalion reached its assembly point, only to find that it had already been cleared. Pushing on to its final objective, it found this also cleared, courtesy of the 1st Battalion of the 507th. Digging in was organized and patrols were set up.

Cpl. Bill Highfill was in the Machine Gun Platoon of the 3rd Battalion's HQ Company:

I led the left stick and was in the door as we descended over the Rhine. . . . Many of the troopers were new replacements, and this was their first combat experience. Most of the battle of the Bulge veterans were telling them what to expect and reassuring them to trust their training and use their own good judgment.

We jumped at 400 feet but were in the wrong zone. Because of the heavy ack-ack fire and disorientation of the pilots, they dropped us in a British glider zone. When we hit the ground, it was chaos.

The first person I teamed up with was a British trooper. We joined forces because we were both lost. As he and I were working our way across a field, we encountered small-arms fire from a farmhouse. We dropped to the ground and returned fire. After a pause, a white flag appeared and fourteen German soldiers surrendered to us. By now the Germans were giving up all over the area.

The 3rd Battalion was organized into three groups. Two of these, thinking that the regiment was on the correct drop zone, unknowingly marched toward Hamminkeln. Within ten minutes, they realized their mistake and retraced their steps. They then set off for their intended assembly point. The third group discovered its actual position by questioning a prisoner, and was therefore able to march directly to the assembly point.

Jumping with the 513th PIR was the 466th Parachute Field Artillery Battalion's forward observation team, which, because of the misdrop, would now be separated from its unit. Cpl. John Magill describes the situation:

The red warning light came on above the open doorways of the C-46. We stood up and hooked up in our new dual-door fashion, sounded off for equipment check, and stood ready. Then, as the Rhine became visible through the small windows, all hell broke loose! The concentration of antiaircraft fire was beyond all predictions and all expectations. I watched in awesome disbelief as neighboring planes burst into flames and plunged earthward with their human cargo. The sound of shell fragments striking the bottom of our C-46 was almost rhythmic!

Suddenly all the training, all the past combat, and all of the past psychological adjustments went for naught as I was hit with an overpowering premonition of death! Every man has a limit. As I sought to "put it all together" to maintain sanity and to survive, I had hoped that the proper mix of "change forces" and "stabilizing forces" would see me through. But I had exhausted the change forces and was stretching the stabilizing forces that separated me from the animal. "Why was I here?"

For just a brief, fleeting moment I was back at Fort Benning: "One thousand, two thousand . . . opening shock, check canopy, and everybody around you." Then I was back, east of the Rhine River, in flak thick enough to walk on. I hauled down on both front risers, literally collapsing half of my chute to get down through the screaming inferno of shell fragments and small-arms fire. The scene was unlike anything that I had imagined! C-46s on fire! Lifeless bundles hanging limp in their parachutes! Flak everywhere!

For the first time, I looked down, and there were pastures, running horses, and running Germans. A flash hit me! "Keep track of your red equipment chute!" There it was—I noted about where it would drop, then turned back to landing. I let up on the two risers, slowed down, hit the ground, tumbled from the heavy load and great momentum, struck the quick-release mechanism, and slid out of my chute. I had made it down!

There were hundreds of camouflage chutes littering the ground as I made my way to the crucial equipment bundle. It was there, at the bundle, that I would know if the entire section had made it safely through the roaring inferno. En route to the bundle, I helped to clear the immediate area of enemy resistance. Except for well-protected snipers and machine gunners in protected positions, the enemy was surrendering in large numbers. The overwhelming display of airborne might seemed to have paralyzed a great many of the enemy soldiers.

Within fifteen minutes, the local drop zone had been secured, and my section had reported intact to our red-shrouded equipment bundle. Everything was on schedule!

Within five minutes, according to plan, the 466th Parachute Field Artillery would be dropping. With the area cleared of enemy resistance, they should have their 75-millimeter how-itzers assembled in quick time and with minimal casualties for the artillerymen. My section had to be on our way with the infantry now to be ready to call for and deliver artillery fire on the tough enemy positions ahead.

Just as my men and I, loaded with radio and phone gear, were moving out, British Horsa gliders began to land. The harsh, sobering reality hit me: "My God! Something is all fouled up. The 466th had been dropped in an uncleared area by mistake. They'll be shot to pieces trying to put their how-itzers together under direct enemy fire. Where have they landed?"

I had no choice except to move out with the section in a northeasterly direction toward the infantry objective. We had a dual function: to make contact with the British airborne infantry, and to seize and hold the key perimeter positions before nightfall. I had to be prepared to deliver artillery fire for the expected German counterattacks. But the success of the mission would depend upon the 466th getting set up and into action and yet I had no idea where the 466th had landed! [The 466th had landed on the correct zone.]

As we moved through the drop zones of other parachute units and the landing zones of the glider units, there were some horrifying scenes. A portion of one of the parachute infantry units had been dropped over a heavy forest—the nemesis of the combat paratrooper. Tens of slumped, limp bodies were hanging from the parachute-shrouded trees—struck down before they could get out of their quick-release harness. The plight of many of the courageous glider troopers caused me to choke on the words uttered in jest by the para-trooper, "Herman—no motor." The gliders, cut loose from the tow plane and occupied by men, artillery pieces, or jeeps, had to find a landing space in the midst of flak, heavy small-arms fire, and ground opposition. Many of these gliders hit wires, trees, and other obstacles. The impact caused the jeep or artillery piece to tear from its moorings, crushing glider

troopers and glider crews. Other gliders hit the ground only
to become a blazing inferno from an enemy shell. The bitter
realization that their brave sacrifices would go unnoticed left
an empty, hollow feeling in my stomach. Suddenly we were
pinned down by sniper fire. We were separated from our parachute infantry unit by several hundred yards. For the first
time, the entire section realized our inadequacy—all four of
us had only the short-range .45-caliber pistols. We had no
means of countering the devastating sniper fire with our small
arms; in addition, I had no means of securing artillery fire.
The radio calls to the Fire Direction Center of the 466th
went unanswered!

Dismantling the radio, our section developed a quick emergency strategy. The four of us, loaded down with the heavy
communication equipment, seeking whatever natural cover
was available, would alternate in rising, running, and dropping.
Loaded with half of the 610 radio on my back, I rose and ran
forward, only to be knocked to the ground with the shock of
a rifle bullet that struck and ricocheted off the metal radio!
Next, the captain rose, ran, and dropped a few feet back of
me. The young radio operator was next; as he rose to run, he
was hit! By the time my captain and I could reach him, he was
dead. This nineteen-year-old had spent less than an hour in
combat! What had decreed that one boy should die and I
should get a ricochet?

Expediency forced us to strip the radio part and the phone
gear from our dead comrade, to leave him there, and to continue our desperate effort to reach safety. Suddenly an infantry
squad leader, noting our dilemma, brought his squad into play.
Turning their new, recoilless 57-millimeter, they fired it point-
blank into a nearby barn. The exploding shell brought eight
German soldiers out with hands held high. For the first time
in combat, I felt the overwhelming urge to personally kill all
eight men for having killed my friend and radio operator.

Also among the misdropped were Gen. Josiah T. Dalby, CO of the
Airborne Training Center at Camp Mackall, North Carolina, and Gen.
Ridgely M. Gaither, CO of the Parachute School, Fort Benning, who

had been granted permission to participate in the operation. They found themselves in the middle of a German antiaircraft unit that was supported by machine guns and infantry.

"Shortly after they landed," says the FAAA Narrative on Varsity, "an assortment of gliders landed." These were British gliders carrying members of the 6th Airlanding Brigade. The gliders' passengers were most likely from the Devons plus a mixture of gunners from the Light Regiment and 2nd Airlanding Anti-Tank Regiment. Dalby, no doubt thoroughly relieved, organized what he called the Chattahoochee Task Force, consisting of any soldier, of whatever category, in the immediate area. They overran the German battery and troops and took several prisoners. The following day, the task force delivered 3,500 prisoners to the west bank of the Rhine.

Meanwhile, Lt. Col. Ward Ryan had also put together a task force, which never had more than forty men, including medics. It took 100 prisoners in several hours of fighting.

S.Sgt. Lendy McDonald recalls:

> Nightfall found Kenny Segner, Kenny Graan, and me huddled in a little hole in the ground that we had dug at twilight under the wing of a crashed glider. We were all three snugly wrapped in a large piece of camouflage nylon parachute. We munched on a light meal of ham and cheese K rations. Even so, we all agreed that compared to winter in Belgium, this was sheer luxury. No snow, no ice, no howling wind. We tried hard that night to keep one of us awake in rotation all night long. We were unsuccessful, but nothing happened. Maybe Jerry was a little more tired than we.

466TH PARACHUTE FIELD ARTILLERY BATTALION

The 466th Parachute Field Artillery Battalion (PFAB) came in the final serial, A7, which was flown by the 434th TCG. Ground fire never rose above moderate and the unit had a concentrated drop on Drop Zone W. Nine troopers, keen to get down on the ground, jumped over the west bank of the Rhine. Only one C-46 was shot down and another seventeen damaged. One can only speculate as to how the first two serials would have fared had they followed the right course.

With its infantry support 2 miles away, the unit found itself having to clear out the enemy before it could get its guns set up and firing. The order of landing was HQ, A, B, and C.

The battalion CO, Lt. Col. Kenneth L. Booth, and the majority of his HQ, jumped at 1025 and landed about 20 yards from the farmhouse he had chosen for his command post. The farmhouse and its adjoining buildings were quickly overrun and secured.

The executive officer, Maj. C. V. Hadley, was on a mission to find a Luger. He had armed himself with two .45s and a Thompson submachine gun. As Hadley arrived at the battalion command post, Cpl. Robert Hayes, a messenger, opened a cupboard to reveal a haul of Lugers.

One of the HQ members who landed some distance from the farmhouse was T.Sgt. Joseph Flanagan. He came down beside a fixed 20-millimeter gun, which he captured, along with its crew. The 466th later used the gun to destroy more strongly defended emplacements.

Sgt. John Chester was chief of the 1st Section, Battery A:

At ten o'clock, we crossed the Rhine, then flew through eleven minutes of flak. I thought the plane had exploded when it shuddered in unison with a deafening roar. A 20-millimeter shell had crashed through the plane floor and burst in Boatner's leg. Melvin T. Boatner from Bessimer, Alabama, let out a startled little cry, clenched his teeth, and then turned an ashen white, while Perry and Montanino unfastened his chute and lay him on the other side of the plane.

I was was due to jump first but our "go" signal had been knocked out. So I asked the crew chief if he would stand in the cockpit door and yell and wave his hands when it was time to jump. Red machine-gun tracers seemed to fill the sky. Antiaircraft bursts were blooming all around us at the correct elevation. This was not the right place to be. We were cruising at a near stalling speed just 40 feet above those flak guns. I developed a new respect for those Air Force crews who went home every night to hot showers, clean sheets, clean uniforms, and good food while I scrambled around in the mud and the filth week after week. There was nothing up here to hide behind—no cover to take. They were welcome to all those good things.

Just put me back on the ground. Twenty seconds and a thousand near misses later, I was.

Shortly after VE Day, Chester was sent on furlough to Nice, on the French Riviera. Amazingly, his pilot was the one who had flown Chester and his buddies across the Rhine. He told Chester about events after the jump. The "shell" that had hit Melvin Boatner was in fact a .30-caliber bullet. Before hitting Boatner, it had ruptured an oxygen tank, and it was only through sheer luck that the tank didn't explode and take the whole plane with it. The bullet came to rest alongside Boatner's spine. He was not paralyzed, and his leg was saved, although he lost much of the use of it. Chester continues:

We jumped at 400 feet: There was a bare twenty-second interval between the plane door and the ground, but it seemed like an eternity. We were drawing machine-gun fire from seven different directions, I learned later. I was concerned with only two at the time. They both seemed to be quite interested in lowering my blood pressure.

Things looked hot on the ground, but that transport had been moving along at a near stalling speed on an unswerving course just 600 feet above the flak guns. A clay pigeon on a target range had a better chance at survival. We'd all been anxious to "hit the silk."

From the moment my chute opened I could see tracers in the smoke hazy background from both guns. The range was no more than 200 yards—point-blank for machine guns. Those tracers would start out as tiny specks, grow larger instantly, and then arc away just as they had practically reached their destination. I was acting as much like a monkey on a string as I could, considering the bulky equipment I was carrying. I was trying my best to present a difficult target to those gunners.

I wasn't praying, but my thoughts could be classified as a form of prayer. I was quite sure I wouldn't get hurt, yet any law of logic wouldn't be giving me much of a chance right about now. Those tracers were so very real—five and six of them in the air at one time from each gun—and half a dozen solid bullets between each tracer. Why was I so positive I wouldn't be hurt when the firing was so direct? A tracer drops from its course sooner than a solid bullet, and at this range, there would be practically no arc. I should have more holes in me than a sponge. Why did I even hope differently? Soon I was going to be a fairly still target-on the ground, tangled in suspension lines with a range of about 100 yards.

I thought of some awfully nice people at home who were anxious for me to come back alive. I'd assured them I would, and yet this fact ceased to be an issue any longer. It looked as though there would be a rough job to do on the ground. If I got hit, I would actually be letting the boys down who depended on me. It would mean more work for my buddies. I had never feared death. I didn't now, somehow—still, I had no desire to quit before the job was finished.

Perhaps that was part of the reason those bullets just kept missing. It certainly wasn't the gunners' fault. I did an hour's thinking during those few seconds I was suspended helplessly in space. I'd written two letters home while still on the plane: one to my mother and one to my girl. I'd assured them I would not get hurt. Those letters were still in my pocket. They would be ironically out of place if sent home with my personal effects. This happened to be my thirteenth jump. I wondered if thirteen actually was unlucky.

The ground was coming up fast. Where was I going to land? I checked. I was dropping directly toward a barbed-wire fence. I stopped my acrobatics in the shroud lines and pulled one side of the canopy down. When I became still so suddenly, those gunners must have thought they had scored a hit; they directed their fire elsewhere immediately. I missed the barbed wire by 10 feet.

Foulk had caught some shrapnel in the upper part of his right leg just after he landed. I found him just minutes after that. It was a nasty wound, and he was certainly out of the fight. It seemed to be a flesh wound, and he was not bleeding very much. He was fully conscious and quite rational, with no signs of shock. I was able to direct a medic to his location, but I never did see or hear from Ralph Foulk again.

The concentrated fire sweeping the zone prevented the Battery A gunners from getting to the bundles containing their howitzers. The executive officer, 1st Lt. John L. O'Brien, gathered the men closest to him and led the group to recover the bundles. It was a lost cause, as O'Brien and several of the group were cut down. The battery CO, Capt. Charles D. Duree Jr., began to organize the rest of his men as infantry. They made a concerted effort to clear out the enemy so that the guns could be assembled. Duree was severely wounded during this operation, and command passed to 1st Sgt. George R. Grazel.

Through sheer grit and determination, the 1st and 2nd Sections retrieved their bundles and had their guns assembled and firing by 1100. They continued to eliminate enemy resistance, but not without cost, as all the battery officers were either killed or wounded. Lieutenant Colonel Booth, on learning of the situation, placed 1st Lt. James Nammack in command. By 1500, two more guns were assembled and firing.

Two members of Battery B, 1st Sgt. John T. Bennick and Pvt. Dan Morgan, landed hard as they crashed through the roof of a house. They quickly realized that the house was occupied and set about reducing the odds while also taking sixteen prisoners. The occupiers had a clear view of the area where Battery B was to set up, so Bennick and Morgan's courageous action saved many of their colleagues.

Sgt. James E. Guy was directed by the battalion S-3 (operations officer) to set up his gun beside the command post. His target was the building, which sheltered the soldiers who had killed Lieutenant O'Brien and his men. The building was subjected to a concerted barrage until a white flag signaled that its occupants had had enough.

Another two guns were assembled and firing by 1145. A fourth gun had landed by Battery C's position. Because of the sharp resistance, it was not recovered quickly, but it was firing by 1530. An hour later, the final gun was supporting the infantry.

Battery C's transports were last in the column and therefore received the greatest concentration of antiaircraft fire. Despite the pilots' best efforts, the battery's personnel, and most of the guns, were scattered on the drop. Consequently, it was not until 1500 that the first gun that had been brought in by glider was in the battery's position and ready to fire. Three more guns were in action two hours later. The final gun, which had been dropped in German-held woods, was not recovered until the following morning.

On seeing the casualties sustained by the battery, Lieutenant Colonel Booth ordered the other two batteries to send five men each as reinforcements.

John Magill, forward observer, recalls:

> With the artillery unit set up but horribly decimated, we in the FO section accompanied the parachute infantry as they pushed forward toward their objective. We were taking enemy prisoners in huge numbers. By midafternoon, we had accomplished another goal—linkup with the British airborne infantry. My already tremendous respect for the British Tommies took on an added dimension. A British sergeant, with his head bandaged, summed up their struggle in an almost stoic fashion: "We had bloody flak as we landed, and we had a jolly bit of a rough time in yonder woods."
>
> By late afternoon, the objectives were taken and the perimeter defense was established. I reestablished communication with the 466th, setting up an emergency fire line in preparation for the anticipated German counterattacks during the night. The 466th and the huge artillery on the west bank of the Rhine were zeroed in on this emergency fire line. Within moments of a pending attack, I could call overwhelming artillery fire on the enemy.
>
> As night fell, my section gathered a nylon canopy for warmth. The day had seemed like an eternity since we had eaten breakfast in the marshaling area of France. I had seen planes and gliders plunge to earth in flames, paratroopers hanging limp in the trees, glider men crushed to death in their craft, and my friend die of a sniper bullet. Yet I had made it!

For its actions during Varsity, the 466th was awarded a Presidential Citation "for extraordinary heroism, efficiency and achievement in the

face of great odds and a defensively prepared enemy, [which] resulted in
the provisions of adequate artillery support, which assisted materially in
the ultimate success of the operation and subsequent exploitation of the
gains achieved."

General Dalby gave his own commendation in a letter to Major
General Ridgway:

> May I compliment the combat efficiency of your entire 466th
> FA Bn, and its outstanding Commander, Lt Col Booth and
> his Executive, Major Hadley. It was a privilege to have been
> associated with them.

DIVISIONAL HEADQUARTERS

Bud Miley jumped with the 464th PFAB onto Drop Zone W. He established his headquarters in the village of Flüren. Contact was made with
all three combat teams. The glider element of headquarters personnel
came into Landing Zone N with Batteries A and C of the 155th Anti-
Aircraft Battery (AAB). It took some time, but the men eventually
worked their way to Flüren. One of them was PFC John Kormann,
517th Signals:

> Our glider carried a jeep, which the four of us from my sec-
> tion sat in. The antiaircraft fire was intense, and you could
> hear it pinging off the glider. We got to the LZ but crashed
> into some trees. My group was thrown out of the glider, and I
> hit the ground, stunned.
>
> When I regained my senses, I realized that I was alone.
> There was a lot of gunfire, and mortar shells were exploding
> close by. I grabbed my gun and, keeping low, made for the
> wood, where I found a trench running alongside a single-
> track railroad.
>
> As I began to move along the trench, I heard a rustling
> sound and saw a soldier in a camouflaged smock and steel
> helmet. I raised my gun to shoot him, convinced from his
> uniform that he was German. He saw me and shouted, in
> an unmistakable Cockney accent, "Don't shoot, I'm on your

side!" I didn't realize how similar the uniforms of the German and British paratroopers were. He disappeared along the track.

I left the wood and joined a group of our paratroopers in charging some farmhouses, from which the Germans had been shooting at them. When we got there, the farmhouses had been hastily abandoned.

Bringing up the rear as we passed the last farmhouse, I heard noises coming from a cellar. Convinced that some of the enemy were hiding there, I lifted the slanted, wooden cellar door cautiously and was about to toss in a grenade when I remembered the letter which I had received from my mother the previous day.

She sensed that I was going into battle. "Son, I want you to be merciful," she wrote. "Never forget that the young man you are fighting has a mother who loves him and prays for him, just as I love and pray for you." Infuriated, I thought: "Mother, what are you trying to do, bring about my death? I am trained to kill or be killed!"

Now, I was conscious of mother's plea: "Be merciful!" So instead of throwing the grenade, I shouted in German for them to surrender and come out with their hands up. There was silence. My second shout brought stirring.

The first to come up was an elderly grandmother. Then another woman appeared, followed by four or five little children, until fourteen women and children stood before me. I shuddered at the thought of what I might have done, and the burden it would have placed on my life, had I not received my blessed mother's letter.

I left the paratroopers and continued trying to find my unit. After some more firefights, I reached HQ.

The Divisional Headquarters Signals team established wireless communications with all three combat teams, 18th Airborne Corps, FAAA, and 15th (Scottish) Division. The 513th and 194th Combat Teams also had wired links by 1830, but it was the following day before such a link was put through to the 507th.

CHAPTER 9

Securing the American Sector

194TH COMBAT TEAM

The 194th Combat Team (CT), with the 681st Glider Field Artillery Battalion (GFAB) in support, was to land in an unsecured zone and seize and hold two bridges over the Issel, clear its section of the landing area, defend the line of the Issel River and Canal, and prevent enemy incursion from the southwest.

194TH GLIDER INFANTRY REGIMENT

The size of the 194th Glider Infantry Regiment (GIR) meant that it had to be carried in four and one-third serials. The first two, A8 and A9, were a mix of the 1st and 2nd Battalions, while the third and fourth had the 3rd Battalion's companies scattered throughout the two serials' 144 gliders. The 3rd Battalion's HQ Company made up one-third of serial A12.

Lt. Del Townsend recalls:

> Being on the short-tow glider, it is a very uncomfortable feeling to have the long-tow glider bear to their left so that their towrope is on the right wing of our glider. Being in the right seat, I could see their towrope banging on our right wing. Our pilot was frantic and attempted to fly our glider further to the left and avoid the towrope. At that time, our pilot discovered that we had lost communication with the tow plane. For

reasons unknown, we had no communications with the tow plane. The constructions of a glider with the aluminum tubes covered with canvas won't stand many hard knocks. That towrope banging on our wing was a very uncomfortable feeling. This towrope incident happened about three times during our flight.

At approximately 5 to 7 miles from the Rhine River, we saw a British four-engine bomber to our left front. It was at our same altitude, coming directly toward us, and on fire with heavy black smoke trailing from the plane. About 2 miles or so in front of us, we saw several parachutes open up, so we assumed the crew had escaped. About a mile in front of us, the plane went into a steep dive. When it hit the ground, it exploded with a very loud bang. Just seconds later, it seemed like our glider jumped about 10 feet in the air. Why our glider did not disintegrate and crash is a miracle.

As we approached the Rhine River, the sky was full of U.S. fighter planes, C-46s and C-47s loaded with parachutists, and of course, the train of C-47s towing two CG-4A gliders each. With our communication with our tow plane lost all that we could do was just watch and see what the other gliders were doing. The smoke on the river did not bother us, as we were high enough (1,500 feet) that we could see fairly well. On crossing the river and trying to spot our landing zone, we began to see the white puffs of flak all over the area. We could see C-46s and C-47s going down, CG-4A gliders on fire, and several gliders that had crash-landed.

The gliders began landing at 1030 hours. All but 10 of the gliders that had taken off arrived over Landing Zone S. Of these, nearly 84 percent were hit in the air by small-arms or antiaircraft fire. In the first two serials, four gliders pulled out. Only 29 of the remaining 156 gliders reached the ground undamaged. The 3rd Battalion's Company G, which was the lead unit, had every one of its gliders hit in the air, but casualties were relatively light. All but 12 of the serial landed in a concentrated group at the east end of the zone. In the third and fourth serials, 139 gliders arrived, but only 18 landed without being hit. The landings were spread across

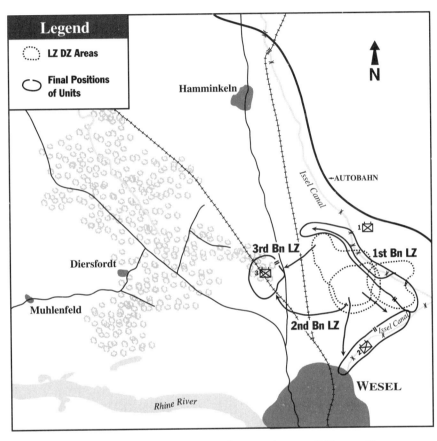

N

Hamminkeln

Issel Canal

AUTOBAHN

1

3rd Bn LZ

1st Bn LZ

Diersfordt

3

Muhlenfeld

2nd Bn LZ

Issel Canal

2

WESEL

Rhine River

194th Glider Infantry Regiment Area of Operations

the zone, and a good number of gliders landed outside it. Serial A12's glid-ers also suffered extreme damage from antiaircraft fire. Nevertheless, the tactical landing suggested by Colonel Chatterton worked extremely well, and the German defenders were thrown into confusion, having to fight on all sides.

Ed Clark, writes in the 26 March 1945 issue of *Stars and Stripes*:

> It's hard to describe a glider landing adequately, particularly when it's made in the heart of enemy territory, with fighting going on all around. Too much happens too fast.
>
> Some lucky gliders made it without a scratch; others became funeral pyres. One glider, ripped through and through with ack-ack, crashes nose on deep into the loamy earth. Not a man comes out. In a few seconds fire started by tracers roars through the fabric.
>
> Trying desperately to land before they are destroyed, other gliders smash through fences, rip through wires, crash into grounded ships. Men who are unhurt tumble out of the last ships.
>
> Despite the losses, the number of glider troops on the field increases. Those who have made it must now reach their pre-arranged assembly point.
>
> Then they start to flush the Jerries out of farmhouse strong-points and the nearby gun positions. Many prisoners are taken, many Jerries are killed.

For Del Townsend, the final approach was not as easy as he had hoped for:

> As we approached our landing zone, for some reason, our tow plane pilot cut us off, and the towrope wrapped around the nose of our glider. Both the pilot and I tried to release the towrope from our glider without success. I could not see the long-tow, but I was concerned the towrope, still attached to our glider, would get snagged on a tree or some other heavy object and cause us to crash. In the midst of all this confusion, we had to spot our landing zone and get the glider on the

ground. With the towrope still attached, I followed the instructions of the pilot on operating the flaps, and we made a hard landing. A bit of dirt piled up in the nose of the glider, but we were able to get out of the glider with no problems. We scrambled to form a defensive position around the glider and to link up with other crews who had just landed.

Of all the gliders that did not land in the zone, quite a few came down on the other side of the Issel River and Canal. Sgt. William Lusk, Company A, reports:

I had three squads of rifleman in three gliders, and one overshot the field and they were all lost. Germans were already approaching and I sent the squad I was with back to the defense area while I kept the Germans at a distance—fire and roll. Then I made my way to the defense area.

Lusk's company seized one of the bridges and prepared it for possible demolition. Farther along the river, a German strong point was making it difficult for Company A and elements of Company C to dig in and consolidate the defensive area. A rifle squad from Company B came to their assistance and cleared out the house, before moving on to capture two 88-millimeter guns and their crews.

PFC Edward J. Siergiej was a rifleman in Company C HQ:

After our glider was cut loose from the C-47 tow plane, we landed in our designated drop zone with considerable damage to the right wing but no injuries sustained by pilots or men on board. The next few hours were spent locating our company's position near the Issel Canal.

The glider of Frank O'Rourke, Company C, went up on its nose as it slowed but quickly settled back to earth. The passengers unsnapped their seatbelts and went out through the door. Right in front of them was the bank of the Issel Canal, which gave them cover from the front. Over to the left was glider Chalk 113, which had been on the short-tow with O'Rourke's glider. He ran toward it and rounded the tail. "A burst of bullets kicked up dirt in front of me," he writes in his article in *World War II* magazine. "I wheeled left toward the source and saw a glider pilot sweeping the field with an automatic rifle. He stopped when he recognized me."

The trooper was part of a machine-gun squad that was sheltering in a drainage ditch bordered by a hedge. O'Rourke got to the ditch and joined the group. The machine gunner, Frank Paskowski, had lost the gun's tripod in the landing. He had managed to find a suitable section of hedge to use as a substitute. He was firing at an 88-millimeter, positioned in a corner of the field, to keep the crew pinned down while a rifle squad worked its way over the top of the canal to flank the gun. One of the squad threw a grenade into the emplacement. The grenade's explosion had the desired effect, and the crew came rushing out with hands raised.

O'Rourke rejoined his group, which continued toward its objective farther along the canal. When they reached it, they began to dig foxholes and prepared to defend their section of the line. "A couple of hundred yards or so farther down, in the corner of the pasture that fronted us, was a German bunker," notes O'Rourke. Keen to capitalize on their first strike, the men set up their mortar and calculated the distance to the bunker, then fired. "The mortar round arced through the air and landed on top of the bunker—a direct hit. Enemy soldiers came pouring out and began running to the woods behind them. We were so surprised that we just stared at each other and at the running Germans."

O'Rourke and his buddies settled into their foxholes and kept watch across the canal, expecting the Germans to attack sooner than later. What they did not know was that the enemy was closer than they thought. O'Rourke continues:

> In the afternoon, some 20 yards across the canal, a small white piece of cloth began to wave from a foxhole. We stared at the flag. We stared at each other. Finally we yelled, "Kommen Sie hier." Two Germans got out of the foxhole and with their hands in the air came over and surrendered. One was an old man who was genuinely happy to be taken prisoner. The other was a young SS man who acted arrogant. We were not impressed. The whole scene was comical. How could these two Germans have been 20 or so yards away all this time and

gone undetected? We sent them back to join the prisoners we had in the pasture.

The rest of the day and night passed relatively peacefully.

Chalk 122 carried Sgt. James Gregory's rifle squad and the platoon leader, Lt. Hymie Glasser. This glider landed well outside the landing zone, to the north, coming to rest at the edge of some woods. The silence and the lack of any other gliders were unnerving. As Glasser was trying to determine where they were, the silence was shattered by machine-gun and mortar fire. The troopers quickly got out of the glider and, with little cover, began to return the enemy fire. They were hit one by one.

Gregory, the BAR (Browning automatic rifle) gunner, Rich Mowrey, and a replacement who had only just joined the company were killed. Glasser was hit in the head, and Bill Whalen, the platoon runner, thought his officer was also dead. But when Glasser opened his eyes, Whalen knew he still had time and treated his wound with sulfur powder, then gave him a shot of morphine. The platoon runner now took charge, and when a German lieutenant called to Whalen's group to surrender, he ordered his men to put down their weapons.

The eleven surviving troopers carried their lieutenant to a bunker, where they came across a German corporal who had received a bad leg wound during the fighting. He was shouting that he wanted to shoot the Americans. The German officer silenced him and explained to Whalen and the others that the corporal had lost a brother in North Africa.

Glasser was hanging on but unable to talk. The troopers made a stretcher for him and carried him back through the enemy lines. They eventually reached a hospital and, on the advice and reassurance of the Germans, left Glasser in the care of German medics. He received excellent treatment and survived the war.

Pvt. Vitautas Thomas was in a Battalion HQ Company glider in Serial A10. He was very nervous. The pilot had had to bank hard and the glider was now heading toward the ground. Thomas's brother had been killed during the fighting in the Ardennes, and he wondered if his own time was about up. He and his five buddies braced for the landing.

It was a hard one. The glider crashed through a fence, jumped a large ditch, and came to rest wedged in an embankment. All six men were thrown around, and their jeep, which was carrying ammunition, broke some of its lashings. Thomas was separated from his helmet and rifle but had no time to look for them. The glider was being fired on from a nearby farmhouse. Fearing that the ammunition would be set off, the troopers piled out of the glider and threw themselves into a ditch.

As the situation calmed down, Thomas gathered himself and went back to the glider to look for his helmet and rifle. He was horrified to find that the helmet had two holes in it. Breathing thanks that his head had not been in it at the time, he reached forward for his rifle. A sniper round thudded into the jeep tire, which was right by his head. That was enough to send him scuttling back to the ditch.

The 1st Battalion was able to orient itself quickly and assembled in good order, but there was sad news almost immediately. Says Lt. Del Townsend:

> One of the first major losses that I learned about was that Major Hundley (the 1st Battalion executive officer) and Lieutenant Loomis (the battalion S-3), plus their entire crew, were killed when their glider was hit and set on fire while landing.

PFC Edward J. Siergiej made a risky run for ammunition:

> When we learned that one of our mortar squads was low on ammunition, I was dispatched to battalion headquarters for a resupply of mortar shells. The net result was that I eventually found myself behind the wheel of a jeep for the first time, loaded with the needed mortar shells. The route back to the company's location was approximately a half mile via an open field to our mortar squad's position on the canal. Mission accomplished with minimum erratic sniper fire en route.

The 2nd Battalion's three companies also assembled quickly. Edgar Bartlett, in the HQ Company, recalls:

> The triangle was crossed with two rows of zigzag trenches. Our glider was put down on the trenches. Allied fighter planes formed an umbrella over our entire drop zone.

PFC James J. "Joe" Rheinberger was in the 1st Mortar Squad, Weapons Platoon, Company D:

> I was an ammunition bearer, so I carried rounds for our 60-millimeter mortar. Our landing was very smooth, but we were under fire immediately and ran for water-filled ditches. We assembled quickly and were off toward our objectives. We were all in place by 2 P.M. We set up our line across the canal. We had houses to stay in, but we dug the deepest foxholes you've ever seen out in the yard. The digging was easy in the sand compared to the frozen soil in Belgium.

Companies were assembled within an hour of landing. Moving toward their objectives, they found the way blocked by tanks. Bazooka-wielding privates first class took care of four of these: Andrew Adams at 10 yards, Robert Geist at 15, William Palowida at 100, and Robert Weber at 600. Their coolness under fire allowed them and their colleagues to reach their final defensive positions.

More Company F troopers showed grit when a group led by Capt. Robert Dukes rushed through a German command post so quickly that the occupants were taken completely by surprise—so much so that the colonel in charge forgot his maps. An aide alerted him to the fact by rushing after him waving the maps and other assorted papers. The aide did not keep them for long, however, as one of the troopers from Company F relieved him of them and passed them to Dukes. The maps were a goldmine of information, showing the positions of defensive strong points and troops. All the papers were passed back to divisional headquarteres.

Edgar Bartlett describes that night's events:

> By evening, we had captured a large metal bridge where the Issel Canal came off the Issel River. That night, German armor with spotlights and infantry support took back the bridge and started penetrating our positions. German infantry came out of Wesel. Our only recourse was to call in our heavy artillery from across the Rhine. This finally broke up the attack by hitting some of the German armor. At daylight, we attacked the

bridge and took it back. We found lots of dead and wounded, both our own and German.

The 3rd Battalion's gliders landed on the eastern side of the zone. Its final objective was the southeast corner of the Diersfordter. German defenses were particularly strong in the battalion's landing sector, and it suffered initial heavy casualties. Assembly by small groups was organized, and these gradually reduced the opposition as the advance to the western side of the zone continued.

PFC William R. Scurlock, Company L, was a former member of the 550th Airborne Battalion:

> We were over the LZ when heavy antiaircraft fire hit the tail of the glider. Despite this, we made a good landing, compared to others, and only went through several fences.
>
> We were briefed that opposition would be light. We took small-arms fire but moved on to the assembly area, where we found German artillery still with shells in the breeches.

In Company I, Lt. Thomas McKinley rounded up fifteen men, and together they rushed an artillery command post, capturing the commanding officer and all his staff.

Company G was tasked to secure the Issel Canal as far as Wesel and to make contact with the British commandos, who had entered the town the previous evening. A platoon led by Lt. Fred B. Wittig tried to work its way through the German lines on the edge of Wesel. It was all to no avail, as the German defense was solid, and the platoon found itself pinned down. Wittig sent a runner back to Company F, and help was soon on the way. The situation was stabilized, and as evening came on, Wittig and his men made it into Wesel and met up with the commandos as planned.

While Wittig and his platoon were on their initial mission, the rest of the company reported by runner that all its communications had been cut and German patrols were breaking through. The German troops had no real idea where the front line was and simply attacked U.S. positions as they came across them. They overran some machine guns, but the Allied line held steady.

Company H, which was acting as reserve company, and the guns of the 681st Glider Field Artillery Battalion dealt with the main thrust of the counterattack. Second Lt. Herman Lemberger, a 681st forward observer attached to Company G, had been calling in the infantry targets when he saw tanks approaching. He moved into the open to get a better view and had just managed to send the coordinates for this new threat when a tank shell killed him. His selfless action meant that the attack was broken up and the tanks dispersed.

The glider pilots of the 435th Troop Carrier Group (TCG) were ordered to move to their defensive positions at about 1530 hours. Once they had cleared houses in the company sector and established defensive positions, there was little activity until late in the evening, as Capt. Fred Goller, CO of the 75th Platoon, explains:

> The early evening was uneventful with the exception of attempts of small enemy patrols to infiltrate through but because of bright moonlight these attempts were discovered very early and repulsed by fire. Lt. Norton's squad stopped an airborne patrol heading toward Wesel. A previous patrol had reported a group of German soldiers near Wesel that wished to surrender and this Patrol was going to take them in. Lt. Norton gave Lt. King permission to accompany the patrol. The patrol accomplished its mission and took 82 prisoners.
>
> At approximately 2300 hours, Lt. Myer's squad halted a British Commando Captain and his patrol. They had made their way from Wesel and wanted to find out what the airborne situation was. The Captain was escorted to our CP [command post] and in turn escorted to the Group CP.

Then a most unusual event occurred. "At approximately 2400 hours a JU88 approached over our CP at low altitude and crashed near the Group CP. F/O Faris, who had been detailed to Group as a runner, made his way to the crash and with the aid of several airborne captured the remaining crew member." The bomber had just missed 1st Lt. Jack E. Lambrecht's 76th Platoon: "[The] JU 88 crash landed a few yards from our platoon CP. A patrol led by Lt. Anderson and Lt. Branch surrounded the plane and took a Luftwaffe Captain prisoner. The other three members of the crew died from injuries."

About the same time, Bill Scurlock was part of a Company I patrol, 194th GIR, which came under friendly fire:

We were to fill in a gap in our lines between a unit of the
194th and the British commandos who had surrounded Wesel
the night before. We took a wrong turn, going right when we
should have gone left. We ended up in Wesel. Suddenly, without warning, all hell broke loose. We were hit with automatic
fire and white phosphorous grenades. Knowing the Germans
didn't use these, we figured that we were under fire from the
British. My squad leader, Sergeant Fox, was hit in the behind
with a grenade. He survived. What saved us was a huge bomb
crater nearby. The British used flares, mortars, and automatic
weapons to keep us pinned down. They didn't know exactly
where we were. We managed to make our way out of the
crater a few at a time. We took casualties.

The Americans had most likely been mistaken for German troops
who were being pursued by the commandos. Joe Rheinberger was on a
mission to find his battalion headquarters "because the radios didn't work
as per usual."

My memory fails me. I am not sure if I ever found it. When I
got back to the company, the Germans launched a counterattack just to our right. They were driven off. I believe that this
event has become known as the battle of Burp Gun Corner.
Most of our troops in that area were glider pilots who had
been formed into a rifle company. (I had helped train them in
infantry tactics back in Marlborough.)

As Joe rightly said, the glider pilots had indeed been involved in a
battle that later entered the U.S. Army Air Forces' annals as "The Battle
of Burp Gun Corner." The 76th Platoon was the first to realize something was happening.

At approximately 2330 hrs, the listening post established
beyond the roadblock reported an approaching enemy tank.
This was relayed to Company CP, and soon after, the approach
of still another tank heading toward the 75th and 77th roads
blocks. Soon after, all hell broke loose in that sector! Our 50

cal m.g. team opened up and slugged it out with a German 20 mm piece for several minutes. In this "trading of shots," two of the A/B men were wounded by enemy fire, forcing them to withdraw their position.

According to Fred Goller, 75th Platoon:

At least one self-propelled 88mm gun and two 20 mm guns approached our position from the SW. After a small exchange of fire and a round from one of the 57 mm guns the enemy changed its course more to the north and attacked the 77th area.

Lt. John I. Love, in charge of Squad 1, 77th Platoon, reports:

They attacked in strength and charged us—yelling and screaming like banshees. We commenced firing as soon as they came in range and continued to do so until they retreated about thirty or forty minutes later.

Their charge was led by a medium or light tank, followed by two flak wagons mounting 20 mm guns. They also had several light machine guns and a quantity of automatic weapons. The number of Germans taking part in this attack is unknown to me, but I'm reasonably sure that more than 200 must have been involved. Amidst much yelling and confusion by the Germans, a small patrol of their men outflanked the 50 cal m.g. and jumped in the same slit trench near Lt. Lee. He thought to eliminate the foe but held his fire for fear of killing part of his own squad. The enemy withdrew to the far end of the trench where the 50 cal. mg had been, and caused no further trouble.

In this firing, Lt. Niblo got a hit on his helmet which put a dent about ¾" deep and 2" long in the helmet, but did not penetrate the steel. A direct hit was scored on the roof of the house in our area by a mortar shell. This shell knocked tiles off the roof into the foxhole of Lt. Davies and me. Lt. Davies was hit in the left eye—either by a shell fragment or a piece of the tile—and was unable to see during the rest of the fight. He was later evacuated to an aid station, and sent from there back to a hospital somewhere in the rear area. I had my helmet knocked off by the falling tile, and while the helmet was off I was creased in the head by a "burp" gun. Some of the weapons jammed, during the fight, due to sand entering the working parts. Lieutenant Niblo had his gun jam on him, as did Lieutenant Dunhoft. Lieutenant Munson fired his carbine until the barrel burned out on it. Lieutenant Norgate, Lieutenant Davies, Flight Officers Jella, Jensen, Jackson, Barthelemy, Benowski, and Lieutenant Kiesling all stood their ground like the brave men they are. They gave a splendid account of themselves.

The 78th Platoon reorganized to make the best use of man and firepower. The two .30-caliber machine guns were resited to give a more effective arc of fire. Lieutenant Prewitt and Flight Officers Avery and Rischel took a bazooka and worked their way along the trench, which paralleled the railway line. They reached a position where any armored vehicle that swung toward the 78th's sector would be exposed.

The enemy force continued to approach the 77th's position. Lieutenant Love takes up the story:

> The tank reached a point slightly west of the center of the crossroad, at which time the bazooka man in Squad 1, Flight Officer Elbert Jella, took dead aim and let fly with his bazooka, getting a direct hit low on the right side of the tank. This shell stopped the tank cold and he turned around and tore down the road in the direction from which he had come. His flight was so rapid that he ran over the two flak wagons in his haste.

The men of the 76th Platoon were also ready. As Jack Lambrecht reports:

> All eyes and ears were alerted and strained for enemy activity across the vast open expanse of field, which they would have to come to reach us. We were in a precarious position and cut

off from news of our other platoons, but stuck and sweated it out. About 0130 hrs the Germans had enough and commenced to withdraw. Listening to them rumble away licking their wounds and not knowing where they would again strike, it was decided to withdraw and strengthen the next line of defense with the 436th Group to the north.

Word was sent at 0200 hrs to all squad leaders from the platoon CP to prepare for an orderly withdrawal. All firepower was carried with us, leaving all but some of the necessities. A patrol was sent ahead to the 436th to prepare for our passing through their line. The whole maneuver was carried out in an excellent manner, with the minimum of exposure to all personnel. The platoon dug in with the 436th Group, in and about an apple orchard, and there spent the night. A listening post of F/O Gallimore, F/O Collier, Lt. Knowlton and Lt. Taylor were left in the old sector to warn us of further enemy activity.

681ST GLIDER FIELD ARTILLERY BATTALION

The 681st Glider Field Artillery Battalion (GFAB) made up the bulk of serial A13, the second flown by the 435th TCG's glider pilots. Six of the sixty-nine gliders had problems over France and had to cut loose. Chalks 119 and 120 were in double-tow. The Divisional Report states that the rope of the former snagged the wing of the latter, thus causing both to crash. All occupants of 119 were killed.

For Curtis Edwards, Battery B, and his buddies, it was a heavy landing. Edwards had traveled to Germany sitting in the jeep, which would be the tow for a gun in another glider. He is not sure whether it was anti-aircraft fire that caused the crash, but the result was injuries and fatalities. Edwards's legs were badly cut, and he sustained blood poisoning because of this. With the other survivors, he hid out for three days. Edwards does not remember the chalk number of his glider, but one, another 122, landed to the southeast of the landing zone and therefore some distance from the others. This may have been his.

As soon as they exited their gliders, the 681st's gunners were under steady fire from German positions, but they were able to get their howitzers into action under the cover of their gliders' wings. Battery A was first off the mark and supported the 194th GIR as this unit made its way to its objectives. By 1400 hours, the battery was established in its planned firing positions. By 1600, Battery B was also in position and a total of ten howitzers were firing. Both batteries continued to give support to the 194th, particularly in the part of the defensive line that was occupied by the 1st and 2nd Battalions.

Around 1900, the 681st GFAB received infantry support from the 435th TCG glider pilots. When the Germans attacked the 435th's positions, the 681st's guns played a vital part in maintaining the integrity of the line.

680TH GLIDER FIELD ARTILLERY BATTALION

The liaison party was the first group of the 680th Glider Field Artillery Battalion (GFAB) to land. It had jumped with the 513th's 3rd Battalion and this had become caught up in the confusion following the 513th's drop off-zone.

The ninety-seven gliders that carried the rest of the battalion and its 105-millimeter howitzers fared better, though two had to abort. The others began landing at 1140 hours, with minimal casualties caused by enemy fire. On the ground, though, it was a different matter, as guns were zeroed in on the landing zone. The men had to make a hasty assembly and even speedier evacuation as small-arms, machine-gun, and mortar fire swept the area. So intense was this fire that close to forty gliders were destroyed, some with their ammunition or transport loads.

Despite the conditions, within five minutes of landing the battalion had guns laid and firing on strong points and artillery positions. By 1245, about half the battalion had assembled in firing positions and six howitzers were engaged in a fire plan. Five hours later, another three guns were also firing and some 900 rounds of ammunition had been collected. The command post was established, with a complete wire net, at 1345.

During that day, the 680th captured three batteries and took 150 prisoners. Its medics treated more than 100 casualties. For its actions, the 680th GFAB received a Distinguished Unit Citation, which says in part:

> [The 680th] is cited for extraordinary heroism, efficiency and achievement. . . . With complete disregard for their personal safety, the members unloaded their gliders under a withering

cross-fire, assembled in small groups, and fought their way through occupied enemy strong points and field fortifications to the assembly area, using howitzers, bazookas, grenades and carbines to reduce enemy positions. With 19 killed, including both battery commanders, and 56 wounded during the assembly, the aggressive action of all members ... in the face of great odds and a defensively prepared enemy ... assisted materially in the ultimate success of the operation.

139TH ENGINEER BATTALION

The gliders of the 139th Engineer Battalion were in two serials, which were to land on the unsecured Landing Zone N. Serial A16 was to land on Landing Zone 1, in the western half, while Serial A17 would be in Landing Zone 2, in the eastern half. They arrived at 1200 hours. The unit's mission was to clear the landing zone and defend it from the north. As the landing zone ran along the north flank of that of the 513th PIR, the 139th was attached to this unit to allow a better coordination of the defense line.

Both serials were provided by the 440th TCG. Flight Officer Don Urcutt was a flight leader:

> On that day, I led three other C-47s, each with a glider in tow and echeloned to my right. The run into the LZ was mostly uneventful until we approached German territory. Flak began to pepper the sky around us, and I recall that I saw one C-47 get hit and then dive straight into the ground. I received only some small-caliber holes in my airplane, but upon landing, we counted some forty-plus. Nothing vital was hit, fortunately. Other than that, the mission was what could be called routine. Of course, blood pressure and heart rate reached some elevated highs while over the combat area.

Flight Officer George Theis, piloting a CG-4A, had on board a jeep and troopers:

> As we approached the Rhine, I could hardly see the river because of smoke, and when the pilot gave us the signal to

cut, I knew that it was no longer practice—it was the real thing.

The first glider in our echelon turned left, followed by the second glider to my left in a flat 270-degree overhead-landing pattern. I followed number two and hoped that the fourth glider on my right would follow us. As we made the second left turn, losing altitude, I saw a church steeple almost directly in my path. I'm sure that I had plenty of clearance, but it looked like I would hit the steeple if I didn't raise the wing. The landing field had been ahead on my last left turn and was now straight in front of the glider. Except for the smoke, the landing was no different than in training.

The nose latch lock had been unlocked as we came to a stop. We all got out as fast as possible. We removed the two poles and immediately raised the tail. The driver started the jeep engine as one of the other troops cut the ropes. As the jeep moved forward, the cable mechanism started the nose to the upright position. The jeep driver stalled the engine and the friction lock slipped, allowing the nose hatch to fall onto the jeep hood. Another soldier helped me raise the nose high enough for the jeep to slip under. We dropped the nose onto the wheel ramps attached to the glider and started looking for the number-four glider that was carrying the trailer loaded with ammunition. It was nowhere to be found.

Dodging small-arms fire, the jeep driver found another glider nearby that had a howitzer that needed a tow. I saw them heading toward their checkpoint as I took cover along a hedgerow. Later, I found out that the number-four glider's ailerons had been damaged so badly by ground fire that the glider pilot could not follow me. He just happened to be lined up with a row of trees in an orchard as he landed. The trees took off both wings of his glider, and I don't know how they got the trailer out. He reported to our GP checkpoint later to report his accident.

After the small-arms fire subsided, I headed along a road toward a farmhouse, looking for signs to take me to our GP checkpoint. Along the way, I met up with a glider pilot who, before the war, was the professional photographer who took the pictures of Betty Grable doing the manual of arms with a rifle for the cover of *Life* magazine. He was with a paratrooper brigadier general [most likely Josiah T. Dalby] who had dropped outside of his DZ. He was lost from his troops, had no maps with him, and asked me if I could help him get to his command post. I realized that I had left my maps in the glider.

He asked me to go back to retrieve them. Along the way, as I was dodging small-arms fire, I went through a hedgerow of bushes that I was using for cover. Out of the bushes came two young German soldiers with hands raised, shouting, "Kamerad, Kamerad." They wanted to surrender rather than be killed. So I took them with me to my glider. Later I was told that the German officers had told them that they would be killed rather than captured. I guess I was as young as they were, and they must have thought they could trust me. They were correct, because I never fired my gun during the whole mission, and I don't know to this day if I could have raised my gun on another human being. Fortunately, I never had the chance to find out.

At the glider, I saw another soldier nearby, so I asked him to hold his gun on my prisoners while I took their picture standing next to my glider. I retrieved the maps and made my way back to the general officer along with my prisoners. I turned them over to the military police, who were collecting prisoners. The general asked me to stay with him as one of his staff. I told him that my orders were to report to the GP checkpoint. He noticed that I was Army Air Corps, not airborne, and let me go. I finally found the GP checkpoint and reported in.

On the day prior to the mission takeoff, I had been sharpening my knife when I cut my finger, requiring a bandage. When I checked into the GP checkpoint, the bandage needed replacement, so I found the first-aid station nearby. After the medic replaced the bandage, he gave me a slip of paper and told me to turn it in when I returned to my unit. I asked him

what it was for, and he said it was for my Purple Heart. I told
him that the cut had not happened in combat and gave it back
to him. Several months later, I learned that had I accepted this
medal, I would have earned enough points to qualify for early
return to the USA. Instead, I had to stay in Europe in the
Army of Occupation in Germany for another year before
returning home.

Returning to the GP checkpoint, we were assigned an area
in the Diersfordter Forest along a road to dig in for that
night. Glider pilots were not regular infantrymen, although
we had infantry training. We were to be evacuated as soon as
army forces secured the landing zones after their breakthrough. During the first night, before the breakthrough, we
were assigned to man the inner perimeter of defense. Our
task was to prevent any German infiltrator from penetrating
the second line of defense.

After digging in, we tried to go to sleep in our foxholes. It
was very cold and damp so some of us retrieved scraps of
glider fabric and parachutes to line our foxholes. I remember
getting an empty .30-caliber ammunition can to place in the
bottom of the hole to sit on for the night.

Company A's gliders were fairly well scattered on landing, with ten
landing close to Landing Zone R—hence George Theis's meeting with
the brigadier general and members of the 513th. The company CO suffered a broken arm from flak shrapnel. A section from the 1st Platoon,
which included its commander, was riding with him. On landing, the 1st
Platoon's commander took charge of the company, whose gliders had
landed on both landing zones and consequently had the hardest job
assembling in good order. Company A's missions were, first, to clear the
southern part of Landing Zone N and, second, to protect the battalion
command post, remaining in reserve in that area. Directed by its new
commander, the company made for the position chosen for the command post. On the way, it met with fire from strong points and snipers.
The men dealt with all of these and took eighty-five prisoners. On
reaching the command post position, the company cleared all enemy
resistance and prepared a defensive perimeter.

All Company B's gliders landed, as planned, in good platoon patterns on Landing Zone 2. The troopers assembled rapidly and went straight into combat against heavily defended strong points, established in farmhouses and barns. They steadily overwhelmed these through the use of grenades and small arms. A battery of 105-millimeter howitzers had been set up in a house, and the 1st Platoon and HQ Company made it their objective. They captured the battery along with its personnel, ammunition, and transport, which consisted of three half-tracks, three one-and-a-half-ton trucks, three cars, and two motorcycles. As the company's sector was cleared, its members were able to settle into defensive positions. A count showed ninety-five prisoners taken.

Company C landed in Landing Zone 1, but its gliders were so widely dispersed that assembly was by squad rather than platoon. Under intense fire, the company cleared its sector of the zone, took seventy-five prisoners, and was assembled at its designated position by 1700 hours.

The battalion's medical personnel were carried in two gliders, one of which landed right beside a defended house. The glider was carrying a medical officer, a medic staff sergeant, a jeep and its driver, and much of the battalion's medical supplies. The forty occupants of the house brought concentrated fire to bear on the glider. A direct hit from mortar fire destroyed the supplies and the jeep and killed the driver. The other two men managed to escape the burning wreckage. With limited equipment, the battalion surgeon had an aid station up and running in no time.

The battalion command post was operational by 1630, in the building that had been selected from aerial photographs. The situation then settled down until about 2300, when Company B reported seeing an enemy group, of about a platoon and a half in strength, moving through the company sector and heading toward the left of the battalion sector. Fifteen minutes later, the enemy group made a frontal attack on Company B's position. The company held its fire while watching the Germans crossing a moonlit patch of open ground. The lead scout was allowed to come as close as 15 yards before the company opened fire. The enemy was thrown into complete confusion, and those not hit continued their advance, only being forced to halt and retreat when white phosphorous grenades fell among them. Company B took no casualties but killed fifteen of the enemy, wounded twenty-three, and took thirty prisoner.

Company A, which was occupying the outposts for battalion command post, was busy taking prisoners throughout the night. Its job was not an onerous one, as the Germans, trying desperately to get back to their own lines, came straight to Company A's positions. Company C reported all quiet in its vicinity up until 2400.

155TH ANTI-AIRCRAFT BATTALION

Batteries A and C of the 155th Anti-Aircraft Battalion were attached to the 507th PIR and 513th PIR, respectively, and were also to provide antitank support. Batteries B and E were attached to the 194th GIR. Battery B was to provide antitank defense, and Battery E was to fulfill any mission given to it by 194th HQ. The four batteries were spread across three airfields and carried within four serials: B and E with the 435th TCG (A12 and A13) and A and C with the 440th (A17) and 441st (A18) TCGs.

Batteries B and E were in gliders flown by pilots from 77th TCS, 435th TCG. One glider for Battery B had to abort but landed safely in Belgium. All the rest arrived on Landing Zone S. The gliders of Batteries A and C reached Landing Zone N, with only one casualty being reported by Battery C.

As part of Battery C, Eugene Howard's crew should have found its way to the 513th, but things did not work out that way:

> I was looking for the zone, which would be near a highway and a railroad. With no warning, the C-47 cut our glider loose. As the glider lost airspeed, the pilot nosed it over and headed for a field. We were only about 300 feet above the ground when I saw the railroad. It appeared that we were going to crash into the earth, when at the last moment, the pilot nosed it up and we pancaked to a landing with a loud crash.
>
> The glider nosed over and skittered sideways, losing a wing in the process. The front end came loose at the bottom and partially opened as the glider came to a stop. The crew scrambled out of the glider. The nose part had warped in the impact and would not open enough to get the jeep out. We managed to all get on the remaining wing, which was cocked up at a crazy angle, and pulled it down. The nose still would not

budge. Part of our crew equipment was an axe, which was stored in the trailer. I hastily retrieved the axe and went to work on the overhead hinges that were partially pulled loose as a result of the impact. A few well-placed blows severed the front end of the glider from the body. As we pulled the front end of the glider aside, the tail section fell to the ground, making it impossible for the jeep to make an exit. We all got on the back end and raised the tail section high enough so that Charlie Martin drove the jeep out of the glider with no trouble at all.

As the jeep and trailer came out, we began to pick up some small-arms fire from the railroad track. Pete had Charlie Martin to pull the jeep and trailer behind the glider as we prepared to do battle. Pete called for five rounds of WP (white phosphorus). We had not had WP with the 57-millimeter. White Phosphorus is an element that burns when it comes into contact with oxygen in the air. It burns with an intense heat hot enough to burn a hole in metal. Immersion in oil the only way to extinguish the flame. When the shell explodes, it scatters the white phosphorus over a wide area.

I quickly loaded the 75-millimeter while Pete was looking for the source of the small-arms fire. Slowly Charlie pulled the jeep from behind the glider.

The enemy made the fatal mistake of firing on the jeep. We laid five rounds of rapid-fire WP on top of them at a distance of about 350 yards. As the white phosphorus did its work, we heard a lot of yelling and screaming from the railroad track. The yelling and screaming receded as they fled.

About 150 yards to our left was a patch of scrubby bushes that made excellent concealment for the 75-millimeter. In the confusion, we made a dash for the bushes.

Other gliders were landing near us with 57-millimeters and gliderborne infantry. A self-propelled 88-millimeter cannon boldly pulled up on the railroad track and blasted the glider we had just vacated. Pete nailed the 88-millimeter with the first round of AP [armor piercing] and then laid a round of HE [high explosive] on top of them. The 88-millimeter began to burn and then exploded as the flames reached the ammo bin.

The glider infantry had formed a skirmish line and began advancing upon the railroad track. Any resistance to their advance was met by a withering fire from the 75-millimeter. As the glider infantry reached the railroad track, a violent battle broke out. We moved out to the track, keeping a low profile. Carl Saggich ran to the railroad track to take a look. In a few minutes, he returned and told us that there were a "million Krauts over there!"

We found a low place that hid the jeep and allowed the 75-millimeter to fire just across the top of the railroad track. Slowly we began picking off vehicles and automatic weapons. We moved slowly up and down the railroad track and rarely fired more than two rounds from the same place.

The infantry was pouring a murderous wall of small-arms and automatic weapons fire into the enemy. A strong counterattack was made in the late morning. A few of them got within 50 yards of the railroad track before they were stopped. It appeared that 90 percent of those in the counterattack had fought their last battle. The rest retired from the battlefield.

About noon, Lieutenant Gray, who had been on another glider, showed up. He told us that we had all missed the drop zone—that the drop zone was on the other side of the railroad tracks, where all of the Krauts were. We also found out that we had landed near a small German town named Diersfordt.

On a high hill near Diersfordt was a medieval castle, which provided an excellent observation spot for artillery observers. A hotly contested battle was taking place around the castle. We were ordered to proceed toward the castle and support the infantry in taking the castle. The castle was not more than a mile or so away. We moved rapidly along a large highway toward the castle. The parachute infantry of the 507th was holding the road. We found a hill about 800 yards from the castle that afforded a good field of fire.

As we took up our position, we noticed that some German artillery, both light and heavy, seemed to surround the castle.

They were sustaining a good rate of fire as though they had plenty of ammo.

Lieutenant Gray surveyed the castle for the longest time with his field glasses. At last he said that he saw two artillery observers in the castle towers. He gave Pete the field glasses to take a look. Lieutenant Gray asked Pete if he could take out the towers. Without the observers, the eyes of the artillery would be gone. Pete allowed that taking out the towers would be a piece of cake.

With unerring accuracy, Pete demolished the towers of the castle. The blinded artillery was thrown into a state of confusion. We laid another four rounds of WP on top of the artillery.

With a wild charge, the 507th took the castle. Over 300 prisoners were captured. Just before dark, the American flag was run up the flagpole of the castle.

Later in the day, one section from Battery C took up positions in and around the sector occupied by Company B of the 139th Engineers, and fire plans were coordinated between the two units.

Eugene Howard's crew had stayed with the 507th:

After securing the area around the castle and the area where we landed, we moved southeast toward Wesel. The Germans were fiercely defending the city. Wesel was another transportation network town. Four major highways and three rail lines came together here. Field Marshal Montgomery's plan was to surround the town, cut all of the roads and rail lines, and disrupt the water and electric supply.

Along with the 507th Parachute Infantry, we were 3 or 4 miles north of the town. We headed east on a small country road. Sometime around midnight, we could hear a hum of traffic to our right front. The small road we were on intersected one of the three main major highways. The Germans had barricaded the small road and established a defensive line about a quarter of a mile from the major highway. The infantry discovered the Krauts. There was a sharp exchange of small-arms fire, and two infantrymen were killed. The infantry withdrew, and we were asked for support.

We moved to a bend in the road about 400 yards from
the barricade. I could see what looked like a dim outline
of the barricade. Pete was not able to see it. From where we
were, the road seemed straight to the barricade. I told Pete to
align the sights down the middle of the road with enough
elevation for 350 to 400 yards. I loaded a round of HE into
the 75-millimeter and we fired on the enemy. We missed the
barricade. A hail of small-arms fire answered from the German position. The 507th Parachute Infantry returned their
fire. I loaded another round of HE. Pete found the barricade
this time. We slammed a round of WP into the barricade. In
the eerie light of the burning white phosphorus, the 507th
laid a withering fire upon the Krauts. We fired two more
rounds of HE, one on each side of the barricade. The Kraut
defensive line grew quiet. A patrol by the 507th infantry confirmed that the Krauts were gone.

The crew was called upon in the early hours of the twenty-fifth to
deal with enemy traffic on the main road out of Wesel.

224TH MEDICAL COMPANY

None of the 224th Medical Company's fifty-three gliders were identified by red crosses or any other marking that would identify them as
medical transports. The 300 medics were carried as part of the last two
serials into Landing Zone N. In A20, one glider was forced to land on
the west side of the Rhine and two collided about 50 feet above the
landing zone. In A21, all eight gliders landed successfully.

Lt John W. Heffner and Lt. Bruce C. Merryman, 62nd TCS, 314th
TCG, were carrying medic Pvt. Wallace E. Thompson and his jeep. Aware
of the dangers awaiting them on the ground, the pilots had briefed their
passenger that as the descent began, he was to start the jeep engine, and
as soon as the glider was on the ground, he was to drive forward, which
would raise the nose section of the glider and allow him to exit. But
things did not quite happen as planned. Bruce Merryman explains in
Thunder from Heaven journal, by Don R. Pay:

As we neared the ground we were hit with a round from an
88mm field piece. It exploded behind the jeep and the shrap-

nel evidently cut the ropes holding the jeep, allowing the jeep to move forward. This caused the nose latches to break. We had an arrangement whereby a cable was fastened to an "A" frame on top of the copilot side of the nose section and over two pulleys and hooked to the rear bumper of the jeep. This opened up the front of the glider and allowed the jeep (with Thompson holding on to the steering wheel) to "fly" the remaining distance to the ground, landing on its wheels, before our glider landed.

Thompson had just finished an extremely rough 3-hour flight from our base in France and was more or less in a daze after his solo flight in his jeep. He later told us that right after his "landing" an officer and one or two enlisted men came by in a jeep loaded with ammo and/or explosives. I'm not sure of the exact sequence of events that followed but while Thompson was still in his jeep a German sniper opened up with a rifle and hit him in his helmet a number of times. At about the same time a mortar round exploded behind the jeep and a piece of shrapnel penetrated the helmet, made a complete circuit inside the helmet between the helmet and liner and then exited. The rifle bullets did not penetrate the helmet, but the shrapnel from the mortar did. Thompson was untouched by any of this and the only wound he received was a scratch on his nose! He wasn't sure what caused it.

He had decided to follow the other jeep, with an officer and enlisted men in it. When that jeep received a direct hit by a mortar round, which destroyed the jeep and killed the men in it, Thompson left his jeep and jumped into a ditch by a railroad track. That is where we found him.

Up until that time we didn't know where he was, or even if he was still alive after the crash. After we took stock of our situation we found that Heffner had been hit in the hand with a piece of shrapnel, which lodged in the knuckle of his hand and was causing him extreme pain. Medic Thompson gave him a shot of morphine for the pain. Thompson then treated my shrapnel wounds with sulfa powders and put bandages on them. We lay there for a short while and then Trooper Thompson said, "This is not getting my job done," whereupon he got

up and strolled out to his jeep as if he were on a picnic, started
the engine, and began picking up wounded and hauling them
to the Aid Station.

Our area was still under fire but-Thompson ignored it and
came to where Heffner and I were to see how we were doing.
He was drawing fire from the Germans so he told us he would
be back for us as soon as the fighting died down some. With
that he left and went back to picking up wounded and hauling them to the Aid Station. The incoming fire didn't seem to
bother him a great deal.

The remaining forty-nine gliders began landing at 1225 hours. The
zone was still not cleared, and the company suffered heavy casualties.

With so much opposition, it took more than an hour to assemble
enough staff for the clearing station, which the men established in the
previously selected area. German prisoners were employed as stretcher
bearers and in the digging of foxholes and stretcher trenches. German
medical staff were given supplies to use in the treatment of their own
wounded. A total of 394 casualties, of which 117 were seriously wounded,
were treated during the day.

Twenty-year-old Cpl. Bill Tom arrived in the Wesel zone by jeep.
Bill had started his military career as a rifleman in the 194th GIR. By
various twists of fate, he found himself on detached training as a medic
and, as he puts it, "orphaned from the 17th Airborne Division." He finally
caught up with the 17th in the Ardennes but was made a medic-at-large.
When the 17th returned to France, Bill remained with the U.S. 9th
Army. His initial orders for Varsity were to take care of troopers dropped
in the wrong area or involved in glider crashes:

All the troopers I came upon in the crashes were all killed. In
one planeload that had caught on fire, the entire load of paratroopers was incinerated. Several had to be buried in one
grave, all tangled up like a bunch of fried chicken wings. I was
not able to eat fried chicken and roasted meat for many weeks
thereafter.

But there were also lighter moments as a medic:

Later in the day, I had to care for a wounded German soldier who was shot in the head. Even though he must have weighed over 200 pounds, his head was swollen disproportionately larger than his body frame. Whatever projectile hit him did some very bloody damage to his head. He was still alive, but he was triaged out of his favor since such a massive head wound was beyond our level of care. He had to be evacuated further back. Meanwhile, I had many of our own wounded troops to care for.

In time, the German soldier died. I was told to move his body to the morgue, which was a tent located among many other tents in the dark. It was midnight, and no flashlight was permitted in a combat area. As was the usual case, I carried the head end of the litter (the heavy end), and Private Booker had the feet end. The morgue tent was the eighth one in the back. We trudged very slowly in absolute darkness with that heavy load. My arms, back, and neck were in such excruciating burning pain that I lost count of the tents. I approached one tent, which I was certain was the morgue. I kicked the canvas flap open and stepped inside. I stepped on something hard and round, and I fell down. The German body was pitched off the litter and fell heavily on something to make a grunt noise, like a German ghost. Booker and I took off like two bats out of a cave, running back to the aid tent in total darkness.

What I thought was the morgue was actually the kitchen supply tent. Next morning, I was severely chewed out by the sergeant for scaring his cooks half to death to find a dead body on top of their breakfast potatoes!

GENERAL RIDGWAY CROSSES THE RHINE

Just before 1500 hours, Gen. Matthew Ridgway crossed the Rhine in a British amphibious vehicle. As it climbed onto the east bank, the machine gunner fired a few bursts in a sweeping arc, but there was no return fire.

The jeeps were offloaded, but Ridgway continued on foot, his Springfield rifle in hand. Turning the bend in the road he saw, about 50 feet ahead, a German in a foxhole staring straight at him. The general stopped, waiting for the crack of the enemy's rifle, but the man was dead. It was a heart-stopping moment, and Ridgway carried on, but with greater caution.

Hearing a noise, he waved his men into cover just as the strangest of sights came into view. It was a paratrooper on a horse, but instead of his helmet, the trooper was wearing a silk top hat. To the trooper's amazement, his commanding general suddenly appeared on the track. Completely flustered, he did not know whether to salute where he sat or to dismount and salute from the ground. Ridgway burst out laughing, the tension was broken, and the trooper, grinning, went on his way. It was a sign that this part of the landing area was secure.

The first stop was 17th Airborne commander Gen. William Miley's headquarters, where Ridgway received a brief rundown of the day so far. Miley was concerned that he had yet to hear from Eric Bols at Kopenhof farm, so as the light began to fade, Ridgway, Miley, and escort set off for Kopenhof.

The convoy's route ran through the 194th's sector and then the 513th's. Ridgway stopped to get a report from each CO. At Coutts' HQ he heard about the misdrop and the ease with which the C-46's had caught fire. He later gave instructions that the aircraft would never be used again to carry paratroops. At Kopenhof, the American party also met General Gale. The atmosphere was good.

Ridgway and Miley left the farm about midnight. In the ensuing period, since their passing through the area the first time, a battle had broken out. The jeeps ran headlong into a German patrol. All was confusion as the two groups engaged in a fierce gunfight. Ridgway emptied his magazine and got down on the ground to reload. At that moment, a German grenade exploded under the jeep. Ridgway was hit in the shoulder by a piece of shrapnel. The front wheel, against which he had come to rest when he twisted to get a new magazine, saved him from certain death. The men soon drove off the Germans, and the jeeps and passengers continued to Miley's headquarters.

CHAPTER 10

The Second Day

BRITISH SECTOR

3RD PARACHUTE BRIGADE

During the remainder of the night, considerable traffic from the Rhine started to pass through the 3rd Parachute Brigade's area. Visitors to its headquarters included the COs of the 4th Royal Tank Regiment and 3rd Scots Guards.

Soon after first light on 25 March, the Germans launched a counterattack with infantry and four tanks against the 1st Canadian Battalion but were easily driven off. The rest of the day passed comparatively quietly.

5TH PARACHUTE BRIGADE

At first light, fighting patrols were sent out to close the gap between the 5th Parachute Brigade and the Airlanding Brigade. A warning was also issued to the 5th to be prepared to relieve the Airlanding Brigade of responsibility for the defense of Hamminkeln, should it prove necessary to use the Devons to restore the situation in the Oxfordshire and Buckinghamshire Light Infantry (OBLI) sector. This did not prove necessary, however.

The brigade then spent a quiet day watching the battle by the 15th (Scottish) Division to the northwest and the Airlanding Brigade to the southwest.

Lt. "Dixie" Dean, 13th Parachute Battalion, 5th Parachute Brigade, describes his day:

> After a wash, shave, and breakfast, I felt much better, and since there was nothing happening, I walked across to battalion HQ, inquiring after the missing members of the platoon. I was surprised to find Jack Watson there, until he explained he was standing in for Roy Leyland, who had been called to help out at brigade, since both the brigade major (Mike Brennan) and Ted Lough (DAQ), were wounded. "Claude" Milman was acting OC [officer commanding] of A Company, with Bill Davidson as temporary adjutant. I asked what other casualties there had been and learned that both my two particular friends in the battalion were out of action: "Joe" Hodgson was missing, and Freddie Skeate was a walking wounded. The only officer known to have been killed was Chris Selwyn of B Company—in action for the first time. Of my missing gunners, the gun team of Cpl. Tony Cabrera and L.Cpl. "Ginger" Langton were dead, while Sgt. Frank Kenny and L.Cpl. Fred Pengelly were reported wounded. Eric Barlow told me later that the two young NCOs had been part of his group, who had all landed in the trees and subsequently fought their way through to join the battalion. He warned them that carrying the gun and tripod on their shoulders made them an obvious target for snipers and advised them to abandon these. They refused to do so and were indeed picked off as a result.
>
> The casualty collecting post was in a large barn across the yard, so I walked over and found Fred Skeate standing outside, unconcernedly smoking his pipe. After his shrapnel wound had been cleaned and dressed the previous day, he returned to his company, but now that all was quiet, was being evacuated to the field hospital, and indeed, as we spoke, his name was called and off he went. Inside the barn, I found Fred Pengelly, lying on a stretcher. He looked pale but was in good spirits, and on my return to the platoon area, I sent Tommy Stephenson, his pal in the section, to have a word with him.
>
> Now that I definitely knew the fate of my missing, there were letters to be written to their next of kin. It wasn't a task

I relished, but it had to be done, and now was as good a time as any, since in the farmhouse alongside the position, I would be able to sit at a table to do so. But first I practiced writing with my left hand. Having satisfied myself that the results were readable, I laboriously finished the task. Next, I performed the much more pleasing duty of promoting Cyril Andrews to lance sergeant, as he was the new section corporal.

Early in the afternoon, friendly armor in the form of Sherman tanks moved through on the road to Hamminkeln, thus confirming that the linkup with the waterborne assault had been made. Later in the day, we too were on the move, following in their tracks, and now we saw what terrible havoc the ack-ack guns had caused the gliders. Hardly a one escaped damage, but the railway yard on the outskirts of the town was the scene of indescribable chaos. The yard had tall trees on three sides, and several Horsas of 2ndOx and Bucks had hit these and then, seemingly out of control, flopped heavily to the ground, breaking up as they did so. The gliders were simply heaps of firewood, and the casualty rate doesn't bear thinking about.

However, they had succeeded in their main task of seizing intact the bridge over the River Issel and, indeed, of holding it against any counterattack. Over the bridge we passed a Panther, knocked out by a 6-pounder off the RUR [Royal Ulster Rifles]. It had slewed off the road and into a ditch. We didn't advance much further that evening, before occupying a farm and settling down for the night, but were on the move again at first light.

Recalls Capt. David Tibbs:

As was my custom after a battle, I walked widely over the area to make sure that all casualties had been gathered in. In the wood into which I had seen our men dropping at the initial assault, I found, to my distress, about twenty-five dead parachutists who had been caught in the trees and, while struggling to free themselves, had been shot by Germans who had been gathered there in large numbers. Most of the parachutists were still hanging in their harnesses, but some had reached the ground, and one young officer (Selwyn, son of the dean of Winchester) still had an automatic in his hand, but with the side of his face blown away by a grenade. They were all from our battalion, and many I knew well. It was then I realized how fortunate we had been that Sergeant Webster had held off jumping until we had cleared the trees. I continued my walk across the open area and came across, perhaps, eight gliders that had attempted to land in full view of German ack-ack guns. Each was a tangled wreck, some burnt out, and all surrounded by dead men, everyone in the glider, thirty in each case. It was deeply upsetting to know that these men had died without any opportunity to fight back and without any chance of surviving, but such is the penalty for being the attacking force with no element of surprise.

AIRLANDING BRIGADE
2nd Battalion Oxfordshire and Buckinghamshire Light Infantry
Pvt. "Nobby" Clarke describes how his unit decimated an attacking enemy force:

Shortly after dawn on 25 March, enemy infantry were observed moving towards our area, supported by several tanks. Now, with fully effective radio communication, we were able to call for support, so that within a very short time our heavy artillery shells, now reranged, began exploding among the advancing enemy.

This was quickly followed by several rocket-firing Typhoon aircraft—in what the pilots called a "cab-rank" formation—swooping in low, in line one behind another. They seemed to take no time at all to destroy all the tanks, an awesome demonstration of the decisive power of this very effective weapon.

From an upstairs window in our small house, I saw the enemy force virtually annihilated as I watched. It was with some awe that I saw a lone enemy medic moving around his dead and wounded comrades. The courage and devotion to duty of this very brave man, under that hellish fire, held my attention for many minutes.

Lt. Hugh Clark also witnessed the counterattack:

Sunday morning dawned clear and bright, and it was not long before we again heard tracked vehicles moving in the area of Ringenberg to our front. We had overhead a "cab rank" of rocket-firing Typhoon aircraft. We called them into action, and they proceeded to give a wonderful display as they dived over our position, firing their 20-millimeter cannon and releasing their rockets. We had no way of checking their effectiveness, but clouds of oily black smoke arose over Ringenberg, and we assumed they had scored hits on the tanks. The road junction was still under sniper fire, which resulted in the death of Capt. Clive Moncrieff, second in command of the Support Company. At the time, he was being driven to regimental headquarters in a jeep and hoped to get around the junction by driving at speed. Unfortunately, the sniper was too quick for him, and he was hit and killed and the jeep crashed. Two wounded men were brought into my platoon position on stretchers, but there was no way we could get them across the road until after dark.

David Rice spent some time in the morning sharing my slit trench. He and I were both practicing Christians, and we were able to pray and read a Psalm together. We were both looking for something to eat and drink as we had nothing apart from our water bottles and chocolate carried in our pockets since leaving England the previous day. Two other incidents I remember that happened during the morning. An American artillery spotter plane came over and ventured too near the Germans to have a go at it and shoot it down.

During the afternoon, we heard that the ground troops who had crossed the Rhine the previous day had linked up with our division and that we would be relieved that night.

Sgt. Pilot Eric Ayliffe recalls his unit's pullout and return to England:

Hamminkeln was still receiving the occasional shell as we began to pull out. When we drew near the pontoon bridge across the Rhine, the commandos who had crossed the river in boats lined up to cheer us on our way out. We were taken to Helmond, where the Dutch people looked after us very well.

Then to Eindhoven and flown back to RAF Down Ampney on 30th March. There we were met by HM Customs, who wanted to know where we had spent the last few nights! The answers they received were varied, to say the least. Tempers were short, and they soon diplomatically ran out of forms. Maybe the threat to burn their hut down helped.

Those of us from F Squadron who returned were taken to RAF Fairford. Our kit was laid out for us, but the empty beds in our hut were a sad reminder that life for us would never be the same again.

Denis Edwards's story did not recommence until the twenty-sixth, but it is worthy of space:

At some time on the morning of the 26th, D Company had moved some distance beyond the railway station and was preparing to launch an attack on a large wood which, according to intelligence reports, was heavily defended.

In the usual way, as a prelude to the attack, our artillery put down a heavy bombardment on the wood. Then the shelling ceased as our lads were preparing to attack, when a lone figure emerged from the wood, wandering through the early morning mist and greeting them with a wave of his hand. I was that lone figure, and the lads all agreed later that I was very fortunate not to have been shot before I was recognized. When they saw me, they were convinced that they were seeing my ghost. In reply to their urgent questioning, I was able to assure them that there were no Germans in the wood, which was then occupied without a shot being fired.

When our company commander saw me, his face turned white before changing to red as he bellowed, "Where the hell have you come from?" "I don't know, sir," I replied with complete honesty. "I was in that wood." "Good God, man," bellowed the company commander, "I've sent off a signal that you had been killed in action. I saw your body lying on the embankment."

Others who were standing around nodded their agreement and also said that they too had seen me "killed."

No one was ever able to explain how I could have been wandering around alone in heavily occupied enemy territory for some thirty-six hours without being captured or shot. Nor could they understand how I had managed to survive our own massive shelling of the wood and emerge completely unscathed.

I have no definite answer to the mystery; the last thing that I could remember was diving for the shelter of the railway embankment when the shelling began, and then emerging from the wood a day and a half later. The period between is a complete blank.

I can only surmise that I must have been very severely concussed; the blast of the shell burst certainly killed several men all around me. I must have been completely unconscious when our company commander and the others saw the bodies, and I was presumed to be dead and was left with the others to await a burial party. On regaining consciousness, in the midst of a pile of broken and bloody corpses, I would have been the only living person in the area. I suppose that I would have hurried off in search of my company, driven by instinct and fear of being left alone, this latter condition probably aggravated by having been temporarily deafened by the effect of the shell blast. The direction in which I chose to wander could only have been determined by chance, and it was our own shelling of the wood that caused me to leave it and thereby to encounter my own company advancing to attack it. But this is only to surmise and to offer an explanation that is at least logical.

12th Battalion, the Devonshire Regiment

From dawn throughout the hours of daylight, members of the Intelligence Section and Mortar Group of the 12th Battalion, the Devonshire

Regiment, manned a brigade observation post in the church steeple. Generally, the day was quiet and uneventful.

At about 1000 hours, a troop of M10 Achilles tanks from 15th (Scottish) Division arrived in the town. They were a welcome sight and were quickly factored into the antitank plan.

Six hours later, the CO of 5th Kings Own Scottish Borderers (KOSB) arrived, accompanied by his reconnaissance parties. He spoke with Gleadell about the KOSB taking over the management of the town. During the evening the main body of the 5th Parachute Brigade arrived and arrangements were made for a handover early the next morning.

1st Battalion Royal Ulster Rifles

The 1st Battalion Royal Ulster Rifles was preparing breakfast when, at 0730 hours, two Panther tanks with infantry aboard attempted to rush the bridge. Coming at full speed down the road, the tanks were set to break through the line. A 6-pounder crew from the Support Company swung their gun to face the threat. Their first shot was a direct hit and left the lead vehicle knocked out and on fire. Their second damaged the other vehicle. This action lifted morale and the men ate breakfast with relish and in peace.

By 0930, reports showed that no enemy troops or vehicles remained in the battalion sector. Typhoons kept watch overhead and were on call for the rest of the day. Air reconnaissance reports told of little enemy movement on the roads in the area.

53rd (Worcestershire) Yeomanry

The 53rd (Worcestershire) Yeomanry's first incident of the morning was the heavy shelling of E Troop. The troop's members moved about 250 feet away and reestablished their howitzers. The 25-pounder, for which they were also responsible, had to stay where it was, however, since there was no transport to move it. The troop took the inconvenience of the move as a golden opportunity to rid itself of the large gun, which was most unpopular. So there the gun stayed until its owners reluctantly had to collect it as the march into Germany began.

The 212th Battery had a busy morning dealing with small parties of infantry and some tanks, which Typhoons finally dispersed. Late in the afternoon, there were signs that the enemy was attempting to build up a force on the eastern bank of the River Issel for a counterattack. Again, Typhoons with the batteries' help ensured that no such attack was made.

Lt. Douglas Harper of the 53rd had also been occupied with letter writing. His words speak volumes:

> My Dear All at Home
>
> At last I have a few minutes rest in which to write and tell you that I am safe and well, fit and happy.
>
> Well, as you have guessed and will no doubt have read in the papers by now, I am now in Germany, having landed by glider in the recent airborne landings east of the Rhine. Yes it was a marvellous experience and I was glad to get down safely.

U.S. SECTOR

During the day, Gen. Matthew Ridgway organized a partial develop-ment and amalgamation of the River Issel sector, putting the 513th Para-chute Infantry Regiment (PIR) on the left, the 194th Glider Infantry Regiment (GIR) in the center, and the 507th PIR on the right, with its right flank fixed on the Issel Canal. The 680th Glider Field Artillery Battalion (GFAB) continued to act as division artillery.

507TH PARACHUTE INFANTRY REGIMENT

The commandos were having problems in the northern part of Wesel, and the 507th Parachute Infantry Regiment was ordered to go to their assistance and make firm contact. This it did at 1330, and at 1400, 1st Commando Brigade came under the command of the 18th Airborne Corps and was attached to the 17th Airborne Division in a reserve capacity.

513TH PARACHUTE INFANTRY REGIMENT

S.Sgt. Lendy McDonald, Company A, 513th Parachute Infantry Regi-ment, describes the events of 25 March:

> All [that] day, we moved further into Germany, meeting with little resistance and taking more prisoners. Late that evening,

after clearing a large wooded area, we came to another large clear field with another large wooded area on the other side. As we gathered on the edge of the woods we were in, and peering across the clear field to the woods on the other side, we got a radio order for A Company to clear the woods on the other side. Dennison, Pinder, and I told Lieutenant Beckett we felt it was too dark, with poor visibility, and with no idea of what we might run into, we should wait until morning. If we got into a firefight, we probably would end up shooting each other in the dark. Beckett agreed. We stayed put. In a few minutes, the radio order was repeated. Lieutenant Beckett told the radioman our situation and our decision and ordered him to relay the message. We got an immediate reply again, ordering A Company across the field to clear the woods on the other side. Lieutenant Beckett took the radio, identified himself, and said, "You tell General Miley that if he wants those woods cleared tonight, he better hurry on down here." We heard no more from them that night.

On the night of 1 April, a Panzerfaust hit the tank on which McDonald was riding. His buddies, thinking he was dead, moved his body to the side of the road. He had only been knocked out, though, and regained consciousness sixteen hours later in a field hospital. A visit from his CO, Colonel Coutts, who was wounded in the shoulder, still brings a lump to McDonald's throat.

194TH GLIDER INFANTRY REGIMENT

During the late afternoon, the 194th Glider Infantry Regiment worked with the 507th PIR to seize a new defensive line across the Issel. The units met little enemy resistance and were established in their objective by 1800 hours.

For the 194th's fighting pilots, it was nearly the end of their time in Germany. Capt. Fred Goller, 75th Troop Carrier Squadron (TCS), 435th Troop Carrier Group (TCG):

It was necessary to reclear the houses in the area in case some enemy had infiltrated through our lines during the night. The clearing was accomplished without any events, no enemy had infiltrated through. At 1000 a patrol consisting of Lt. Crocker, F/O Julian, F/O Brockman and F/O Klootwyk was sent out to find any information on the missing men. The entire LZ was patrolled, field hospital records checked, and many dead bodies examined but no information was obtained concerning the two missing men. F/O Jacobson's body was later found in the field.

At 1700 the group started on its evacuation. The 75th platoon furnished the rear guard protection. The march to the Rhine and subsequent ferry across in assault boats was uneventful. The Group remained overnight in the town of Xanten on the west bank of the Rhine and proceeded on "Ducks" to the Glider Pilot Rest Area at 0900 hours the following morning.

Transportation was furnished from the rest area to B-86. As aircraft became available, the glider pilots were evacuated to A-48.

According to 1st Lt. Jack Lambrecht, 76th TCS:

Early morning, 25 March '45, a patrol of Lt. Anderson, Lt. Steen and myself reported to 436th Group CP and were told to attach the 76th Platoon with them and dig in as part of their own sector. Word was given that they would send out a runner to Regimental Hdqs. and notify 435th Company of our location. Later the same morning, our own patrol was met and it was decided to take up our old positions.

In taking up our position it was again necessary to send patrols into the adjacent German houses and clear them out. Several more prisoners were taken on these patrols. Several breaks in the field phone line were mended and contact was made with Company CP.

All went well during Sunday morning and afternoon. At 1630 hrs, word was received from Captain Gordon, Company Commander, to prepare the 76th platoon for immediate evacuation, and to stand by for further orders. Both 30 cal machine guns, bazookas, grenades and ammunition were turned into Company CP for distribution to A/B. Soon after word was received to move up to Company CP, where we joined the other platoons of the "fightenist [sic] body of GP's in the Troop Carrier Command." Thus we marched out of the Wesel area and on to the Rhine River.

Says 1st Lt. Garnett F. Holland, Squad 2 Commander, 77th TCS:

The next morning a few snipers fired on our area. About 0830 to 1030 all surrounding houses were searched. Wounded Germans that were found were given first aid and others were taken to the P.W. area.

During the day all men of the 77th were preparing for another night's stay. Their fox-holes were prepared in much better fashion, and were made more comfortable. At about 1730 word was passed around that we were to evacuate.

Flight Officer Gency, one of the boys in my squad, complained of his leg being sore, and his stomach bothering him. He had hurt himself on landing his glider the day before. He said it didn't bother him enough to go to the hospital. But as we were leaving, he was found unable to do any walking, and we sent him to the hospital. We joined with the rest of the 77th and evacuated.

Recalls 1st Lt. Earl Davis, 78th TCS:

The next morning word was received that the 76th had found it necessary to withdraw and had not been contacted. A patrol was formed from the 78th to contact them and this was accomplished.

At 1800 the evacuation got under way and a march was made to the river where the men were taken across in boats. They marched on to the town of Xanten. Then the confusion of evacuation really began. It was dark and past midnight, so the men scattered to the four winds when they were told to sleep anywhere they could. They never were assembled again and the return trip to the Rhine camp for glider pilots, then to B-86 and finally back to A-48 by C-47 was made in small irregular groups.

On 27 March, Miley gave the final order: "Advance to Dorsten. This is a pursuit." The Last Drop was over.

EPILOGUE

Varsity was an operation of "firsts" and "onlys":
- the first and only time in the war that the Curtiss C-46 Commando was used to carry paratroops operationally
- the first and only time that the WACO CG-4A glider was successfully double-towed operationally
- the first and only time that the Airspeed Horsa Mk II glider was used operationally
- the first and only time that ground troops began assaulting an objective before airborne troops had landed
- the first and only time in the war that airborne troops landed, in daylight, in a heavily fortified and defended area
- the first and only time that U.S. glider pilots were used in an organized infantry role

But was Varsity a success? Answering this question for any military operation generally elicits a counterquestion: Were the planned outcomes of the operation met? In the case of Varsity, the answer is yes.

The 6th Airborne's parachute brigades fulfilled their tasks: They secured the left flank and captured and held the vantage points in the Diersfordter. The coup-de-main glider troops captured both bridges and held them. The Oxfordshire and Buckinghamshire Light Infantry and Royal Ulster Rifles secured all their objectives in and around Hamminkeln station, and the Devons did the same for the village itself.

The 17th Airborne troopers also completed their tasks. They secured the right flank and cleared and held Diersfordt castle and village. They also secured the center and southeastern sectors of the landing area and swiftly dealt with any German incursions. They held bridges intact and created links with the 1st British Commando Brigade and 15th (Scottish) Division.

Overall, the accuracy of the drop was much better than in Normandy and Holland. The vast majority of paratroopers and gliders landed on their zones, and those that did not were no more than 2 miles from where they should have been. In the case of the 513th, its misdrop was most fortuitous for the 6th Airborne Division's Airlanding Brigade.

The smokescreen caused huge problems for transport and glider pilots. As they often had little view of the ground above 200 feet, it is understandable that landings did not occur as briefed. That said, the skill and courage of the glider pilot regiment and troop carrier command pilots in poor visibility and under intense antiaircraft fire must be commended. For the most part, the tactical landing theory worked well. The Germans were thrown into confusion as gliders surrounded them on all sides. All their previous experiences had been of gliders landing en masse.

For the pilots in the 313th Troop Carrier Group, flying aircraft, without self-sealing tanks into the maelstrom of ground fire is also worthy of commendation. Despite its shortcomings, the double capacity of the C-46 over the C-47 made a great difference to the operation.

Giving the 435th Troop Carrier Group pilots extra field and weapons training to equip them for employment as an infantry company proved to be a sound decision. With the RAF pilots, their thoughts on their military training vary. There simply wasn't enough time to train them to the level of their army comrades, a good many of whom, having survived Normandy and Holland, brought a huge amount of battle experience to this operation.

The bringing together of two organizations, the army and the air force, both in joint command and flying, worked extremely well. The mixed crews quickly established a great camaraderie, and many RAF pilots, like Brian Latham, enjoyed the opportunity of talking to and learning from the flying soldiers.

The success of the antiflak program is open to debate. There is no doubt that the huge artillery barrage on enemy positions prior to the landing caused a great deal of damage. Still, there were sufficient antiaircraft units untouched by the barrage to cause considerable damage to the transports, tugs, and gliders.

The use of air support, controlled by FVCPs, had been tried in Normandy and Holland. Its success in Holland had been moderate, and it was employed only to aid the XXX Corps in its advance to Arnhem. The "cab rank" for Varsity worked with FVCPs attached to each division, and over the two days, it was used against thirty targets. The work of its aircraft assisted greatly in both divisions' defense of their sectors.

So was Varsity necessary? In his report, Gen. Matthew Ridgway said he believed that "the airborne drop was of such depth that all enemy artillery and rear defensive positions were included and destroyed, reducing in one day a position that might have taken many days to reduce by ground attack alone."

Was he correct? With the sometimes jaundiced eye of hindsight, it can be easy to criticize the planners, who could work with only the information they had available at the time. Although battered and bruised by the Allied onslaught, which had forced them back across the Rhine, the Germans still posed a threat to the follow-up crossing, knowing it would not be long in coming. So, to protect the bulk of the troops that would have to come across the Rhine, the Germans in the immediate crossing area had to be contained and subdued, while their comrades who were in striking distance of Wesel and Hamminkeln had to be prevented from reaching them. The answer, for the Allied planners, was to place a blocking force between the opposing armies. That force was an airborne one.

Charles B. MacDonald believes that Varsity "unquestionably aided British ground troops." Yet he also wrote in *The Last Offensive: United States Army in World War II, European Theater of Operations* that "although the objectives assigned the divisions were legitimate, they were objectives that ground troops alone under existing circumstances should have been able to take without undue difficulty and probably with considerably fewer casualties."

Was he correct? The U.S. 30th and 79th Divisions sustained only forty-one fatalities in the river crossing. Casualties in Operation Varsity are shown in the following table:

Unit	Killed	Wounded
6th Airborne	248	738
17th Airborne	393	834
RAF	7	20
9th Troop Carrier Command (includes glider pilots)	41	153
Glider Pilot Regiment	98	77

In percentage terms, for the two airborne divisions, the 6th had 12 percent casualties and the 17th had 13 percent. Senior medical staff had been warned to expect casualties in the region of 10 percent, which even the medics thought was a high figure.

In contrast, for the glider pilots, the Glider Pilot Regiment had a staggering 27 percent casualty rate, whereas the Troop Carrier Command had 11 percent. This statistic is partly accounted for by the height of glider release: the British at 2,500 feet and Americans at 600 feet.

In the end, whether Operation Varsity was necessary or the river crossing should have included the two airborne divisions as ground troops, as in the Ardennes, is left to conjecture. Varsity happened, the Rhine was breached, and the end of the war was brought closer.

Perhaps some words of Winston Churchill, written in Field Marshal Bernard Montgomery's autograph book at his tactical headquarters, might help in drawing a line:

> The Rhine and all its fortress lines lie behind. Once again they have been the hinge on which massive gates revolved. Once again they have proved that physical barriers are vain without the means and spirit to hold them.
>
> A beaten army, not long ago master of Europe, retreats before its pursuers. The goal is not long to be denied to those who have come so far and fought so well under proud and faithful leaderships.

APPENDIX A

Resupply

The initial resupply plans called for a number of missions to be flown, which would maintain supplies over the first three days in Germany. But in reality, only the first mission was flown.

At 1300 hours, 240 B-24 Liberators, from the 8th Air Force's 2nd Air Division, arrived at the Rhine. Each aircraft carried two and a half tons, which had been packed into twenty bundles, distributed in three locations: twelve in the bomb racks; five in and around the ball turret, which had been removed; and three by the emergency escape hatch in the tail. Most of the bundles were fitted with parachutes. Half the aircraft flew to Drop Zone B to resupply the 6th Airborne Division and half to Drop Zone W for the 17th.

Tom Wallis, 2nd Airlanding Anti-Tank Regiment, witnessed the resupply drop:

> Later that day, we had stopped for food when suddenly above the general sound of small-arms fire was a deep rumbling sound, which got louder and louder then appeared the most magnificent sight I have ever seen, when Liberator American bombers with bomb bays wide open roared across, directly above us—the captain of the lead aircraft leaning out of his window smiling and waving. At that moment, it seemed the aircraft released canisters fitted with parachutes. The sky was

black with chutes, and there was a need to be quick on your feet as these containers came whizzing down. This was the resupply drop, one of the things that regretfully went wrong at Arnhem. This time supplies were available. No one who ever witnessed that resupply drop will ever forget it. Those planes came in at 100 feet high. What a wonderful and impressive sight! Sadly, many of those planes could be seen turning around to go home with smoke trailing from engines. We all hoped they made it back safely.

Lt. "Dixie" Dean, 13th Parachute Battalion, also recalls the drop:

Our prisoners were still hard at work when the division's resupply arrived. We knew from the briefing that it was expected, but had no idea what a show we were about to witness, every bit as spectacular in its own way as the glider fly-in on the evening of D-Day.

Once again it was heralded by the growing roar of multiple engines, this time approaching at a much greater speed. The ever-mounting crescendo of noise came from the rear and was overhead almost as soon as the first whisper, and a long line of four-engined Liberators, flying abreast, flashed over, and immediately the sky below was filled with multicolored chutes, floating gently to earth. Suddenly one of the left-hand planes rose almost vertically skywards, hung there for a moment, and then plunged to the ground, exploding in a mass of flame and black smoke. Then all was silence again.

The Liberators came in low and slow. Some power-line and tree hopping was necessary, which caused obvious problems with dropping bundles accurately. Nevertheless, the 17th reported collecting 50 percent and the 6th 80 percent. Undoubtedly, bundles dropped in the trees were collected and used, so the 17th likely retrieved more than officially reported.

As with the transports, the bombers were vulnerable on the turn for home. Fifteen were shot down and 104 damaged.

Problems arose with the collection and distribution of the supplies, particularly ammunition. For the 6th, loss of Royal Army Service Corps carriers and men sustained in the landing meant that to begin with, there were only a handful of soldiers and two carriers. By late afternoon, thirty men and six carriers were working. A request to the Airlanding Brigade and Royal Artillery produced another ten jeeps and trailers, and supplies began to move to areas of greatest need.

APPENDIX B

Orders of Battle

U.S. XVIII Airborne Corps	Maj. Gen. Matthew B. Ridgway
	Maj. Gen. Richard N. Gale
	(deputy)
British 6th Airborne Division	Maj. Gen. Eric Bols
3rd Parachute Brigade	Brig. S. H. James Hill
1st Canadian Parachute Battalion	Lt. Col. Jeff Nicklin
8th Parachute Battalion	Lt. Col. George Hewetson
9th Parachute Battalion	Lt. Col. Napier Crookenden
224th Parachute Field Ambulance	
RAMC	Lt. Col. A. D. Young DSO
3rd Parachute Squadron RE	
5th Parachute Brigade	Brig. J. H. Nigel Poett DSO
7th Parachute Battalion	Lt. Col. Geoffrey Pine-Coffin
	DSO
12th Parachute Battalion	Lt. Col. Ken Darling
13th Parachute Battalion	Lt. Col. Peter Luard
225th Parachute Field Ambulance	
RAMC	Lt. Col. Bruce Harvey
591st Parachute Squadron RE	

6th Airlanding Brigade — Brig. Hugh Bellamy DSO

1st Battalion RUR	Lt. Col. Jack Carson
2nd Battalion OBLI	Lt. Col. Mark Darrell-Brown DSO
12th Battalion Devonshire Regiment	Lt. Col. Paul Gleadell
195th Airlanding Field Ambulance RAMC	Lt. Col. M. W. "Bill" Anderson
6th Airborne Armoured Reconnaissance Regiment	Lt. Col. Godfrey Stewart
2nd Airlanding Anti-Tank Regiment RA	Lt. Col. F. E. Allday
53rd (WY) Airlanding Light Regiment RA	Lt. Col. R. A. Eden
2nd Forward Observation Unit (Airborne) RA	Lt. Col. Harry Rice

US 17th Airborne Division — Maj. Gen. William M. Miley

507th Parachute Infantry Regiment	Col. Edson D. Raff
464th Parachute Field Artillery Battalion	Lt. Col. Edward S. Branigan Jr.
513th Parachute Infantry Regiment	Col. James W. Coutts
466th Parachute Field Artillery Battalion	Lt. Col. Kenneth L. Booth
194th Glider Infantry Regiment	Col. James R. Pierce
681st Glider Field Artillery Battalion	Lt. Col. Joseph W. Keating
680th Glider Field Artillery Battalion	Lt. Col. Paul F. Oswald
155th Anti-Aircraft Artillery Battalion	Lt. Col. John Paddock
139th Airborne Engineer Battalion	Lt. Col. Stanley T. B. Johnson
517th Signals Company	Capt. David Jesberg
224th Airborne Medical Company	Maj. James Kenny

APPENDIX C

Divisional Orders

17TH AIRBORNE DIVISION

Issued 18 March 1945

1. b. (2) XVIII Corps (Abn) consisting of 6 Br Abn Div and 17 US Abn Div will drop in the WESEL area at P–Hour, D–Day to assist the assault crossings of 15 Div (Br).

    (4) NINTH AIR FORCE will accompany the 17 US Abn Div air lift to WESEL SECOND TAF will accompany US air lift to DZ's and LZ's and continue to work in cooperation with 17 US Abn Div.

    (5) IX TCC will transport parachute troops, glider troops and equipment of the 17 Abn Div and will effect air resupply to the 17 Abn Div.

2. 17 ABN US DIV will drop at P–Hour, D–Day; seize, clear and secure the div area with priority to the high ground just E of DIERS-FORDT, and the bridge over the ISSEL R from (253458) to (235458) (both incl); protect the right (S) flk of Corps; establish contact with 1st Commando Brigadier (Br) NE of WESEL at (to be announced), with 15 Div (Br) at (to be announced) and with 6 Br Abn Div at (161456), (169462), (219477) and (196467).

6TH AIRBORNE DIVISION

3 PARA. BDE. GP.

Clear and hold the area road junction 168462—road junction 168473—road junction 168462—feature 157461—road junction 158465—bridge 154470.

Patrol out to and be prepared to hold area road and rail crossing 185476—road and rail crossing 189474—road and track junction 182467—cross roads 179473.

5 PARA. BDE. GP.

Clear and hold the area road junction 197499—road junction 197496—road junction 201492—buildings at 187483—road junction 187497.

Patrol out to and be prepared to hold area road junction 169493—buildings 177488—buildings 170486—road junction 167490

6 AIR LANDING BDE. GP.

To seize and hold the following areas in order of priority:
  a) Bridges over R. ISSEL at—railway bridge 216500—road bridge 217497—road bridge 223485 by special Coup-de-Main parties.
  b) Capture and clear the town of HAMMINKELN.
  c) To clear the area required for Div. H.Q. vicinity 189479.

GLIDER PILOT REGIMENT

  a) To land the 6 A/L Bde Gp in area HAMMIKELN.
  b) To land the support Glider-borne elements of 3 and 5 Para. Bdes within their DZ's.
  c) To land Div H.Q. and Div Tps in the area East of DIERS-FORDTER WALD.

Aircraft Specifications

DOUGLAS C-47 DAKOTA

The C-47, probably the most recognized of all World War II transport aircraft, was adapted from the DC-3 commercial airliner and was used to carry personnel and cargo, tow gliders, and drop paratroops. Affectionately known as the Goony Bird, the Dakota, or Dak for short, gave sterling service in all theaters of operation.

CURTISS C-46 COMMANDO

The Curtiss Commando was a true workhorse of the U.S. Army Air Forces, especially in the Pacific theater. The type first flew on 26 March 1940 and was powered by two Pratt and Whitney R-2800s, which gave the aircraft a top speed of 269 miles per hour (433 kilometers per hour). The double-door C-46D was that used in Operation Varsity. The C-46 was prone to hits in the fuel tanks.

AIRSPEED HORSA

Airspeed Limited's twenty-eight-seater was named Horsa, after the fifth-century German mercenary. The prototype took to the air on 12 September 1941, with the first production model appearing in June 1942. In all, some 3,500 were produced during the war.

With a wingspan of 88 feet (27 meters) and a total length of 67 feet (20 meters), a fully laden Horsa weighed in at 15,250 pounds (6,917 kilograms). It was constructed almost entirely of three-ply wood. The pilots sat side-by-side. Visibility was excellent through the large Perspex windscreen.

Passengers entered the Horsa through two doors—one forward of the port wing and one aft of the starboard wing—which slid up inside the fuselage. They sat facing each other on benches.

The tail section was designed to be removed, and ramps were then attached to the fuselage to allow the load to be taken out. Occasionally, the enemy used a cordex explosive to blow the tail off.

The Mk II was available in time for Varsity. In fact, this was the only operation in which it would be used. The nose section was hinged on the starboard side to allow loading and unloading of equipment.

GENERAL AIRCRAFT HAMILCAR

The specification for the fourth glider was given the code X.27/40 and called for one capable of carrying a light tank. This was not a new idea. As early as 1935, the Russians had slung pallet-borne T-37 tanks under TB-3 bombers. The Air Ministry and War Office gave the X.27/40 contract to General Aircraft without going to tender. Initially designated GAL49, the new glider was soon known as the Hamilcar, named after a famous Carthaginian general and father of Hannibal.

A total of 412 Hamilcars were built during the war. Only a foot longer than the Horsa, the aircraft had a mighty wingspan of 110 feet and weighed in at 36,000 pounds fully laden.

The pilots sat in tandem some 25 feet above the ground. Passengers were rarely carried, but a total of forty troops could be accommodated in the barnlike cargo area. The glider's main load was the Tetrarch light tank.

WACO CG-4A

The Weaver Aircraft Company (WACO) of Troy, Ohio, did not begin construction of its CG-4A, rechristened Hadrian by the British, until mid-1941. The first was delivered in April 1942, and by the end of the war, close to 14,000 had been built. Of these, 750 were supplied to the Glider Pilot Regiment.

The CG-4A had a wingspan of 83 feet (25 meters), was 48 feet (14 meters) long, and had a total weight of 7,500 pounds (3,400 kilograms). Its fuselage was built of steel tubing. The wings were of a wooden rib construction and covered in plywood. The floor was a honeycombed plywood pattern. The whole aircraft was covered in cotton fabric. The cockpit lifted to allow loading and unloading of the cargo section.

APPENDIX E

Air Movement Tables

17TH AIRBORNE DIVISION

AIRFIELDS

Wing	Group	Airfield Name	Airfield No.	Aircraft Type
50th	439	Châteaudun	A-39	C-47
	440	Orléans/Bricy	A-50	C-47
	441	Chartres	A-40	C-47
	441	Dreux/Vermouillet	A-41	C-47
	442	St. André-de-l'Eure	B-24	C-47
		St. Cyr		
	Pathfinder	Chartres	A-40	C-47
52nd	313	Achiet	B-54	C-46
	314	Poix	B-44	C-47
53rd	434	Mourmelon-le-Grand	A-80	C-47
	435	Brétigny	A-48	C-47
	436	Melun/Villaroche	A-55	C-47
	437	Coulommiers/Voisins Courcy	A-58	C-47
	438	Prosnes	A-79	C-47

SERIALS

Serial no.	Unit	TCC unit	No. of aircraft	Chalk no.	DZ
	Parachute				
A1	507th PIR Regt HQ & HQ Co	PF	46	1–3	W
	1st Bn 507th PIR			4–45	
	G-2 Div HQ			46	
A2	2nd Bn 507th PIR	438th	45	1–42	W
	507th PIR HQ & HQ Co			43–45	
A3	3rd Bn 507th PIR	438th		46–87	
	507th PIR HQ & HQ Co		45	89–90	W
A4	Div HQ	434th	45	1–3	W
	464th PFAB			4–45	
A5	2nd Bn 513th PIR	313th	36	1–21	X
	3rd Bn (-Co. H) 513th PIR			22–36	
A6	Co H 513th PIR			37–42	
	Regt HQ & Service Co 513th PIR	313th	36	43–51	X
	1st Bn 513th PIR			52–72	
A7	Div Arty HQ	434th	45	46–48	X
	466th PFAB			49–90	

Serial no.	Unit	TCC unit	No. of gliders	Chalk no.	LZ
	Glider				
A8	Co G 194th GIR	437th	80	1–14	S
	Co F			15–28	
	Co H			29–50	
	HQ Co 2nd Bn			51–79	
	G-2 Divn			80	
A9	Co E	437th	80	81–93	S
	Regt HQ Co			94–98, 160	
	Co A			99–112	
	Co C			113–126	
	Co D			127–157	
	Recce Platoon			158–159	
A10	Anti-tank Co	436th	72	1, 2, 5, 6, 9	S
	Co B			3, 4, 7, 8, 11, 12	
	Co I			10, 13, 14, 17, 18, 21, 22, 25, 26, 29, 30, 33, 34	

SERIALS

Serial no.	Unit	TCC unit	No. of gliders	Chalk no.	LZ
	Co K			38, 41, 42, 45, 46, 49, 50 53, 54, 57, 58, 65	
	Co M			63, 69, 70	
	HQ Co 1st Bn			15, 16, 19, 20, 23, 24, 27, 28, 31, 32, 35, 36, 39, 40, 43, 44, 47, 48, 51, 52, 55, 56, 59, 60, 64, 67, 68	
	Reg HQ Co			71, 72	
A11	Anti-tank Co	436th	72	88, 91–92, 95–96, 99–100, 107–108, 111–12, 115–16, 119–20, 123–24, 127–28, 131–32	S
	Co M			73, 74, 77, 78, 81, 82, 85, 86, 89, 90, 93, 94, 97, 98, 101–106, 109	
	Co L			110,113, 114, 117, 118, 121, 122, 125, 126, 129, 130, 133	
	HQ 3rd Bn			138, 141	
	Reg HQ Co			75, 76, 79, 80, 83, 84, 87	
A12	HQ Co 3rd Bn	435th	72	1–26	S
	Regt HQ Co			27–41	
	HQ Detachment & Medical Det 155th AAB			42–47	
	Battery B			48–54	
	Battery E			55–72	
A13	Battery E 155th AAB	435th	72	73–81	S
	Batteries A & B 681st GFAB			82–144	
A14	HQ Battery 681st GFAB	439th	72	1–7	S
	Battery A 680th GFAB			8–72	

SERIALS

Glider *continued*					
Serial no.	Unit	TCC unit	No. of gliders	Chalk no.	LZ
A15	Battery B	439th	72	73–96	S
	HQ Battery			97–104	
	Transport 507th PIR			105–125	
	Transport 464th PFAB			126–139	
	Supplies [Engineers]			140–144	
A16	Recce Platoon	440th	45	1–2	N
	9th TCC FCVP			3–8	
	Co B 139th AEB			9–45	
A17	Co's A & C	440th	45	46–77	N
	Battery A 155th AA Bn			78–90	
A18	Battery A	441st	48	1–8	N
	Battery C			9–29	
	Div HQ			30–48	
A19	Div Artillery HQ	442nd	48	1–20	N
	517th Signals Co			21–48	
A20	517th Signals Co	441st	48	1–6	N
	224th Medical Co			7–48	
A21	224th Medical Co.	314th	40	1–8	N
	Transport 513th PIR			9–29	
	British Air Support			30–37	
	G-4 Support [Ordnance]			38–40	
A22	Transport 466th PFAB	314th	40	41–54	N
	G-4 Support [QM]			55–60	
	G-4 Support [Ordnance] 61–79				
	Phantom			80	

6TH AIRBORNE DIVISION

IX TROOP CARRIER COMMAND PARATROOPS

Wing	Group	Airfield name	Aircraft type
52nd	61st	Chipping Ongar	C-47
	315th	Boreham	C-47
	316th	Wethersfield	C-47

		Parachute			
Serial no.	Unit	TCC unit	No. of aircraft	Chalk no.	DZ
B1	8th Parachute Battalion	61st	35		A
	3rd Parachute Brigade HQ		9	36–44	
	224th Parachute Field Ambulance		1	45	
B2	1st Canadian Parachute Battalion	61st	35	46–80	A
	224th Parachute Field Ambulance		1	81	
B3	9th Parachute Battalion	316th	35	82–116	A
	3rd Parachute Squadron RE		4	117–120	
	224th Parachute Field Ambulance		2	121–122	
B4	5th Parachute Brigade HQ	316th	9	123–131	B
	13th Parachute		31	132–162	
B5	13th Parachute Battalion	315th	3	163–165	B
	12th Parachute Battalion		34	166–199	
	225th Parachute Field Ambulance		5	200–204	
	591 Parachute Squadron RE		3	205–207	
B6	7th Parachute Battalion	315th	34	208–241	B
	591 Parachute Squadron RE		2	242–243	

ROYAL AIR FORCE GLIDERS

Group	RAF Sdn	GPR Sdn	Airfield name	Aircraft type
38	296	B	Earls Colne	Halifax
	297			
	190	G	Great Dunmow	Halifax/Stirling
	620			
	ORTU	G (Serial B14)	Matching	Stirling
	295	A	Rivenhall	Stirling
	570			
	196	D	Shepherds Grove	Stirling
	299			
	298	C	Woodbridge	Halifax
	644	D (Serial B15)		
46	48	E	Birch	C-47
	233			
	437			
	271	F	Gosfield	C-47
	512			
	575			

		Gliders				
Serial no.	Unit	GPR Sdn	No. of gliders	Type	Chalk nos.	LZ
B7	2nd Ox & Bucks (Coup de Main)	F	8	Horsa	1–8	O
	1st RUR (Coup de Main)		7		9–15	U
	2nd Ox & Bucks		15			O
B8	2nd Ox & Bucks	E	33	Horsa	31–63	O
B9	2nd Ox & Bucks	F	9	Horsa	64–72	O
	1st RUR		21		73–93	U
B10	1st RUR	E	27	Horsa	94–120	O
B11	1st RUR	A	11	Horsa	121–131	U
	12th Devons		15		132–146	R
	12th Devons		6		147–152	P
	Divisional HQ		2		315–316	P
B12	HQ 6 A/L Brigade	B	15	Horsa	153–167	R
	3rd A/L Anti-Tank Bty RA		5		168–172	R
	53rd (WY) Light Regt RA		3		173–175	R
	195th Field Ambulance		7		176–182	R

Serial no.	Unit	GPR Sdn	No. of gliders	Type	Chalk nos.	LZ
B13	12th Devons	G	24	Horsa	183–206	R
B14	12th Devons	G	20	Horsa	207–226	R
B15	4th A/L Anti-Tank Bty RA	D	12	Horsa	227–238	B
B16	3rd A/L Anti-Tank Bty RA	C	6	Hamilcar	239–244	R
	3rd A/L Anti-Tank Bty RA		2		245–246	P
	3rd A/L Anti-Tank Bty RA		8		247–254	B
	53rd (WY) Light Regt RA		4		255–258	P
	6th AARR Tanks		8		259–266	P
	716 Company RASC		12		267–278	P
	3rd Parachute Brigade		3		279–281	A
	5th Parachute Brigade		3		282–284	B
	Royal Engineers		2		285–286	P
B17	53rd (WY) Light Regt RA	D	28	Horsa	287–314	P
B18	Divisional HQ	A	26	Horsa	317–342	P
B19	53rd (WY) Light Regt RA	B	30	Horsa	343–372	P
B20	4th A/L Anti-Tank Bty RA	G	6	Horsa	373–378	B
	3rd A/L Anti-Tank Bty RA		6		379–384	A
	3rd A/L Anti-Tank Bty RA		9		385–393	P
	53rd (WY) Light Regt RA		9		394–402	P
	6th AARR Mortars		6		403–408	P
B21	3rd Parachute Brigade	D	12	Horsa	409–420	A
	53rd (WY) Light Regt RA		1		421	A
	Royal Engineers		2		422–423	A
	5th Parachute Brigade		12		424–435	B
	53rd (WY) Light Regt RA		3		436–438	B
	Royal Engineers		2		439–440	B

Gliders *continued*

BIBLIOGRAPHY

Alanbrooke, Viscount. *War Diaries, 1939–1945*. Edited by Alex Danchev and Daniel Todman. Berkeley: University of California Press, 2001.

Blair, Clay. *Ridgway's Paratroopers: The American Airborne in World War II*. Garden City, NY: Dial Press, 1985.

Brinson, William L. *Airborne Troop Carrier Three-One-Five Group*. Edited by George Cholewczynski. New Orleans: Walka, 2003.

Crookenden, Napier. *Airborne at War*. London: Ian Allan, 1978.

Farrar-Hockley, Anthony. *The Army in the Air: The History of the Army Air Corps*. Phoenix Mill, U.K.: Sutton, 1994.

Graves, Charles. *The Royal Ulster Rifles*, Vol. 3. N.p.: Times Printing Co., 1950. Used by kind permission of the Royal Ulster Rifles Museum.

Hamlin, John F. *Support and Strike: A Concise History of the U.S. Ninth Air Force in Colour*. Peterborough, U.K.: GMS Enterprises, 1991.

Harclerode, Peter. *Go to It: The Illustrated History of the 6th Airborne*. London: Bloomsbury, 1990.

Hawkins, Desmond. *War Report: A Record of Dispatches Broadcast by the BBC's War Correspondents with the Allied Expeditionary Forces, 6 June 1944–5 May 1945*. London: Oxford University Press, 1946.

Hils, Randolph. *DZ Europe: The Story of the 440th Troop Carrier Group*. Tallahassee, FL: Self-published, n.d.

Ingrisano, Michael. *Valor without Arms: A History of the 316th Troop Carrier Group, 1942–1945*. Bennington, VT: Merriam Press, 2001.

Jewell, Brian. *Over the Rhine: The Last Days of War in Europe*. London: Spellmount, 1985.

MacDonald, Charles B. *The Last Offensive*. Washington, DC: Office of the Chief of Military History, United States Army, 1973.

Neville, Lt. Col. J. E. H. *The Set War Chronicles: The Ox. And Bucks Light Infantry*, Vol. IV. London: Gale and Polden, 1949.

O'Donnell, Patrick K. *Beyond Valor: World War II's Ranger and Airborne Veterans Reveal the Heart of Combat*. New York: Free Press, 2001.

Pay, Don. *Thunder from Heaven: Story of the 17th Airborne Division, 1943–1945*. Nashville: Battery Press, 1980.

Smith, Claude. *The History of the Glider Pilot Regiment*. London: Leo Cooper, 1992.

Warren, John C. *Airborne Operations in World War II, European Theater*. Maxwell Air Force Base, Ala.: USAF Historical Division, 1956.

Wilmot, Chester. *The Struggle for Europe*. Westport, CT: Greenwood Press, 1972.

VETERANS PERIODICALS

The Eagle, the journal of the Glider Pilots Regimental Association.
Thunder from Heaven, the journal of the 17th Airborne Division Association.

PUBLISHED PERSONAL ACCOUNTS

Bullard, Charles Everett. *Little One and His Guardian Angel*. N.p.: Williams Assoc., 2001.

Edwards, Denis. *The Devil's Own Luck: From Pegasus Bridge to the Baltic*. London: Leo Cooper, 1999.

Guttery, D. R. *The Queen's Own Worcestershire Hussars, 1922–1956*. London: Mark & Moody, 1958.

Tucker, Ron. *A Teenager's War*. London: Spellmount, 1994.

UNPUBLISHED SOURCES

Personal Account of Rifleman Paddy Devlin RUR.
17th Airborne Historical Report of Operation Varsity.
Narrative of Operation Varsity, 24 March 1945—FAAA.
Over the Rhine: A Parachute Field Ambulance in Germany, by members of the 224th Parachute Field Ambulance.
Tibbs, David. "The Doctor's Story."

No. 38 Group Report on Operation "Varsity," WO 205/951.

6th Airborne Division Report on Operation "Varsity" and the Advance from the Rhine to the Baltic, WO 205–947.

Operation Varsity Report by Commander Glider Pilots, GPR/65/25/0/00/60.

Battlefield Tour: Operation "Varsity," 18th U.S. Airborne Corps Operations in Support of the Crossing of the River Rhine 1945 March 24–25, by Headquarters British Army of the Rhine, WO 106/5847.

War Diary 1st Battalion RUR, WO 171/5728.

War Diary 716th Company RASC (Airborne Light), WO 171/6344.

INDEX

Page numbers in italics indicate illustrations or tables